MW01123742

Heart to Heart With God -

The Jesus Way

Heart to Heart With God -

The Jesus Way

Claudia Grace Stayton

Cover Art. The beautiful painting on the front cover was done specifically for this book by my gifted artist friend Lianna Soulitzis. Lianna, a recent university graduate, has been painting since she was a young girl. She not only has great skills (art, music, language) but a heart well worth knowing — a beautiful combination. Lianna loves God and he hugs her right back! To contact her, email her at lianna17@gmail.com — or reach her at — Lianna Soulitzis Art on Facebook https://www.facebook.com/search/str/Lianna%20Soulitzis%20Art/keywords_top

My earlier book, *Day by Day the Jesus Way,* is in many ways a foundation for this present work. Copyright © 2003 by Claudia Grace Stayton. Published by Good News Connections, and printed in the United States of America by Armstrong Printing, Austin, Texas. All rights reserved. No part of this book may be used or reproduced in any manner whatsoever without permission, except in the case of brief quotations embodied in critical articles and reviews. First printing in 2003 ISBN 0-9728900-0-9; second printing 2005 ISBN 0-9728900-1-7; third printing 2006.

Copyright © 2015 Claudia Grace Stayton
All rights reserved.

ISBN: 1512297828
ISBN 13: 9781512297829
Library of Congress Control Number: 2015908145
CreateSpace Independent Publishing Platform
North Charleston, South Carolina

COPYRIGHT NOTICES – BIBLICAL REFERENCES We quote from many Scripture versions for balance and enjoyment! Unless otherwise noted, the Scripture quote is from the English Standard Version of the Holy Bible (2001).

AMP THE AMPLIFIED BIBLE, Old Testament ©1965, 1987 by the Zondervan Corporation. The Amplified New Testament © 1958, 1987 by The Lockman Foundation. Used by permission. Its introduction says that it is a rigorous attempt to go beyond the traditional "word for word" concept of translation, to bring out the richness of the Hebrew and Greek languages

CEV THE CONTEMPORARY ENGLISH VERSION. ©1995 by the American Bible Society, 1865 Broadway, NY, NY 10023. Used by permission

CONTEMPORARY PARALLEL NEW TESTAMENT, John R. Kohlenberger III, Gen. Editor, Oxford University Press, New York, , NY, 1997. pp xi - xiv, Quoted by editor's written permission.

ESV Scripture quotations are from The Holy Bible, ENGLISH STANDARD VERSION, © 2001 by Crossway, a publishing ministry of Good News Publishers. Used by permission. All rights reserved.

ESV GTB ESV GOSPEL TRANSFORMATION BIBLE – Study Notes, introductions, index, concordance, and all other included materials, © 2013 Crossway.

H-G KEY WORD STUDY BIBLE Notes from Hebrew-Greek Key Word Study Bible (NASB) edited by Executive Editor Spiros Zodhiates, and Assistant Editors Warren Baker and Joel Kletzing. Printed 1984,1990, 2008 by AMG International Inc., Chattanooga, TN.

KJV KING JAMES VERSION OF THE HOLY BIBLE

MSG Scripture taken from THE MESSAGE. © by Eugene H. Peterson,1993, 1994, 1995, 1996, 2000, 2001, 2002. Used by permission of Tyndale House Publishers, Inc.

NASB Scripture taken from the NEW AMERICAN STANDARD BIBLE. ©1960,1962, 1963, 1968, 1971, 1972, 1973, 1975, 1977, 1995 by the Lockman Foundation. Used by permission.

NCV Scriptures quoted from THE HOLY BIBLE, NEW CENTURY VERSION, © 2005, 1987, 1988, 1991 by Word Publishing, Nashville, Tennessee 37214. Used by permission. All rights reserved.

NIV Scripture taken from the HOLY BIBLE, NEW INTERNATIONAL VERSION, ©1973, 1978, 1984 by the International Bible Society. Latest version (2011) used by permission of Zondervan Publishing House. All rights reserved.

NKJV Scripture taken from the NEW KING JAMES VERSION. © 1979, 1980, 1982 by Thomas Nelson, Inc. Used by permission. All rights reserved.

NLT Scripture quotations marked (NLT) are taken from the Holy Bible, New Living Translation, © 1996, 2004, 2007, 2013 by Tyndale House Foundation. Used by permission of Tyndale House Publishers, Inc. Carol Stream, Illinois 60189. All rights reserved.

NRSV NEW REVISED STANDARD VERSION OF THE BIBLE (NRSV), ©1989, Division of Christian Education of the National Council of the Churches of Christ in the United States of America. Used by permission. All rights reserved.

RSV REVISED STANDARD VERSION OF THE BIBLE (RSV), © 1946, 1952, 1971, Division of Christian Education of the National Council of the Churches of Christ in the United States of America. Used by permission. All rights reserved.
WMF THE WORD MADE FRESH – A "down to earth version" of the New Testament by Andy Edington, WMF Foundation, Inc. Dallas, TX © 1988. (Andy is what he preferred to be called). This is neither a commentary nor a new translation, but a paraphrase of Scripture — a layman's challenge, full of genuine humor and much wisdom." Edington was 37 when he assumed the presidency as the second president of Schreiner Institute (now Schreiner University), in Kerrville, Texas. He served as the second president 1950 to 1971.

USING THE REFERENCE LIST LOCATED AT THE BACK OF BOOK.

I have included quotes and ideas from a variety of authors. So to help you track the source of an idea or quote, I use a simple system called in-line or in-text references (a.k.a. the author-date system). This is instead of traditional footnotes, which can waste space.

After each quote in the text, in parentheses you will see the last name of the author or source. Following the name, there may also be a page number. Or in the case of Chambers, there will be a date for the entry from his daily devotional book, *My Utmost for His Highest.*

If I quote an author who has several books on my reference list, the citation will have the last name of the author and then the year the book was printed. This makes it easier for you to know which resource I am citing. For example, the citation in parentheses shows that while I refer to several Beth Moore books, this particular quote is from her book written in 2014, page 145 ((Moore 2014, 145). Then, if you need more detail, you can consult the Reference List at the back of the book.

CITING BOOK, CHAPTER, AND VERSE

- If I mention a book of the Bible in a sentence, without using a direct quote, I won't abbreviate the book name.

- All biblical quotes are accompanied by the name of the book (often abbreviated), chapter number, and verse. For example, when Jesus says he wants to gather his children to him for protection, the citation is Matthew 23:37 Luke 13:34. This means that the remark was quoted in Matthew and the same situation was repeated in Luke.

* At other times, Jesus expresses the same idea in several different situations, with perhaps slightly varying words. So, for example, when Jesus talks about the importance of faith in accomplishing mighty works, the citation is: Matthew 17:20–21. Also in Luke 17:6; in Mark 11:22–23; and in Matthew 21:20–22. This means that the quote is from Matthew 17:20–21. A very similar idea is found in Luke 17:6. And another similar idea is in Mark 11:22–23, and repeated in Matthew 21:20–22.

* In many cases, a quote may be a single line drawn from a larger passage, say, John 16:13–15. By doing this, I high-light certain words as particularly important, but I am also referring you to the longer passage(s) to get the entire idea in context.

* Various Bible translations treat capitalization and punctuation differently. For example, some capitalize "He" when referring to Jesus or God. Most do not. Whenever I quote from a particular translation, I remain faithful to its particular format. That includes the *Amplified Bible*, which often puts words in parentheses, brackets, and/or italics to clarify or amplify the original text.

* Many of the translations use italics, not for emphasis as a modern text would, but to indicate that the words are not in the original text but are implied by the context. *The Message*, however, uses italics for emphasis. To learn more about this, check each translation's introduction.

TABLE OF CONTENTS

Love is the foundation, the pivotal element of our faith. God invites us into a two-way loving relationship, and everything builds from there. We are so fortunate that Jesus invites us to *come to him*, even though we are the wayward ones . . . Four major threads in this book: (1) Basic truths; (2) God, who do you say I am?; (3) When your ox is in a ditch; and (4) If you truly love God, you will allow him to transform you, and your life will show it. You will say yes to God.

Introduction: Two ships on the horizon
Topics: One true God . . . We can know God and Jesus personally . . . He invites us into a loving personal relationship . . . God wants all to be saved . . . Our Creator . . . God is Praiseworthy, good, faithful, wise, powerful and so much more . . . God is enough and I can trust him .

Topics: Jesus, the Christ, the Messiah . . . God sends him to live and die for us, and to save us . . Jesus and the Kingdom of heaven/Kingdom of God . . . Jesus is the vine, I am the branch . . . Believe, Do, and Become what God says. . . Serve God and follow him . . . Jesus was crucified, died, was buried and resurrected.

God is ever-present and active, even when my ox is in a ditch and life is very hard. And surprisingly, there are little gifts — hard to spot, I'll admit — in the cart, even when the ox, the cart, and we are all in the ditch! Topics: God is always present and working in our lives . . . God permits trials and suffering in our lives – and discipline when we need it . . . In all cases, we can share our sorrow and grief with God . . . God's peace can saturate us . . . God is our comforter . . . Cherish God's help as we endure and cope with our struggles . . . Part of God's help is his God's faith-building gym, which is always open in good times and bad

Be alert to the inevitable obstacles and stumbling blocks that can thwart a life with God. And be confident in God's power to help.
Topics: A recap of two big "S" words: Sin and Satan . . . God gives me power and authority to see things his way and overcome evil . . . Never underestimate the enemy . . . How do I know if I'm hearing from God or from Satan? . . . No matter what trouble, Jesus can provide "living water" and draw us into a life of freedom and following God . . . Strongholds . . . Some common stumbling blocks to life with God . . . Gain new ground and God will help you defend it.

Topics: God knows and wants what is best for us . . . Jesus is the light of the world. And with his help, I can be a light, too . . . God offers us a clear choice: spiritual life or spiritual death . . . Cooperate with God's plan to transform and mold me into the image of Christ . . . Ask God for the tools to do the job . . . God is never done with me . . . But he is not a magic genie fixing every problem . . . When I am cooperating, I admit my mistakes, turn away from sin, and toward God . . . Blessed to be a blessing . . . God is my foundation, my courage as I follow his path . . . Remember, it is not God's job to fix my every problem . . . My motto: God, you are great. God, take my hand. And God, take my mouth!

Topics: He calls and equips us to do all of this: Love others . . . Do good, give, and tend his sheep . . . How does Jesus deal with people who struggle? . . . Seek peace and pursue it . . . Love your enemies . . . Treat others as you want to be treated . . . Live with reasonable expectations . . . Forgive, and don't take offense.

Topics: Jesus wants to break down relational barriers, so that he can have a dialogue between the "lost" and the "found" . . . He addresses our brokenness and desires to fill the emptiness of our lives, where we live on the edges of deceit [and defeat] and fill us with himself. . . . Jesus is relentless in his pursuit of humanity — and that's you. . . . What is it like to have God's call on your life? . . . God plans to reach the world and I am part of that . . . Share the Good News of God . . . Then make disciples, baptize, and teach . . . Some real life examples

Topics: God created every one of us capable of accepting Jesus, who can bring us to the Father. Jesus promises us eternal life with God as soon as we believe and follow him. (Our choice remember?) And that life begins the day we accept him, not when we die and go to heaven. So I live in the kingdom of God now, not just later in heaven . . .

There is nothing like enjoying God's presence and finding satisfaction in him . . . The truth about your spiritual life is between you and God alone, from today until the end of your life on earth and beyond . . . God promises us eternal life as soon as we believe . . . He has prepared a banquet and gifts for us . . . There are consequences for following, or not following God . . . It is an amazing privilege to know, believe, and trust God . . . We can experience the joy of the Lord, his peace, his wisdom . . . God shares his wisdom and power with us if we are following Jesus . . . And when we do fall, he is there to help pick us up . . . Sadly, some may never experience all of this, but that can change if they choose . . . Life with God isn't all sunshine and merry-go-rounds. But God is with me on the mountaintops and in the valleys.

AT THE END OF EACH CHAPTER

There is space at the end of each chapter for you to write your own prayer and meditation. God has prompted me to give you this space and encouragement — for your sake and for mine as well. May it inspire you to write your own thoughts for each section, slowly, as you go through.
I use the first person "I" so it seems present and more real, but of course, you can use any form or style you like. I know God looks forward to hearing from you, whether you are a seeker or a seasoned veteran!

AND AT THE END OF THE BOOK

HEART TO HEART WITH GOD –
THE JESUS WAY

AN OUTLINE FOR THE INTRODUCTION

> The only way to live an undefeated life is to live
> looking to God.   Oswald Chambers, March 6 entry

> The steadfast love of the LORD never ceases, his mercies
> never come to an end; they are new every morning; great is your
> faithfulness.   Lamentations 3:20-23, 31--33

1. Love is the foundation, the pivotal element of our faith
2. God's invitation to you is: "Come to Me"
3. Ours is a simple faith: believe, do and become. So, say yes. Come and enjoy the whole party
4. Four major "threads" from my life that wind through this book
   * First thread – the basic truths of our faith
   * Second thread – God, who do you say I am?
   * Third thread – when your ox is in a ditch
   * Fourth and final thread: if you *truly* love God, you will allow him to transform you, and your life will show it.
   * Henry Blackaby's "seven realities of experiencing God"
   * Bottom line? I can't stay where I am and go with God at the same time! There are core steps I need to take, regardless of my situation.
   * A key part of the process is obedience.
   * God gives us free will – to say yes or no to him. But caution: 'No' decisions can become "declarations of independence which are essentially atheistic"

5. Getting fit, faith-wise
6. Some final words before we begin chapter 1
   * First: no matter who tells you what, make sure to check it out with God's Word and his Holy Spirit.
   * Second: knowledge is a wonderful thing, but *wisdom* — knowing how to use that knowledge for God's glory — is even more wonderful. And let's restrain our inner "know it all".
   * Third: there will be people who tell you that God doesn't produce miracles today. *Don't you believe it!*
   * Fourth: your fellow travelers on this Christian journey may disappoint you from time to time. But no worries; we're all human.
7. And finally, a little bit about me

HEART TO HEART WITH GOD –
THE JESUS WAY

INTRODUCTION

The only way to live an undefeated life is to live
looking to God.   Oswald Chambers, March 6 entry

The steadfast love of the LORD never ceases, his mercies
never come to an end; they are new every morning; great is your
faithfulness.   Lamentations 3:20-23, 31--33

LOVE IS THE FOUNDATION,
THE PIVOTAL ELEMENT OF OUR FAITH

God invites us into a loving, two-way, "up close and personal" relationship with him. He loves us. We love him. And everything builds from
there. You may have heard 1 Corinthians Chapter 13 (called the love
chapter) read at weddings: "Love is patient, love is kind . . . " and so on.
But I see the *entire* Bible as the "love book", because everything between
believers and our God is based on love. For instance, this book is my
passionate-to-the-core love for God poured out on paper. And it is his
astonishing and extravagant love for us that drives the whole project.

And who is this all for? YOU! And why? Because God loves you.
Surprised? I am praying that, through this book, you will let God show
his heart to you and open your heart to him in ways you've not yet
experienced.

The love between our God and his followers is the key, the beginning, and the heart of Christianity. But this love between us is no sen-
timental greeting card. *It is the very foundation of our faith.* And this love,

like any other true love, is to be treated, not like some fragile flower, but like a sweet and healthy child that needs to be fed, nurtured, and taken out and exercised often! Beyond that, we need to give this love the honor, respect, and obedience it so deserves. Otherwise, the robust and satisfying passion we have for Father and Son can fade into a pale version of its former self and become our first love, now lost.

Everything we discuss in this book — faith, prayer, obedience, conversation with God, evangelism, and much more — is vital to our faith and our personal relationship with God. Each experience with God is evidence of our love and helps us to grow that love day by day. But none of these alone is the foundation of our faith. And when we act as if they are, we may have problems.

We come from many different countries and cultures. Some of us are atheists (not many, really), while many are fervent believers in Judaism, in Buddha or Muhammad, or the almighty dollar (or the British pound or Euro). And many of us are faithful Christians. We are of different ages, occupations, incomes, and backgrounds. Maybe you are a happy-go-lucky person, or someone who is facing great sadness. Maybe you drink too much, talk too much, or hide too much. Maybe you've just happily retired. Or you've been out of work for months and afraid that nothing good is ever going to come. You may have been raised in a church where Jesus was rarely mentioned and no one truly knew God. Or you may be devoted in your Christian faith.

Whatever our background, some of us have no idea what's up in the divine department. But we all yearn for "what God provides, whether we know it or not. Believers and nonbelievers, even atheists, search for what only God can give" (Jacob 2012).

And, we all have things we believe, or *say* we believe. Some of the things we do track perfectly with our stated beliefs. Others, not so much! Most of you reading this will know some Christians, and so you will also know that some Christians seem to follow Jesus, and some don't. You may also know some Jewish followers, Muslims, Buddhists, and so on. Some of them may be following their faith more with their mouths than with their lives. But we are not here to judge *anyone.* We are here to help bring light to us all.

GOD'S INVITATION TO YOU: "COME TO ME"

Regardless of our differences, nothing is as important as getting right with God and staying right with God (Chambers Aug 19). And there is only one – simple but not necessarily easy – way to do this. God, through Jesus, is saying to each and every one of us: COME TO ME (Matthew 11:28, 19:14, 21, and elsewhere). "Me?" you gulp. Yes, you! Now some good and well-meaning religious folk would have you believe that while God does say, "Come to me," he always adds something else. They'll try to persuade you of this, but you mustn't be fooled. Consider this carefully:

GOD DOES *NOT* SAY:
Come to me, once you have answers to all your questions.
GOD DOES *NOT* SAY:
Come to me when you are completely clean, pure, without sin.
GOD DOES *NOT* SAY:
Come to me only when you fully understand and accept Jesus' virgin
birth (and the Trinity, and the resurrection, and so on).
GOD DOES *NOT* SAY:
Come to me and then have every material possession you crave.
GOD DOES *NOT* SAY:
Come to me only when you have mastered the Bible.
GOD DOES *NOT* SAY:
Come to me so you can sit in a fancy church with other fancy people,
and congratulate one another on how smart and perfect you all are.

Now some of you may be thinking, "It *might* be great to come to Jesus and his Father. But I don't know how to do it. And I'm still not sure that I would be welcome, given all my mistakes and terrible choices — these things I now hear you call 'sin'." I understand those doubts. But if you come along with me, you will find many assurances that God wants you to come to him, through Jesus, just as you are.

Recently, I met a new friend, Tye Barrett, who has written a number of great songs as part of a praise group called The Gladsome Light (see Reference List for details). His voice is warm and good, and his style is comfortable and moving. But most of all, I can feel God's Spirit coming closer and closer as Tye draws us into worship. *That* is a real gift! His song "Wayward Ones" portrays so well what Jesus is saying to us. No matter what your past sins are, no matter how you have trampled on yourself or those you love, Jesus says, over and over, "Come to me. I have given my life for you and you can now become a child of God."

[We say] We are the wayward ones. Liars and beggars, those who betray. We hand you over. Deny your name. Cast you aside, yet still you say [And Jesus replies, twice] This is my body. This is my blood. Broken and shed to show my love. [We say] We are the broken ones. Tired and foolish, filled with disbelief. We forsake you, deny your name, cast you aside, yet still you say [And Jesus replies, twice] This is my body. This is my blood. Broken and shed to show my love. Remember me. Remember me. Come to the table. Take and eat. Remember me. Remember me.

Please carefully consider everything I've said so far and what's ahead as well. No matter where you are in your journey, would you agree to hold off repeating to yourself some of the strange things you've heard from people? Instead, ponder God's invitation: "Come to me!" You have *nothing* to lose, and *everything* to gain! God is saying to you, "Come to me." Period. No qualifiers. No ifs, ands, or buts. No requirements at all, other than just *"COME.*

We've talked – and will talk more – about God inviting us into a personal love relationship with him. So just for a moment, close your eyes and imagine walking to your front door and finding a beautifully wrapped package. It has your name on it, along with an invitation on the outside from God which says, "Come to me". What will you do with the gift? Will you open it immediately or will you leave it on the porch for months or years? Or maybe you will set it inside your front door and walk by it several times a day, without opening it? For a week? For a year or even more? If that's you, ask God to help you discover this delightful package, with its personal invitation, and then show you what to do with it. I promise, you won't be disappointed.

If you open the package and accept God, you can go to heaven. But this promise is just the beginning of your walk with God, and there is

so much more to follow! So as you walk with me through this collection of ideas and thoughts about God, I encourage you to ask yourself
a question, drawn from Dallas Willard's thought-tingling book, *The
Divine Conspiracy*: "It is good to know that when I die all will be well,
but is there any good news for life here and now? [Or] Does Jesus only
enable me to 'make the cut' when I die? *Can I not have both?*" (Willard,
12)

These are questions many of us have asked at one time or another.
The good news is that we *can* experience God's love and life in this
world, *and* in the world to come. It's like having your cake – a beautifully
decorated cake, a glorious homecoming in heaven at the end of our
earthly life. *And* we can also eat it too – enjoy the cake every day, along
the way, experiencing God's love, comfort, peace, wisdom, and guidance on every step of our earthly journey.

What we believe about God is foundational to our entire belief system. God is all-loving and wants what is best for us, which is a holy and
submitted relationship with him. He has a plan, but he does not force us
to do things his way. In fact, we are free to choose our own way, rather
like deciding to negotiate our own way through a minefield instead of
following a trained guide.

OURS IS A SIMPLE FAITH: BELIEVE, DO AND BECOME.
COME AND ENJOY THE WHOLE PARTY

People may tell you that if you say "Yes" to Jesus, then you are set. And of
course, accepting Jesus (who describes himself as the door to the Father) is
certainly the first and key admission into a life with God. But is there more?

What if someone told you that you were invited to a marvelous party,
and all you had to do was to slip just inside the tent and cling to the edge.
You'd be in the party, yes! But would you be experiencing everything that
the host had planned for you? As you enter the party, you might notice
that there are some good people huddling just inside the entrance. They
have said yes to Jesus, and God is delighted! But many of these people may
never move forward, or follow Jesus, or walk with God, or hear his voice.
They have gained admission to the party, which is indeed a wonderful

thing, but they have not yet discovered the glories and joy that await them if they would just get up, take God's hand, and start exploring.

But wait! Didn't the invitation to the party explain what wonderful things would happen there and even afterwards? Consider that the Bible was written for believers as well as nonbelievers. And there are endless verses with advice on following God and living his way. So why not look again at that party invitation (and this book, for that matter) and crawl from the edge into the center, where the party is in full swing? Imagine the conversations, the warm hugs, the great projects and superior advice, the thrills of energy, love, and wisdom running through the place! Oh, and did I mention the music? And over it all is a sense of peace that passes all understanding. That is what God has in mind for our life on this Earth. And that is what this book is all about: saying, "Yes" and then saying "Let's Go!"

My husband and I "found" Jesus fairly late (as if poor Jesus was lost). And from that first moment, our love has driven us to share him and his Father with everyone we meet. So whenever I say or write *anything,* my prime determination is to share God and Jesus with you, and to tell the truth as I know it, in a direct and unvarnished manner. I don't favor the fortune cookie kind of fluff you can find in some books. So here, together, what you and I share will be *all truth in love.*

THERE ARE FOUR MAJOR "THREADS" FROM
MY LIFE THAT WIND THROUGH THIS BOOK

First thread – The basic truths of our faith
The first thread that weaves through this collection began in 1993, the year we met Jesus. Our focus then, and now, is the basic truths about God the Father, Jesus the Son, and the Holy Spirit. As a new Christian, I was very curious about what Jesus told us to do, because, frankly, I had no idea (although I had sat in church most of my life)! Over the years, those answers became my little book *Day By Day The Jesus Way.* And I began to understand that God has equipped us, and continues to equip us, for whatever he calls us to do and to be. But actually trusting that, and living it every day, is a daily decision for me, not a one-off deal.

So Step #1 for us will be to get the basics straight, OK? Whether we're dancing along a scenic mountaintop, or stuck with our ox in a ditch, the basics are always the same. And they will ground us in the truth daily.

Second thread – God, Who Do You Say I Am?

The second thread is a phrase that Jesus asks his disciples in Matthew 16:13–20 (Mark 8:29; Luke 9:20). And I believe it is a question we all need to ask God as well. "God, who do *you* say I am? Who am I in *your* eyes, God? What am I capable of? What have you formed me to be? What is your vision for my heart, mind and soul? What gifts and abilities have you placed within me?" This isn't a quick or easy process, and there are still times when I cling to my old view of myself instead of God's view of me. But I am a determined work in progress. And the journey is worth taking!

But how do I do that? Where do I start? Have you asked yourself these very questions? Then come along with me, as we explore "Who am I, God?" As you and God grow closer and as we learn to see things *his* way, our faith grows. And more and more of our entire personality leans on God in absolute trust and confidence in his power, wisdom, and goodness (faith as described in Hebrews 4:2 AMP). But please note: My objective here isn't to think better of myself. If that were the case, I could just hire a hypnotist or surround myself with professional flatterers. No, my goal is to grow closer and closer to God, and to see things, including myself, the way *he* sees them.

Trying to understand myself without first understanding God is backwards and, in my view, impossible. So, before I can find out who I am, I need to accept who God is and what his relationship is to me. That is where you and I will begin. I have just one small word of warning, though. I don't know how this part will turn out, but I'm pretty sure it won't be some Hallmark card on steroids. I expect that we will explore, and God will provide answers that are rich in truth and simple, but not necessarily easy to live out. But that's what we want, isn't it? Truth, the truth that will set us free!

Third thread – When Your Ox is in a Ditch
This third thread comes from the verse in which Jesus talks about rescuing an animal that has fallen into a pit or a well (Luke 14:5 and Mt 12:11–12). In those days, oxen were big and useful creatures that people depended on for all manner of things. So when I use the phrase "an ox in the ditch", I'm describing a situation that is both urgent and difficult, perhaps even desperate!

"But I don't own an ox", I can hear you say. Maybe not, but do you have a teenager who is off the rails, or a boss who rages at his staff, or an aging parent, or a job that is about to be eliminated? Is your spouse drifting from you, mentally if not physically? These are just a very few of "the oxen" that can come crashing down, burying you and it in a deep, deep ditch. No major disasters on the horizon? Good for you! But are there any little oxen wandering about in your life? Are they growing? Hmm?

This third thread began during the hardest trial of my life, my darling husband's long journey with Alzheimer's disease. Unlike some other hard times in my life, I definitely did not bring this on myself, and neither did my husband. Am I an expert in all of this, a wise observer who used all her free time researching Alzheimer's? Am I sitting on a little princess chair now, spouting platitudes, never having had a disastrous time? No, and no again! I write with a serious track record of having been in the ditch. And I write from a place of true love for God and love for anyone going through devastating times. That, plus what God can show us, is a great place to be. And I hope you'll consider standing there with me.

We all know that life can be great, and life can be not so great! It's sometimes easy and sometimes hard. When life is easy, we tend to get lazy and cruise along, enjoying what we consider our just rewards. Then whoops! Something goes wrong and we're eating dirt instead.

Fourth and final thread: If you *truly* love God, you will allow him to transform you, and your life will show it. Say yes to God!
This is inspired primarily by Henry Blackaby's study "Experiencing God", which we took a few years after accepting Jesus. He describes seven realities of experiencing God. And these faith elements influence my life – and this book – to this day (Blackaby 1996).

- ❖ God is always at work around you [and in you and through you].
- ❖ God pursues a continuing, intimate love relationship with you that is real and personal. [And through this relationship, God does amazing things:]
- ❖ God invites you to become involved with him in his work.
- ❖ God speaks by the Holy Spirit - through the Bible, prayer, circumstances, and the church — all to reveal himself, his purposes, and his ways.
- ❖ God's invitation for you to work with Him always leads you to a crisis of belief that requires faith and action.
- ❖ You must make major adjustments in your life to join God in what He is doing.
- ❖ You come to know God by experience as you obey him, and he accomplishes his work through you.

Bottom line? I can't stay where I am and go with God at the same time! There are core steps I need to take, regardless of my situation. And I talk about them throughout this book. Chapter 2 talks about the steps from repentance to life with God. Chapter 8 talks about the sequence to defeat Satan's strongholds in our lives. And Chapter 9 talks about steps to cooperate with God's plan to transform us into the image of Christ.

A key part of the process is obedience. Elisabeth Elliot says, "Whatever God says, my answer is yes" (Elliot p 16)! Now I'll admit obedience wasn't my strongest suit before I met Jesus, and there are times when I struggle with it now. But I love God wildly and see the logic in putting my 'obedience' where my mouth is, regarding that love. I am not referring "to faultless obedience, but to a new trajectory of life that springs from a radical transformation of having been born again (see 1 Jn 2:1-6; 3:9). John is *not* saying that our obedience . . . earns God's love, since we are saved by Jesus' sacrifice, not our own efforts . . . But he *is* saying that those who have God's love show it . . . [So] we cannot confidently claim that his grace [his unmerited favor toward us] is ours if we show no evidence that our lives are his" (ESV-GTB).

God doesn't want puppets. He wants us to follow him willingly. So our all-powerful and loving God decided to create us capable of saying yes *or no* to him. We call that "free will" – freedom to accept or reject his gifts, his plans, his guidance, even his great love for us. Poet John Milton, in his epic poem *Paradise Lost, Book 3,* calls this being created "sufficient to stand yet free to fall" (Milton 1667). But if we say no and refuse to acknowledge God's supremacy and our dependence on him, there are consequences. Elisabeth Elliot points out that our 'no' decisions then becomes "declarations of independence which are essentially atheistic" (Elliot pp 15-16).

GETTING FIT, FAITH-WISE

Most of us, including Christians, can be pretty smug about our lives at times, although we may not recognize it or own up to it. We feel sympathy and maybe a little cockiness, watching as other people's children fall down a hole, or other marriages fail. It's tempting to think *I'm doing the right thing. That's why my life is so good.* But it's important to remember that Jesus himself said that God makes his sun rise on the evil and on the good, and sends rain on the just and on the unjust (Mt 5:45). So even undeserving people can have good times. And good people can have bad times, at least here on Earth!

Naturally, we all *love* our good times. And we are usually frightened by the notion of terribly tough times. But if we can accept that bad times are part of life, then where do we go from there? I've been giving this thought and wondering what are the essential faith-training elements we need to incorporate into our lives, while things are good, that will help us face the bad times that inevitably come. We definitely are *not* super-humans who glide through tragedy with nary a tear! But we have a captain on our team who is with us every step, guiding, wiping tears, hugging, or when necessary, saying, "Have courage. Get back up! You are not alone."

In my life, I can see, with God's help, the gaps in my faith, the weakness of my trust in God, and my tendency to get shaky when things seem insurmountable. All of these need shoring up. And wouldn't it be far better to do more of that spade work before the tsunami hits? Also, let's always remember that, in God's eyes, we are a work in progress. Or as my wise friend Evy says, "It takes a lifetime." So, there is no condemnation here — just some words that might help you and me as we follow God through this amazing minefield called life. As my dear friend Oswald, says, "Preparation is not suddenly accomplished. In fact, it is a process that must be steadily maintained. It is dangerous to become settled and complacent in our present level of experience, because the Christian life requires preparation and then more preparation" (Chambers, Sept 24).

SOME FINAL WORDS BEFORE WE BEGIN CHAPTER 1

First: No matter who tells you what, make sure to check it out with God's Word and his Holy Spirit.
Be wise and discerning, because people can say anything, but that doesn't make it true. Indeed, someone can pull one or two lines of scripture to make a somewhat dubious point. So ask yourself, is this comment consistent with Scripture overall. Is it consistent with the character and truth of the Creator, the Father of the Universe? Is it consistent with the life and words of Jesus, the Savior of Mankind? Does it fit with everything I know so far?

I have heard people talk about God as if he were a luxury car dealer, just waiting to provide them with the latest toy. And I have heard people say that if your loved one dies, it's because you didn't have enough faith in God. So in short, people can say all sorts of outrageous things, and some of them say them from very fancy podiums and pulpits. But that does *not* necessarily make what they say true. It is up to you, consulting with God's vast wisdom and love, to discern what is true, whatever the source.

Stayton and I once led a group of third graders (mostly boys) at a week long Vacation Bible School. Now this was pretty soon after our experience at YWAM, so we were well-schooled in how to hear other people when they talked about faith. There was a curriculum of course, but Stayton and I also made a little list of things we wished we'd known about God when we were these kids' ages. And one main thing on our list was this: If a grown-up tells you something about God or Jesus that doesn't quite fit what you've heard or read elsewhere, ask the grown-up *very politely:* "That is so interesting. Can you show me where that is in the Bible?"

Now I give the same advice to you! You are surrounded by great information about God, in church, in books, in Bible studies, etc. But I have learned that even in Bible studies, leaders and fellow classmates can present things that seem somewhat off track – or just flat wrong! (see "About Me" for a personal example) We are all human after all. Don't be shy about commenting, in a gentle way. But also don't be shy about leaving a particular study – again gently – if it's not leading you closer to Christ.

Second: Knowledge is a wonderful thing, but *wisdom* — knowing how to use that knowledge for God's glory — is even more wonderful.
Let's resist the impulse to take the knowledge we have and use it to push our own biases and agendas on other people. Let's focus on God, not our own infallibility. After all, God is a whole lot smarter and bigger than you and I are, and isn't that a comfort?

The Bible, God's Word, is a marvelous thing, a large collection of books written by various men at various times, all under the guidance of God. Naturally, there are different views, different audiences, and different ways of expressing God's truths. Some things are the backbone of our faith, nonnegotiable in a sense. But there are many other things on which there is a healthy diversity of viewpoints among faithful Christians. My advice, whether you are an inquirer, someone new to the faith, or even a seasoned veteran, is to allow room for diverse opinions. Seek unity, not division, in your discussions and relationships. But keep focused on the central truths, which do not vary.

Sometimes discussions can become heated debates, because we are human and want desperately to "win". But that is not what you and I are going for, and it certainly isn't what Jesus is hoping for. So use wisdom, and pray for *more* wisdom. If we focus on pleasing God, whom we love, rather than one-upping people, we'll be on solid ground. Come back and back to this whenever you are tempted to think your particular viewpoint is the only one to consider. So let's keep a tight rein on our "know it all" spirit! And don't get involved in foolish arguments that only start fights . . . Be kind to everyone . . . teach effectively and be patient with difficult people . . . gently teach those who oppose the truth. 2 Timothy 2:23–26 NLT

Third: There will be people who tell you that God doesn't produce miracles today. *Don't you believe it!*

Of course, folks can be quite serious and well-meaning when they say that miracles ceased at some point, never to return. But in the strongest way possible, let me suggest that when people tell you that, you should smile, say "That's interesting", and immediately toss it into your mental trash basket. God is *not* giving up on miracles, as if they were some out-of-style kitchen from the 1970s. Just ask me sometime, because I can give you examples! Or ask God! He's got lots of miracles he can tell you about.

Fourth: Your fellow travelers on this Christian journey may disappoint you from time to time. And you may disappoint them.

But we are all human, and we must not let this derail us. I learned this shortly after I met Jesus, from a wise woman named Emily Mockovciak who had learned this early in her own Christian life. Emily also said that God will never disappoint you or let you down. And my wise friend, Scott McCracken, has lately deepened this for me. He points out that there *may* be times when we *think* God has disappointed us, but in truth he is acting according to his own good plan.

God is looking at the prize – helping us become more Christ-like and advancing his Kingdom. So *his* moves may not fit exactly onto *our* wish list. But is that God's fault? Or is it *our expectations* of God — not rooted in reality or Biblical truth — that are the problem? Perhaps when you read chapter 10, about living with reasonable expectations for your fellow man, you'll see that we have the same problem in *other* relationships, when our expectations are out of whack!

AND FINALLY, A LITTLE BIT ABOUT ME
(OKAY, MAYBE NOT A "LITTLE" BIT, BUT I DID TRY!)

First of all, you may or may not realize that different churches teach different things. They each have their strengths, of course. But just because you sit in a McDonald's (as Nicky Gumbel says) doesn't make you a hamburger. In fact, I once heard a very "successful" retired pastor speak, as he returned to his large, posh former home church for a visit. He stood before hundreds and hundreds of his former flock, and began with these words: "The first thing I want to do is to apologize to this congregation for not preaching Jesus from this pulpit." I knew he was telling the truth, but I wept when I heard his words, bravely spoken after all those years. They were dramatic proof that God is always pitching when it comes to our lives and his plan for our Christ-likeness. Whether you are young or old, ignorant of Jesus or a professional preacher, God is still working with you, loving you, and showing you the truth, if you will only listen!

My husband and I came late to the whole Jesus party. For years we sat in a church where there wasn't a lot of "preaching Jesus", but we didn't know enough to spot it. We went to Sunday School and even a year-long Bible study on the Old Testament. There the teacher (who was very bright and impressive) told us that the book of Isaiah was written by two men, so there was a First and Second Isaiah. The way we know that (she said) was that the second half of Isaiah occurred *after* Isaiah lived – so he couldn't possibly have written about it. Imagine our shock when we learned later in our mission school training (YWAM) that of course this was false. But it showed how our church handled Isaiah's prophecies from God – as impossible. We just hadn't known enough to challenge her assertions about Isaiah and biblical prophecy (a phrase – by the way – that was never mentioned in class or in the study materials).

So to say the least, we lacked a first-hand true knowledge of God, Jesus, and the Holy Spirit. To us, God was far off and fancy. And we had no idea that the Father wanted a relationship with us. Although we yearned to know him, we didn't know how. I was trying to understand it all intellectually, but having limited success, (to say the very least). Could he have dropped a "wisdom bomb" on us then? Yes. But I now believe that he knew we would come to him later, and because we'd been stupid so long, we were the perfect ones to talk about him and Jesus – frankly, simply, and without any self-congratulation.

Were my husband and I pure and perfect when we met and embraced God? Oh, ha! So far from it! Like many people, we had each made serious mistakes in our lives. But despite our sin and ignorance, God still pursued us, although we didn't know it at the time. Later, I would say to anyone who would listen: "We are proof that God recycles garbage!"

Am I proud of our entire past? No. But I am beyond grateful that God proves (through us and so many others) that he still loves us and is in there pursuing us, until the very end, despite our many imperfections.

In the midst of all this, God had given us a strong desire to help people. So, in 1993, we retired early and enrolled in a five-month Youth With A Mission course to equip us for mercy (service) work. The Father was so gracious to entice us to this course, knowing that we knew almost nothing about faith! And I still imagine him delighted and slapping his knee with laughter, as we enrolled in what was really a discipleship and missions training course, even though we had absolutely no firsthand knowledge of Jesus.

Three weeks into that school, we discovered the God who loves us personally! And we connected with his precious son Jesus, who lived and died just so we could have an abundant, eternal life with the Father and with him. And we met God's Holy Spirit, alive and well, in and around us. We still are amazed every day! No surprise, then, that the essence of God for me is the massive love I have for him and the amazing love he has for me. Truly the sweetest love ever! And I know every one of you is fully capable of experiencing that in your own unique way.

Through the years since I met Jesus as a Friend, Lord, and Savior, I've given a lot of thought to what I believe. I'm no guru, philosopher, or theologian. And I've learned that talk, even religious talk, can be cheap! But I am a lover of God, so I know it is important for me to do three things: KNOW what I believe; DO what I believe; and BECOME what I believe! Then, when I find a disconnect anywhere, I need to ask God, "Show me what's wrong."

At the very beginning of my walk with God, I was drawn to focus on Jesus' words, because he is the center of our faith, *and* I knew so little of what he'd said during his life. Later, I realized that this was God guiding me – like a laser beam – to what Jesus said. I've been glad for it ever since! Eventually, my notes became a little book called *Day By Day the Jesus Way*, which is used by lots of people. In fact, that little book is the backbone of what you are reading today.

My husband and I were very ordinary people pursued by an extraordinary God, and our lives have never been the same. Like Jesus, our goal is to help people meet and know our heavenly Dad! We were able to travel and do two or three months of overseas mission work annually, for ten-plus years, until Stayton became ill.

Life is not all ponies and ice cream cones, of course. In fact, just today as I begin to wrap up this book (August 2015), almost two years to the day since Stayton's death, I still miss him terribly. And I miss overseas missions. But I know that for now, I am where I should be – finishing this book. And I know most certainly that God is with me. And that is very good news!

Oh, one more little thing about me. People always ask about our last names because they're different and confusing. Before we married, Stayton recommended I get a different last name, because many of his friends couldn't spell or pronounce his last name: Roehm (pron. Reem). But I was in a romantic cloud and so I took his name, despite his advice. But he was right, so a few years later, when I was trying to start a consulting business (emphasis on the 'trying'), we agreed that I needed a name people could spell and pronounce. So I decided on the name Stayton, which was his mother's family name. And I had another reason which I didn't tell him. I wanted his name in mine for all of my life, especially if he died first. So I am happily CLAUDIA STAYTON.

Okay, now, back to you and this book. Read about living "Heart to Heart with God – The Jesus Way", but please don't take my word for it! Read the Bible. (That's why I have included far more scripture here than you'll find in most books.) Ask God to show you the truth of his words in your life. Talk to him and listen to him. Day by day, month by month, spend time with Jesus and his great Dad. And enjoy the vast number of books and authors I've quoted throughout. I promise I won't be pumping any sunshine or fancy talk up your shirt! There's no need for that when you are meeting and embracing the real deal: the Creator and C.E.O. of the universe and his precious Son! I pray that you will come with your heart as well as your mind, and let Jesus teach you his ways.

Jesus, help me convey through this book how very good you are and how much you and your Father love us. I pray for all those who pick up this book, whether they yearn to know more about you and Father God — or whether they are just curious. Open their hearts and minds as we share the truth about you! Then they can understand more about your amazing love and about your will for their lives.

I am writing to those who are seekers and even skeptics and doubters. I am writing to Christians who attend church, but wonder "Is there more to God than what I'm experiencing?" I am writing to those who will use this book to reach others for Jesus. And finally, I am writing to every friend who helped me during the seven years — from Stayton's diagnosis to his death. My thanks for being God's hands and feet and heart during that sad but rich time. I wouldn't have wanted to be anywhere else!

Father, help me to hear you and follow you. Only with your help are these behaviors – my Christian walk –possible: I hear when you are speaking to me. I clearly identify your unmistakable activity in my life. I believe you to be and do everything you have promised; I adjust my beliefs, character, and behavior to you and your ways; I recognize a direction you are taking in my life and identify what you want to do through my life; I clearly know what I need to do in response to your activity in my life; I experience you doing through me what only you, Father and Son, can do (all drawn from Blackaby p 8). *CGS*

CHAPTER 1 OUTLINE: WHO'S YOUR DADDY? WHAT IS GOD LIKE? AND CAN I REALLY KNOW HIM?

God says: I have loved you with an everlasting love. Therefore
I have continued my faithfulness to you. Jeremiah 31:3

Faith is the heroic effort of your life.
(Chambers May 8 classic version)

"Fill your mind with the thought that God is there . . . [Then] when
you experience difficulties it will be as easy as breathing
for you to remember, 'My heavenly Father knows all about this!' . . .
God is my Father, He loves me'" (Chambers July 16).

Introduction . . . Two Ships On A Horizon

1. There is one true God, real and alive right now, not just in heaven when we die. He is our Father. He gave us Jesus. He is Spirit. He wants to connect with us, heart to heart. We know about God because he tells us his true story in the Bible. And God's truth can set us free.

2. God invites us into a loving, personal relationship with him, through Jesus. So we can know God and Jesus up close and personal, heart to heart and face to face. Don't be content to just know about God or about Jesus – like someone who might have read all about your

mother but never met her, never talked to her, never embraced her, or even fussed with her.

- God is love
- God's love is perfected in us
- We love him because he first loved us.

3. God loves us and wants all to be saved.
4. Our God is praise-worthy. He is faithful, good, and righteous. And I have confidence in his character.
5. God is Creator. He's the potter. We are clay. He created and he is still creating today. Jer18:1-6
6. He is our God of hope
7. God is patient, steadfast, and encouraging.
   He is just and merciful. He is our God of peace.
8. God is my shepherd. He is my strength, fortress, savior. He is my shield, the power that saves me.
9. God is wise and powerful.
   And he is so much more!
10. God is enough and I can trust him completely, because of all he is and all he has said and all he has done. He is with me always. He will never leave me or forsake me. I do not fear.

WHO'S YOUR DADDY? WHAT IS GOD LIKE?
AND CAN I REALLY KNOW HIM?

God says: I have loved you with an everlasting love.
Therefore I have continued my faithfulness to you. Jeremiah 31:3

Faith is the heroic effort of your life.
(Chambers May 8 classic version)

Dear Father, help me to always fill my mind with the thought that
you are here with me, in good times and bad . . . [Then] it will be as
easy as breathing for me to remember: MY HEAVENLY FATHER
KNOWS ALL ABOUT THIS!' . . . GOD IS MY FATHER,
HE LOVES ME'" CGS (drawn from Chambers July 16).

INTRODUCTION:
TWO SHIPS ON THE HORIZON

Let's begin by asking who God is and what he's like. We understand God
in various ways, and we encounter him as Father, Son, and Holy Spirit.
So we'll talk about those roles, in a way we all can understand. But you
may be wondering why we need to do this at all. Why do we need a 1-2-3
or A-B-C discussion of God? And what does any of that have to do with
helping me if I am drowning *now*?

Let's look at it this way. Imagine you are bobbing in the ocean with
the tiniest of life jackets. You are alone, wet, hungry, and scared. Then,
on the horizon at quite a distance, two large boats appear from separate

directions. One is a vessel with a captain and crew dedicated to helping you. The second boat has pirates onboard, eager to enslave and/or kill you. Would it be useful to know the difference between these two ships? What if someone could tell you in advance which boat you should swim to? Who can you trust? Who will not only help you, but stay with you in difficult times? Isn't that information you would want and need? Well, that's why we are covering the basics here of who God is and what he is like — because one of those "boats" is God!

Am I promising that God will always deliver you from your trial or difficulty? Jesus doesn't say that, and neither do I. But God does promise that he will be with you during your tough times and offer you love, wisdom, and comfort that are unparalleled in this world. In fact, God promises many things to those who follow him. And I'm going to highlight one promise early on that I want you to burn into your brain and say out loud — IF I SEEK GOD, I WILL FIND HIM! Scripture is ripe with this promise, including 2 Chronicles 28:9, Psalm 24:3–6; Leviticus 26:12 (and cited later in 2 Cor 6:14–7:1; and James 4:8–10). So, let's move on and learn more about God and what a relationship with him means to you and to me.

THERE IS ONE TRUE GOD: REAL, ALIVE, AND ACTIVE NOW, NOT JUST IN HEAVEN WHEN WE DIE

God is our Father. He gave us Jesus. He is Spirit. He wants to connect with us, heart to heart. We know about God because he tells us his true story in the Bible, which is my guide for how to relate to God and how to live my life. God offers life-giving water now and into eternity, unlike a mirage in the desert that promises drinks for the thirsty but only delivers mouthfuls of sand. (Thank you, nine-year old Conner Andrus for that visual.)

In the many years before Christ, God patiently revealed his nature to the prophets and other characters of the Old Testament. "The Jews were the primary vehicle through which God chose to reveal himself to the world . . . [But] slowly, as the scriptures were written and compiled, the character and love of God were being revealed for the whole of mankind, not just the Jewish people" (Horrobin 71).

Twice in the Spring of 2015, I heard speakers say that the Bible is not about us. It is about God, not us. I understand what they were trying to get at, in the sense that all of life is about God. But God wrote this book, through men, to teach us about him and about his plan for us. He is the Supreme Being, and we are his creation. So of course, the Bible is about him, but he *and* the Bible are also about us.

GOD INVITES US INTO A LOVING, PERSONAL RELATIONSHIP WITH HIM, THROUGH JESUS. SO WE CAN KNOW GOD AND JESUS UP CLOSE AND PERSONAL , HEART TO HEART AND FACE TO FACE

Taste and see that the Lord is good. Ps 34:8

[15] All who declare that Jesus is the Son of God have God living in them, and they live in God. [16] We know how much God loves us, and we have put our trust in his love. 1 John 4:15–16 NLT

Don't be content to just know *about* God or *about* Jesus, like someone who might have read all about your mother but never met her, never talked to her, never embraced her, never even fussed with her. "Knowing God is a matter of personal involvement — mind, will, and feeling. It would not, indeed, be a fully personal relationship otherwise. To get to know another person, you have to commit yourself to his company and interests, and be ready to identify yourself with his concerns. Without this, your relationship with him can only be superficial and flavorless" (Stanley 2000). And it is the same with God.

God is love.
Both the Old and New Testaments are full of God's love for us, and his efforts to bring our hearts "'home'" to him. This was one of Jesus' major themes, as he pointed us always to the Father and his great love for us. And in case we miss the point, Psalm 136 repeats this phrase twenty-six times: "His steadfast love endures forever." Remember, relationship with God — the love between us — is the basic element, the pivotal word of our faith (as we said in the Introduction). God loves us as sons and

daughters, even before we know or love him. He gave us Jesus, his Son, to show us the way to the Father and his ways (1 John 4:8, 16). But God's love is a phenomenon we can barely fathom from a human perspective.

God is patient and keeps his eye on the long game, so he doesn't withdraw his love every time we make a mistake or disappoint him. Still, loving us doesn't mean God gives us everything we want or ask for. No wise father would do that. In Hebrews 12:10 and elsewhere, scripture tells us that God will use circumstances and consequences to teach, correct, discipline, and direct us, when we need it. That is because he cares about us, is committed to us, and wants us to grow.

And God's love is perfected in us (1 Jn 2:5 and 4:7–21).
Here, "John speaks of love being brought progressively to its full god-like character in us, as the gospel continues its ongoing transformative work through God's abiding presence with us" (ESV-GTB Notes). This love is not something we imagine or create. It is the work of the Spirit within (Romans 5:5). Like a wide-open faucet, God's love flows to us and through us, as we yield to the Spirit and abide in his love. The more it flows, the more we experience God's love!

We love him because he first loved us. 1 Jn 4:19
I engage whole-heartedly in a loving, personal relationship with God, which is his desire and will. Not because I am afraid of him, but because I am so very grateful for his love! "My love is a thankful and joyous response to the love which has already embraced us and provided for us by the sacrifice of his Son. The gospel is indeed news of great comfort and joy" (ESV-GTB Notes).

More verses about God's love.
I trust in the steadfast love of God for ever and ever. Ps 52:8
God sees us as his children. Isa 45:11
Who shall separate us from the love of Christ? . . . I am sure that neither death nor life, nor angels nor rulers, not things present nor things to come, nor powers, nor height nor depth, nor anything else in all creation, will be able to separate us from the love of God in Christ Jesus our Lord. Rom 8:35–39

For more on love – God's and ours – see Introduction and every single chapter in this book!

Jesus was the first to continually refer to God as our "Father". And perhaps the best-known scripture passage is John 3:16 KJV: For God so loved the world, that he gave his only begotten Son, that whosoever believeth in him should not perish, but have everlasting life.

Jesus says: As the Father has loved me, so have I loved you; abide in my love. If you keep my commandments, you will abide in my love [or make yourself at home MSG], just as I have kept my Father's commandments and abide in his love. Jn 15:9–10

Jesus says: The Father himself loves you, because you have loved me and have believed that I came from God. Jn 16:27 NRSV

Jesus says: O Jerusalem, Jerusalem, the city that kills the prophets and stones those who are sent to it! How often would I have gathered your children together as a hen gathers her brood under her wings, and you would not! Luke 13:34 Mt 23:37

Jesus says: Surely I am with you always, to the very end of the age. Mt 28:20b NIV (affirming God's promise: "Never will I leave [or fail] you; never will I forsake you." in Deut 4:30–31; 31: 6, 8; Josh 1:5; and repeated in Heb 13:5)

Jesus says: [speaking in John's vision] Behold, I stand at the door and knock; if any one hears my voice and opens the door, I will come in to him and eat with him, and he with me. Rev 3:20

And Jesus' "lost and found" parables (Lk 15) show us that God takes the initiative in seeking the lost (That's us before we accept Jesus!)

GOD LOVES US AND WANTS ALL TO BE SAVED

The Lord is not slow about His promise . . . but is patient toward you, not wishing for any to perish but for all to come to repentance. 2 Peter 3:9 NASB

God takes no pleasure in the deaths of the wicked, but wants them to turn back from their wicked ways and live. Ezek 33:11

Repeatedly in the Bible, God demonstrates his love for us and calls us to him, even when we have failed him. And he takes no pleasure in the spiritual death of anyone, urging us to "turn and live" (Ezek 18:23–32 and 33:11). Of course, there are those who ignore this verse, saying that in the beginning of time, God picked all the winners and losers in the "who gets saved" sweepstakes. But I am convinced otherwise. Yes, God *knows* from the beginning what will happen, but that is not the same as picking winners and losers before the race even begins. Likewise, a few verses in the Bible seem to imply that God can withdraw his love or not love one of us in the first place. Again, that's not how I see it! Here are some more examples of God's love and how invested he is in our lives:

God says: [15] "Can a mother forget the baby at her breast and have no compassion on the child she has borne? Though she may forget, I will not forget you! [16] See, I have engraved you on the palms of my hands; your walls are ever before me. Is 49:15-16 NIV

God says . . . Return, faithless Israel, declares the LORD. I will not look on you in anger for I am merciful . . . I will not be angry forever. Only acknowledge your guilt, that you rebelled against the LORD your God . . . You have not obeyed my voice . . . Return, O faithless children . . . And I will give you shepherds after my own heart, who will feed you with knowledge and understanding. Jer 3:12–15 ESV

God says: [33] For this is the covenant that I will make with the house of Israel after those days, declares the Lord: I will put my law within them, and I will write it on their hearts. And I will be their God, and they shall be my people. [34] And no longer shall each one teach his neighbor and each his brother, saying, 'Know the Lord', for they shall all know me, from the least of them to the greatest, declares the Lord. For I will forgive their iniquity, and I will remember their sin no more. Jer 31:33–34

God says: [25] I will sprinkle clean water on you, and you shall be clean from all your uncleannesses, and from all your idols I will cleanse you. (citing Jer 33:8) [26] And I will give you a new heart (see Ezek 11:19,20), and a new spirit I will put within you. And I will remove the heart of stone from your flesh and give you a heart of flesh (see Ezek 11:19-20). [27] And I will put my Spirit within you, and cause you to walk in my statutes and be careful to obey my rules. Ezek 36:25–27 (and see Ezek 37:24,27)

Ezekiel 33:11 God takes no pleasure in the death of the wicked, but wants them to turn back from their wicked ways and live!

Zeph 3:17 . . . he will renew you in his love; he will exult over you with loud singing.

Rom 5:6–10 . . . [8] God shows his love for us in that while we were yet sinners, Christ died for us . . . [10 AMP] If while we were enemies we were reconciled to God through the death of His Son, it is much more [certain], now that we are reconciled, that we shall be saved (daily delivered from sin's dominion) through His [resurrection] life.

God says I will live in them . . . (Going further than he did in the Old Testament, where he promised to live among his people.

2 Cor 6:16. Also see Ex 29:45-46; Lev 26:11-12; Jer 31:1

OUR GOD IS PRAISE-WORTHY. HE IS FAITHFUL, GOOD, AND RIGHTEOUS, AND I HAVE CONFIDENCE IN HIS CHARACTER

The LORD reigns, let the earth rejoice . . . Righteousness
and justice are the foundation of his throne. Ps 97:1–2

[33] I will sing to the Lord as long as I live [Ps 63:4]. I will sing
praise to my God while I have being. [34] May my meditation be
pleasing to him, for I rejoice in the Lord. Ps 104: 33-34 ESV

In fact, God has so many amazing qualities that I've had to alphabetize many of them just for this section! And he shares these qualities with us, his children. God has good thoughts and plans for each of us, and when I trust in this, I can reject crippling fear and embrace courage! God is my Shepherd, my Father, and so much more. He is with me, now and always. But he is not, repeat not, my fairy godmother or Santa Claus! And contrary to some, "he is not a mean, smiting guy!" (my grandson Jacob's phrase, June 2012). Instead, God gets down to our level, through Jesus, and then pulls us up toward his level (Jacob again).

God is wise, all-knowing, and all powerful, here and now! He has no equal. He is the source, and he shares his wisdom and his power with us. He gives us strength and can make us *all* overcomers! God doesn't want us to worry about tomorrow, but to do our best —combined with his best — and count on him always.

Charles Spurgeon says, "There are some who get a wrong idea of Him [God the Father] . . . They imagine that love dwelt in Christ, rather than in the Father, and that our Salvation is rather due to the Son and the Holy Spirit, than to our Father God . . . [But] the Truth of God is that we are as much indebted to the Father as to Jesus or the Holy Spirit. He truly loves us as much and is as worthy of our highest praise as either the Son or the Holy Spirit" (Spurgeon 1860). Certainly, that's how Jesus felt, and he said often that everything flowed from God the Father to him, and on to us. In fact, Jesus says, "Apart from God I can do nothing. I can do nothing for the kingdom by myself." John 5:19

Isa 40:12–31 NLT [12] Who else has held the oceans in his hand? Who has measured off the heavens with his fingers? . . . [18] To whom can you compare God? . . . [28] Have you never heard? Have you never understood? The LORD is the everlasting God, the Creator of all the earth. He never grows weak or weary. No one can measure the depths of his understanding. [29] He gives power to the weak and strength to the powerless. [30] Even youths will become weak and tired, and young men will fall in exhaustion. [31] But those who trust in the LORD will find new strength. They will soar high on wings like eagles. They will run and not grow weary. They will walk and not faint.

Ps 11:7 For the LORD is righteous; he loves righteous deeds; the upright shall behold his face.

Ps 34:8 Oh taste and see that the LORD is good.

Ps 71:19 Your righteousness, O God, reaches the high heavens. You have done great things. [Ps 126:2; 1 Sam 12:24; Lk 1:49]

Ps 36:5-6 Your steadfast love, O LORD, extends to the heavens, your faithfulness to the clouds.

Ps 57:10 Your steadfast love is great to the heavens, your faithfulness to the clouds.

Ps 100:5 NIV For the LORD is good. His steadfast love endures forever, his faithfulness continues through all generations.

Ps 106:1 Praise the LORD! Oh give thanks to the LORD for he is good.

Ps 145:9 NKJV The Lord is good to all, And His tender mercies are over all His works.

1 Cor 1:9 NIV God is faithful [Deut 7:9; Isa 49:7; 1 Cor 10:13; 1 Thess 5:24; 2 Thess 3:3; 2 Tim 2:13; Heb 10:23; 11:11] who has called you [Rom 8:28] into fellowship with his Son, Jesus Christ our Lord·

1 Cor 10:13 No temptation has overtaken you that is not common to man. God is faithful, and he will not let you be tempted beyond your ability [Dan 3:17; See 2 Pet 2:9] . . . But with the temptation he will also provide the way of escape, that you may be able to endure it.

GOD IS CREATOR. HE'S THE POTTER. WE ARE CLAY. HE CREATED AND HE IS STILL CREATING TODAY JER 18:1-6

> . . .Trust your lives to the God who created you,
> for he will never fail you. 1 Peter 4:19 NLT

> [24] O Lord, what a variety of things you have made!
> In wisdom you have made them all. The earth is full of your crea-
> tures . . . [27] They all depend on you to give them food as they need
> it. [28] When you supply it, they gather it. You open your hand to feed
> them, and they are richly satisfied. [29] But if you turn away from
> them, they panic. When you take away their breath, they die and
> turn again to dust. [30] When you give them your breath, [or when you
> send forth your Spirit - ESV] life is created, and you renew the face
> of the earth. Ps 104:24-30 NLT

We can see God in all things. He made everything and everyone special. And I must remain in God's hands, the potter's hands, to be effective. Then he can continue to mold me and use me as he chooses. God originally saw us as companions, but somewhere along the line, many of us forgot that. If you are looking for the perfect soul mate, look to God (see Ps 139). Friends and counselors, best friends and spouses can be wonderful, and even life-giving, at times. We need those dear people and are blessed by them, for sure. But no one on this Earth can supply what God can. We can rely on God and we can talk to him about anything — the big things, the great things, the little things, and even the desperate things!

The big picture of the creation story — that God created and he is still creating today — relates, of course, to another big picture: the biblical story of our redemption, and our reconciliation with our Father God. "First Adam, and later Israel, were placed in God's sanctuary (the garden and the Promised Land, respectively), but both failed to be a faithful, obedient steward, and both were expelled from the sanctuary God had created for them. But Jesus Christ, the second Adam, the son of Abraham, the son of David, was faithful and obedient to God. Though the world killed him, God raised him to life, which meant that death was defeated. Through his Spirit, God pours into sinners the resurrection life of his Son, creating a new humanity 'in Christ'. Those who are 'in Christ' move through death into new life and exaltation in God's sanctuary, there to enjoy his presence forever" (ESV Study Bible notes on The Bookends of Biblical Theology located in Rev 21 notes).
For more on our creator, see Genesis 1 and 2.

HE IS OUR GOD OF HOPE

In our everyday language, we use the word "hope" a lot. "I hope it won't rain this afternoon." "I hope we can get to the movie before it's sold out." But in the Bible, the word "hope" means "more than a vague wish that something will happen. It is a sure and confident expectation in God's future faithfulness and presence. The horizon of Christian hope extends beyond death into an eternity prepared by God himself, the reality of which is guaranteed by Jesus Christ . . . [It is] a confident expectation for the future, describing both the act of hoping and the object hoped for . . . A total grounding of one's confidence and expectation in God's goodness and providential care even in the face of trouble. And when grounded in God, hope provides the motivation to live the Christian life even in the face of trouble" (Manser 1999).

Ps 33: 17–19 NLT [17] Don't count on your warhorse to give you victory — for all its strength, it cannot save you. [18] But the Lord watches over those who fear him

[^AMP^ who revere and worship Him with awe], those who rely on his unfailing love . . . ²⁰ We put our hope in the Lord. He is our help and our shield.

Rom 5:5 AMP Such hope never disappoints or deludes or shames us, for God's love has been poured out in our hearts through the Holy Spirit Who has been given to us.

Rom 15:13 NIV Now may the God of hope fill you with all joy and peace as you trust in him, so that you may overflow with hope by the power of the Holy Spirit.

1 Peter 1:3-7 NLT ³ All praise to God, the Father of our Lord Jesus Christ. It is by his great mercy that we have been born again [^ESV^ to a living hope], because God raised Jesus Christ from the dead. Now we live with great expectation, ⁴ and we have a priceless inheritance—an inheritance that is kept in heaven for you, pure and undefiled, beyond the reach of change and decay. ⁵ And through your faith, God is protecting you by his power until you receive this salvation, which is ready to be revealed on the last day for all to see. ⁶ So be truly glad. There is wonderful joy ahead, even though you must endure many trials for a little while. ⁷ These trials will show that your faith is genuine. It is being tested as fire tests and purifies gold—though your faith is far more precious than mere gold. So when your faith remains strong through many trials, it will bring you much praise and glory and honor on the day when Jesus Christ is revealed to the whole world.

For more on hope, see chapters 3-4, 7-8, 11 and 12.

GOD IS PATIENT, STEADFAST, AND ENCOURAGING. HE IS JUST AND MERCIFUL. HE IS OUR GOD OF PEACE.

Ps 145:9; Rom 9:14; 2 Chron 19:7
Rom 15:5–6 NKJV ⁵ Now may the God of patience and comfort grant you . . . ⁶ that you may with one mind and one mouth glorify the God and Father of our Lord Jesus Christ.
1 Cor 1:8 Jesus will sustain me to the end.

God and peace are absolutely linked throughout Scripture!

Rom 16:20 [20] The God of peace will soon crush Satan under your feet. [Gen 3:15; [Luke 10:17–19; Rev 12:11]

1 Cor. 14:33 For God is not a God of confusion but of peace.

2 Cor 13:11 . . . Aim for restoration [Luke 6:40], comfort one another, agree with one another [Rom 12:16], live in peace [Mk 9:50]; and the God of love and peace will be with you.

1 Thess 5:23–24 NLT [23] Now may the God of peace make you holy in every way, and may your whole spirit and soul and body be kept blameless until our Lord Jesus Christ comes again. [24] God will make this happen [Phil 1:6], for he who calls you is faithful. [1Cor 1:9]

For more on mercy, see chapters 7, 8, 10 and 12.

For more on patience, see Introduction and chapters 3, 4, 6, 9, 11 and 12.

For more on peace, see Introduction and chapters 2-7, 10 and 12.

GOD IS MY SHEPHERD
GOD IS MY STRENGTH, FORTRESS, AND SAVIOR.
HE IS MY SHIELD, THE POWER THAT SAVES ME.

Ps 23 . . . [1] The LORD is my shepherd; I shall not want . . .

Ezek 34:30–31 [30] And they shall know that I am the LORD their God with them, and that they, the house of Israel, are my people, declares the Lord GOD. [31] And you are my sheep, human sheep of my pasture, and I am your God, declares the Lord GOD."

God says . . . Ezek 34:11–16 NIV . . . I myself will tend my sheep and have them lie down, declares the Sovereign LORD. I will search for the lost and bring back the strays. I will bind up the injured and strengthen the weak, but the sleek and the strong I will destroy. I will shepherd the flock with justice.

Jesus says, I am the good shepherd. The good shepherd lays down his life for the sheep. Jn 10:11

God says: I am your shield. Gen 15:1

And we say: You, O Lord, are a shield for me, my glory, and the lifter of my head (Ps 3:3). See also Ps 84:11; Ps 119:114

Ps 18:1-2 NLT [1] I love you, lord; you are my strength. [2] the lord is my rock, my fortress, and my savior; My God is my rock, in whom I find protection. He is my shield . . . See also Heb 2:13. Ps 68:19–20; Ps 79:9

Isa 41:10 ESV Fear not, for I am with you; be not dismayed, for I am your God; I will strengthen you, I will help you, I will uphold you with my righteous right hand.

For more on our shepherd, see chapters 2, 7, 10 and 12. And additional scripture pages for ch 1, 7, 12

For more on strength, see chapters 2-10. And additional scripture pages.

GOD IS WISE AND POWERFUL

Christ is the power of God and the wisdom of God . . God has united you with Christ Jesus. For our benefit God made him to be wisdom itself. Christ made us right with God; he made us pure and holy, and he freed us from sin. 1 Cor 1:24, 30 NLT

Ps 18:2 NLT [1] [The Lord is] the power that saves me, And my place of safety. See also Heb 2:13. Ps 68:19–20; Ps 79:9

Eph 1:17–23 NLT [Pray] [17] asking God, the glorious Father of our Lord Jesus Christ, to give you spiritual wisdom and insight so that you might grow in your knowledge of God. [18] I pray that your hearts will be flooded with light so that you can understand the confident hope he has given to those he called — his holy people who are his rich and glorious inheritance.

[19] . . . understand the incredible greatness of God's power for us who believe him. This is the same mighty power [20] that raised Christ from the dead and seated him in the place of honor at God's right hand in the heavenly realms. [21] Now he is far above any ruler or authority or power or leader or anything else—not only in this world but also in the world to come. [22] God has put all things under the authority of Christ and has made him head over all things for the benefit of the church. [23] And the church is his body; it is made full and complete by Christ, who fills all things everywhere with himself. (see more on this passage in the Additional Scriptures pages at the very end of the book.

Col 1:9–12 [9]. . . [May you] be filled with the knowledge of his will in all spiritual wisdom and understanding, [10] so as to walk in a manner worthy of the Lord, fully pleasing to him, bearing fruit in every good work and increasing in the knowledge of God. [11] May you be strengthened with all power, according to his glorious might, for all endurance and patience with joy, [12] giving thanks to the Father, who has qualified you to share in the inheritance of the saints in light.
For more on wisdom, see Introduction and chapters 2-7 and 12.
For more on power, see chapters 2-8 and 10-12.

GOD IS ENOUGH AND I CAN TRUST HIM
COMPLETELY, BECAUSE OF ALL HE IS

Some trust in chariots and some in horses,
But we trust in the name of the Lord our God. Ps 20:7 NIV

My health may fail, and my spirit may grow weak, but God remains
the strength of my heart; he is mine forever. Ps 73:26 NLT

Author Madeleine L'Engle described her husband of forty years and his experience with a terrible, and ultimately fatal, bout with cancer. And I understand her perfectly. L'Engle's faith was not in a Santa Claus or ice cream and pony kind of God. Her God — and mine — is the one true God, who is with us in good times and bad. Having experienced my husband's own terrible illness, I agree with her 100 percent. Here's what she writes:

"I hear different people tell of some good or lucky event and then say, 'Surely the Lord was with me'. And my hackles rise. My husband is desperately ill, so where is the Lord? What about that place of excrement? Isn't that where Love's mansion is pitched? Isn't that where God is? Doesn't such an attitude trivialize the activities and concerns of the Maker? Doesn't it imply that God is with us only during the good and fortuitous times and withdraws or abandons us when things go wrong?

"I will have nothing to do with a God who cares only occasionally. I need a God who is with us always, everywhere, in the deepest depths as well as the highest heights. It is when things go wrong, when the good things do not happen, when our prayers seem to have been lost, that God is most present" (L'Engle 1988, 24). Amen, sister!

Our temptation as humans is to trust in ourselves,
in our own strength and in our own understanding. It's how we were trained as children. And there is nothing wrong with being responsible. But God is very clear on this: We need to trust and rely on him alone. And we can be safe in doing so because we know his character. We know who he is and what he's like! Henry Blackaby sums it up beautifully: "I agree that God is absolutely trustworthy. I agree to follow God one day at a time, even when he doesn't spell out all the details. I agree that I will let him be my way" (Blackaby, 12).

James 4:6 AMP says that God gives us more and more grace (power of the Holy Spirit, to meet an evil tendency and all others fully). So, when you need more, you will have more. This is easy to say, of course, but harder to internalize. Personally, I've had plenty of experience relying heavily on my own understanding and intellect, often failing to ask God (the ultimate intellect) what he wanted. And I've reached for crutches of all sorts to continue my solitary struggles. In all these things, I am fully human and flawed. But if I let it go at that, if I don't mend my ways and learn to fully trust God, am I really building my faith, believing and following him? And if I don't fully grasp the love and grace God showers me with to accomplish this major feat, aren't I selling him short?

"The goodness of God assures us that he will not forsake us utterly, and that he will give me strength to bear whatever evil he has permitted to happen to me. Therefore I resolve to fear nothing" (Brother Lawrence, 24). And Scripture reminds us that our Heavenly Father has grafted us into his family through our faith in Jesus Christ, and that Jesus himself pursues a relationship with us so we could come to know and trust him. Without God, "Trust is a risk. We never learn whether someone is worthy of our trust unless we risk walking with him, and that's what God invites us to do" (Rothschild, 17).

Scripture is emphatic that God is enough and I can trust him completely. He is with me always. He will never leave me or forsake me. So I do not fear.

Jesus says: [9] . . . You have one Father, and he is in heaven. [10] . . . one Teacher, the Christ [the Messiah]. Mt 23:9–10

2 Chron 20:15b,17b . . . Fear not, the battle is not yours but God's.

Joshua 1:6–9 NRSV . . . Be strong and courageous; do not be frightened or dismayed, for the LORD your God is with you wherever you go.

Ps 46 A very present help in trouble

Ps 54:4 My helper . . . the upholder of my life

Ps 55:22 Cast your burden on the Lord and he will sustain you.

Ps 56:3–13 NLT [3] But when I am afraid, I will put my trust in you. [4] I praise God for what he has promised. I trust in God, so why should I be afraid? What can mere mortals do to me? . . .

Ps 62:1–2 For God alone my soul waits in silence; from him comes my salvation . . . my hope. He only is my rock and my salvation, my fortress . . . Trust in him at all times . . . (idea again in v 5–6)

Rom 8:31–32 If God is for us, who can be against us? He who did not spare his own Son but gave him up for us all, how will he not also with him graciously give us all things.

Eph 3:20 . . . [20] I trust God, who is able to do immeasurably more than all we ask or imagine, according to his power that is at work within us.

2 Cor 12:7–10 . . . God's grace is sufficient for me.

2 Tim 1:7 God did not give us a spirit of timidity but a spirit of power and love and self-control.

1 Jn 4:4b KJV (one of my favorites of all time) . . . Greater is he that is in you, than he that is in the world.

For more on: He is with me and will never leave me, see Chap 2, 7, 9, 12

To sum it all up: God is intimate, loving and yet bigger than we can imagine – all at once!

When I met Jesus for the first time, *he* knew that I needed a Father rather than a creator. I needed a comforter, a shepherd, and a brother. So that's how he came to me — or I came to him — or both. And he majored in *love*, which I sorely needed. He knew just how to approach me so that I would finally understand and love him, head over heels. And in one short moment, after years of searching and puzzling, I was completely his!

Later, studying Isaiah 40 (Feb 2011), I realized that I'd unconsciously scaled back my picture of God in the beginning, because I needed a loving Father more than I needed a cosmic giant. And I could see that God had it all well in hand. Now, if you love God (or even if you don't), you probably understand that God is *much* bigger than anything we can grasp or even imagine. I've known that in a big picture kind of way, but in 2011, as I read and pondered Isaiah 40, it struck me as never before. Things that we think are huge — mountain ranges, terrorist plots, people exploiting the helpless, disease, a sunrise, or a lost job — can all fit in the palm of God's hand. And as we know from Isaiah 49:16, God loves me – and you – so much that [16 AMP] he has indelibly imprinted (tattooed a picture of) us on the palm of each of his hands.

Jesus, you know I'm not alone in needing love, comfort, guidance, consolation, and more. It's the human condition. So when you came from your dizzying heights to walk with me, *that* is when I fell in love with you and with our Dad!

Father, when I studied Isaiah 40, I experienced a marvelous rush when I contemplated all the ways you are bigger than and vastly superior to anything or anyone we might compare you to. I've taken a tiny peek under the great tent you cast across the universe, and I am changed forever. Has it taken me a while? Yes, but that's OK. Now, I have an intimate relationship with the up close and personal God I fell in love with *and* the stunningly incomparable God of the universe. It's astonishing that you love me and comfort and guide me, all the while presiding over the whole of creation. Thank you, God, for all of this today and every day! CGS

PRAYER AND MEDITATION FOR CHAPTER 1

CHAPTER 2 OUTLINE: JESUS IS THE CENTER OF GOD'S PLAN FOR US AND FOR OUR WORLD

Jesus, the Son of God, is the way, the truth,
and the life. And he is a loving and
powerful combination: God and Man!

1. Since God wants us all to be saved and takes no pleasure in a person's spiritual death, he sent Jesus to live and die for us. Jesus was — and is — God's rescue plan for us! Through Jesus, God offers forgiveness and reconciliation to a hurting world. But he gives us a choice. Once we say 'yes', we are accepted immediately into God's family. And the adventure begins.
    *   Remember, God takes no pleasure in any person's spiritual death
    *   Early Christians knew that Jesus was (and is) life-giving and life-saving.
2. A quick definition of sin
3. There is a wide red ribbon weaving through the Bible pointing to a Savior, a Messiah, a Lord to come: Jesus.
4. Jesus is the Christ, the Messiah, the Son of God born to a virgin.
    *   Jesus was created by God in the body of a human.
    *   Jesus' public ministry began when he was "baptized" by the Holy Spirit as he came up from the waters of John's baptism of repentance.
    *   Jesus is Messiah.
5. I believe God and I believe in God. And I accept and believe that Jesus is who he says he is: the Son of God, the Messiah, my Lord, and my Savior.

- Remember, God always invites us to live and walk with him. And he sent Jesus to show us how – to BELIEVE, DO, and BECOME.
- We believe that people deceive themselves and you when they say that all we must do is believe.

6. To serve God, I must follow him, and that means turning to and following Jesus. Jesus is my model.
    STEP 1: Repent and believe in the gospel.
    STEP 2: Deny yourself and follow me.
    STEP 3: Jesus says, "If you love me, keep my commandments." Jn 4: 15. This includes honoring the law and teachings of the Old Testament.
    STEP 4: Keep focused on Jesus, as he guides us.

8. Jesus spoke from his heart on the night before he was crucified (John 17). It's an excellent summary, in own words, of what he purposed and did in partnership with his heavenly Father, the one true God.

9. And finally, God permitted Jesus to be crucified, die, and be buried. On the third day, he was resurrected. He appeared to his disciples and to others before ascending to heaven to be with God. By his resurrection, Jesus conquered death and hell. He lived and died for me, and I want to do the same for him.

10. Jesus and the Kingdom of Heaven/Kingdom of God.
    - Jesus talks about the Kingdom from the beginning of his ministry.
    - The Kingdom of God is the message of Jesus.
    - What, Where, and When? is the Kingdom of Heaven?
    - As a believer, I live in the Kingdom of God now.
    - The Kingdom of God is not the kingdom of niceness and it is not the kingdom of safeness.
    - The Kingdom of God and Satan.

CHAPTER 2

JESUS IS THE CENTER OF GOD'S PLAN
FOR US AND FOR OUR WORLD

All the ends of the earth shall see
the salvation of our God. Isa 52:10 RSV

[24] Christ is God's ultimate miracle and wisdom all wrapped up
in one . . . [30] Everything that we have — right thinking and right
living, a clean slate and a fresh start — comes from God
by way of Jesus Christ. 1 Cor 1:24, 30 MSG

Jesus, the Son of God, says he is the way, the truth, and the life. And
no one comes to the Father except through him (Jn 14:6 NKJV). So,
what's he like? And what is he to me? If we look back over all of God's
characteristics — loving, powerful, wise, and with us always — we'll see
who Jesus is, too! So what's the difference? Just that Jesus actually walked
on this Earth as a man for more than thirty years, feeling and hearing
and touching the same things we do. So he is a loving and powerful
combination: God and Man!

**SINCE GOD WANTS US *ALL* TO BE SAVED,
HE SENT JESUS TO LIVE AND DIE FOR US.
JESUS WAS — AND IS — GOD'S RESCUE PLAN FOR US**

Remember, God takes no pleasure in any person's spiritual death.
(Ezek 18:23, 31-32; 33:11 and 2 Pet 3:9). That is why the Father sent Jesus
to die on the cross as a sacrifice to pay for your sins and mine. Through
Jesus, God offers forgiveness and reconciliation to a hurting world. So
Jesus is the Savior, making it possible for us to be forgiven and reunited
with God. In this way, God achieves what human beings cannot achieve
by themselves: forgiveness of rebellious sin against God and restoration
to a reconciled relationship with God. But God gives us a choice!

If we accept and choose life (Deut 30:15, 19–20 and Jn 14:6), Jesus
will show us how to live day by day, starting now! Once we say yes to
God, we are accepted immediately into his family. We don't have to earn
a bunch of brownie points to get into heaven. We're there because of
God's goodness, not ours. Then Jesus teaches us exactly how to build
a solid relationship with him and the Father. And God's Holy Spirit,
sent by the Father and living in us, brings God's awesome power to help
make us the people God intends us to be.

Early Christians knew that Jesus was (and is) life-giving and life-saving.
"Jesus and his early associates overwhelmed the ancient world because
they brought into it a stream of life at its deepest, along with the best
information possible on the most important matters. These were matters with which the human mind had already been seriously struggling
for a millennium or more without much success. [So] the early message
of Jesus was not experienced as something its hearers had to believe or
do because otherwise something bad would happen to them. *The people
initially impacted by that early message generally concluded that they would be
fools to disregard it. That was the basis of their conversion.*

"Sadly, too many of us today don't see Jesus as life-giving and life-
saving. Too many Christians and non-Christians today see Jesus' teachings as mere suggestions, rather than essential. And gradually, the
Christian faith plays a smaller and smaller role in individual character

development and overall personal sanity and well-being. Yet, individual Christians still hear Jesus call them, saying, 'Whoever hears these words of mine and does them is like those intelligent people who build their houses upon rock, standing firm against every pressure of life.' Mt 7:24–25)

"But wouldn't it be glorious and life-giving if we understood the gospel immediately and so well that we answered Jesus: 'Yes, I will do what you say! I will find out how I will devote my life to you, Jesus! This is the best life strategy I ever heard of! Thank you. Thank you!' And then we would race off to churches, fellowships, teachers, and into our daily lives, to learn how to live in his kingdom as Jesus indicated was best" (drawn from Willard xiv, xvi).

A QUICK DEFINITION OF SIN

Before I met Jesus in a real way, the word "'sin" made me feel uncomfortable. It sounded old fashioned and churchy (although I don't remember it being mentioned much in the church where I grew up). But I've learned some things along the way and benefitted from some very wise people. So let me share a few definitions that helped me.

I now describe sin as turning my back on God. Imagine a road going in two directions, as roads have a way of doing. Now picture God at one end of the road, and Satan and sin at the other end. You can't go in both directions, can you? So you must pick a direction and head there. Sin is turning your back on God, either deliberately or unconsciously, and heading in the opposite direction. And when we do that habitually and without growing or changing, then I say that we are no longer just turning our back on God. We're turning our back on God, dropping our pants, and mooning him!

My favorite definition of sin comes, not surprisingly, from Oswald Chambers, who calls sin "red-handed mutiny against God" (Chambers June 23). He also says, "One of the penalties of sin is our acceptance of it. Sin establishes itself in the sinner and takes its toll. You gradually get used to it, until you finally come to the place where you no longer even realize that it is sin. The deadliest attitude that we exhibit today is that which comes from unconsciously living this lie" (Chambers Mar 16). And to that, I say, *Ouch!*

From the beginning of mankind, we have sinned and rebelled against God. But long before Jesus was born, God was concerned about our sin and wanted to save us and forgive us.

"In Jesus, God brings his long-standing, redemptive work through-out the ages to a culmination by sending his eternal Son (Mk 1:11; Heb 1:1). The grace that he has been working out through the ages comes to a decisive climax with Christ. In this way God achieves what human be-ings cannot achieve by themselves: forgiveness of rebellious sin against God and restoration to a reconciled relationship with God

. . . No matter how accomplished or how broken a human being's life might look from a human perspective, from God's perspective the effect of the fall on human beings is so profound that it cannot be redressed by human effort. In God's holy love and righteousness, he relentlessly pursues human beings to reconcile them with himself through Jesus' life and atonement. Being placed into a God-given, righ-teous, and lasting relationship with him lies at the heart of God's love and grace" (ESV GTB notes).

THERE IS A WIDE RED RIBBON WEAVING THROUGH THE BIBLE, POINTING TO A SAVIOR, A MESSIAH, A LORD TO COME. THAT IS JESUS.

"The redemption component of biblical history begins unfolding long before the crucifixion narrative in the Gospels. And even though Jesus' name isn't mentioned until the New Testament, the Bible reveals the dawning light of redemption near the very beginning. Immediately after Adam's and Eve's sin, God says to the one who tempted them, 'I will put enmity between you and the woman, and between your offspring and her offspring; he shall bruise your head, and you shall bruise his heel' (Gen 3:15). Bible scholars refer to this verse as the 'first gospel'. It is God's first promise to redeem his world and people — broken by Adam's sin — by the divine provision of One who would come through a human source to defeat Satan while also suffering an awful attack from him.

"This early verse in Genesis sets the stage for all that follows in the Bible. The rest of human history will be played out on this stage. Thus, every piece of Scripture that follows has a redemptive context . . . Jesus is the chief and culminating figure on this stage. The stage is set for him; all that transpires on the stage relates to him; and we do not fully understand anything on the stage until we have identified its relation to him. Now, it should be emphasized that placing every text in its redemptive context does not mean that every text mentions Jesus. Rather, every text relates some aspect of God's redeeming grace that finds its fullest expression in Christ. . . . [Then we see] how God's Word predicts, prepares for, reflects, or results from the person and/or work of Christ" (ESV-GTB Notes in introduction).

JESUS IS THE CHRIST, THE MESSIAH, THE SON OF GOD, BORN TO A VIRGIN.

Jesus was created by God in the body of a human.
Angels appeared to Mary and Joseph to announce God's plan (Mt 1:18–25, Lk 1:26–38). The angel even told them the baby's name, Jesus (Mt 1:21, Lk 1:31). When Jesus was just a baby, God showed Simeon and Anna the prophetess that he was the Messiah, a fulfillment of prophecy (Lk 2:25–35, 36–38).

Jesus' Spirit and character are God's, so he is the Son of God. He is completely human and completely God. Don't worry about how to understand this. We aren't God so we'll never completely "get" it! Just accept that Jesus is like us and like God. He is the only perfect man who has ever lived.

Jesus' public ministry began when he was "baptized" by the Holy Spirit as he came up from the waters of John's baptism of repentance.
Mt 3:16–17 Mk 11:9–11 Lk 3:21–22
Then he was full of the Holy Spirit and led by him. Lk 4:1

Jesus is Messiah.
Scripture tells us there will be many false prophets, but only Jesus is the Messiah, the Son of God.

Jesus says: Beware of false prophets, who come to you dressed as sheep, but inside they are devouring wolves. Mt 7:15 AMP (using imagery from Ezek 22:27)

Jesus says: Don't let anyone mislead you, because many will come in my name, claiming to be the Messiah. They will lead many astray. Mk 13:5-6 NLT   Lk 21:8 Mt 24:5, 11

Jesus says: I assure you, until heaven and earth disappear, even the smallest detail of God's law will remain until its purpose is achieved. So if you break the smallest commandment and teach others to do the same, you will be the least in the Kingdom of Heaven. But anyone who obeys God's laws and teaches them will be great in the Kingdom of Heaven. Mt 5:18–19 NLT

Jesus says: I tell you the truth, the man who does not enter the sheep pen by the gate, but climbs in by some other way, is a thief and a robber. The man who enters by the gate is the shepherd of his sheep . . . I am the gate for the sheep . . . The thief comes only to steal and kill and destroy; I have come that they may have life, and have it to the full. Jn 10:1–2, 7–10 NIV

Col 2:8 NIV See to it that no one takes you captive through hollow and deceptive philosophy, which depends on human tradition and the basic principles of this world rather than on Christ.

2 Pet 2:1–3 NIV . . . there will be false teachers among you. They will secretly introduce destructive heresies, even denying the sovereign Lord who bought them — bringing swift destruction on themselves.

I BELIEVE – AND BELIEVE *IN* – GOD. AND I ACCEPT
AND BELIEVE THAT JESUS IS WHO HE SAYS HE IS.

> I was unrighteous . . . but when I accepted Jesus as Lord and Savior, I
> was washed, sanctified, and justified in the name of Jesus and in the
> Spirit of God. 1 Cor 6:11

This statement – I believe God and *in* God – is not just an intellectual assent. It is my full-bodied surrender. People talk a lot about "accepting Jesus", and that's a good thing. But let's be clear: "accepting" is not quite the same as "fully partaking". Consider a party invitation as a simple example. You receive the invitation and call the host to say you accept and will be at the party. Maybe you even tell other people you'll be there. But there's another decision that comes *after* you say "Yes". You must actually go to the party. Otherwise, you have given lip service to the host and others, but you have not followed through in any meaningful way. Now, for us, the very good news is that even if we haven't yet gone to the Jesus "party", we can still make that choice. God is yearning for us to come, and he will never give up on us! A very personal thing, but something to consider in your own heart, yes?

Jesus has a lot to say about who he actually is.
Jesus says: I AM THE RESURRECTION AND THE LIFE. He who believes in Me, though he may die, he shall live. And whoever lives and believes in Me shall never die. Jn 11:25–26 NKJV
Jesus says: Believe in God, believe also in me . . . I am in the Father and the Father in me. Jn 14:1, 11 (and earlier in Jn 10:38)
Jesus says: I AM THE WAY AND THE TRUTH AND THE LIFE. No one comes to the Father except through me. If you really knew me, you would know my Father as well. From now on, you do know him and have seen him. Jn 14:6–7 NIV
Jesus says (over and over): I AM THE LIGHT OF THE WORLD; he who follows me will not walk in darkness but will have the light of life. Jn 8:12 and repeated in Jn 9:5 and 12:46. See also Jn 1:4–9 and 3:19–21
   [And then he said] You are the light of the world . . . Let your light shine before others, so that they may see your good works and give glory to your Father who is in heaven. Mt 5:14, 16 (reflecting the imagery of Isa 60:1–3)
Jesus says: I AM THE GOOD SHEPHERD. The good shepherd lays down his life for the sheep . . . I know my own sheep, and they know me . . . I have other sheep, too, that are not in this sheepfold. I must bring them also . . . and there will be one flock with one shepherd. Jn 10:11–16 NLT (reflecting the imagery of God as all-powerful, and yet still shepherd in Isa 40:10–11 and Ezek 34:11–16, 30–31)
Jesus says: The bread of God is he who comes down from heaven, and gives life to the world. . . . I AM THE BREAD OF LIFE; whoever comes to me shall not hunger, and whoever believes in me shall never thirst . . .

I am the living bread that came down from heaven. If anyone eats of this bread, he will live forever . . . Jn 6:33, 35, 51 (reminiscent of Isa 55:2)

Jesus says: If you knew the generosity of God and who I am, you would be asking me for a drink, and I would give you FRESH, LIVING WATER . . . Anyone who drinks the water I give will never thirst — not ever. The water I give will be an artesian spring within, gushing fountains of endless life. Jn 4:10-14 MSG (building on Isa 12:3)

Jesus says: I AND THE FATHER ARE ONE. Jn 10:30

Jesus says: I AM THE DOOR; if anyone enters through Me, he will be saved, and will go in and out and find pasture. Jn 10:9 NASB

Jesus says: Nothing will be impossible for you. Mt 17:20–21 Also in Lk 17:6; Mk 11:22–23 Mt 21:20–22

Remember, God is always inviting us to live and walk with him.

Jesus is the way to the Father. So Christianity is about a heart-to-heart relationship between us and God through Jesus, not just a list of do's and don'ts. Our relationship has three key elements: BELIEVE and DO and BECOME. First, Jesus says, "Believe in God. Believe also in me" (Jn 14:1). This belief is the doorway to our new life with God. But we can't stop there. We go on to become who God intends us to be and to do what Jesus tells us to do. "If you love me, you will obey what I command." (Jn 14:15 NIV) So we each can choose to accept or reject God's invitation, Jesus. We each decide to say yes or no.

People deceive themselves (and you) when they say that all we must do is believe. And we are to let no one deceive us in the faith (Rom 16:17-19 and Eph 5:6-11).

Jesus says very clearly that after we accept him, God expects us to participate with him as he continually works in us, on us, through us, and around us. Any less and you miss the wonderful banquet God has set out for you! We try to do what Jesus tells us to do — not to get a ticket to heaven, but because we love him and are so grateful for his love and presence in our lives. He rescued us from the terrible gulf that separated us from the Father. Why wouldn't we want to follow him and do what he says? We'll talk about this more later, OK?

More good news: Jesus isn't simply giving us high standards. He's giving us much divine help to do what we need to do (see Mt 11:28-30). Fortunately, Jesus promises to love and help every step.

Jesus' commandments have their roots in the Old Testament, the Holy Scriptures which he took seriously.

Jesus says, I have not come to destroy, but to explain, make relevant, and complete the law and the prophets. Basically, there is no change to be made in the law of God until everything is finished in accordance with God's plan. Mt 5:17–18 WMF

So we got the basics from Moses, and then this exuberant giving and receiving, this endless knowing and understanding, all came through Jesus, the Messiah. Jn 1:17 MSG.

Instead of destroying the law, Jesus asks us to look at the heart of the law, at God's intentions for our lives, not just at the letter of the law, and man's interpretations over the centuries. In fact, he warns that our hearts will be far from God if we are legalistic and teach as doctrines the commands of men. Mt 15:3, 8–9 AMP; Mk 7:6–9 (reflecting Isa 29:13)

Some say that Jesus is only an historical figure, with no relevance today. Not so! He is alive today, active in your life (if you'll let him), speaking to you in your language, in your land. Jesus loves you. And he wants to bring you home to meet his Dad!

Sadly, many people try to make the Christian faith too complicated. We begin to think we need an advanced degree in theology to know God. We have long lists of questions and think we can't believe until every last question is answered. But nothing could be further from the truth. The good news of Jesus Christ is simple — read it for yourself! Then ask him into your heart. Once you decide to say yes to Jesus, the basic truths he taught will begin to make sense.

When you give yourself to the One who came to save you, you become a "new creation," and allow God's Holy Spirit to occupy your very core. He will be with you every day, loving you, directing your footsteps, answering your questions, picking you up when you fall, and giving you life everlasting, beginning now! With his help, you will discover true faith, leaning your entire personality on God in absolute trust and confidence in his power, wisdom, and goodness (Heb 4:2 AMP).

Life with God, through Jesus, can be richer than you can imagine.
When you lean on your faith in God, through Jesus, life will change. Some things will happen immediately while others are a longer process. Even so, Jesus is not a magic potion, and God is no divine genie, scurrying around to fulfill our every wish. There will be times when we face troubles and pain. Sometimes, God will pluck us out of harm's way. But even if he does not, we cannot be crushed by these troubles, because God is with us always. He will never leave us or forsake us, no matter how difficult the circumstance.

Even in those times when all seems lost and dark and hopeless, God is there for you. When I can remember to reach out, feel his love, and trust him, the circumstances may or may not change. But by determining to trust God, I reconnect with my Rock and I am instantly better. So either way, we should trust completely in God and his amazing grace. I love the Bible story in Daniel 3:16–18 about Shadrach, Meshach, and Abednego facing the fiery furnace. God is with us, they believed, "whether we are delivered from trouble or whether we are delivered in trouble" (Chambers, Aug 2).

Relying on God isn't easy, because it works against every ounce of self-sufficiency built into us from childhood. But it can happen if we take one small step, then another, day by day, the Jesus way! Then we are truly blessed: spiritually prosperous, with life-joy and satisfaction in God's favor and salvation, regardless of our outward conditions. Mt 5:9 AMP

TO SERVE GOD, I MUST FOLLOW HIM, AND THAT MEANS TURNING TO JESUS AND FOLLOWING HIM. JESUS IS MY MODEL

Jesus says: Whoever serves me must follow me . . . Jn 12:26

Imagine that you are on a trip to Texas, but you begin to see signs for Canada. What should you do? First, you must recognize your mistake. Then you must turn around and head back the right way. If you are tempted to turn back toward Canada — maybe because there was a wonderful diner on that stretch of road — you have to stay focused and remember that your goal is Texas.

It's the same in your spiritual life, and in mine. Ever since Adam, all of mankind has sinned and rebelled against God. My sin separates me from God. To reconnect, I must accept Jesus and his sacrifice for my sins. I must accept him as my Lord and Savior. I must repent: that is, renounce my sins, turn away from them, and ask God's forgiveness. Why is it set up like that? I don't know, because I am not the one who constructed this scenario. God is. So I can't explain it entirely. But I do know it's true, just like I don't have to understand the engineering and construction genius behind the Golden Gate Bridge to trust it and drive over the bridge.

"Today . . . so many people are devoted to causes and so few are devoted to Jesus Christ . . . Jesus Christ is deeply offensive to the educated minds of today, to those who only want him to be their Friend and who are unwilling to accept him in any other way. Our Lord's primary obedience was to the will of his Father, not to the needs of people. The saving of people was the natural outcome of his obedience to the Father" (Chambers June 19). *That* is our model!

STEP 1. Repent and believe in the Gospel.
Repenting is confessing or admitting to a particular sin, accepting personal responsibility for it, and then turning away from it completely. And what is sin? As we said earlier, sin is a heavy-sounding word, but its meaning is pretty clear. Sin is what we do when we rebel against God, when we turn our backs on him and what he wants us to do and be. In effect, when we say, "My way, not God's way." *That* is sin!

Jesus knew quite well that no one, righteous or otherwise, is perfect. We all need help of some sort, and Jesus provides the love and "doctoring" that can transform our hearts, minds, and souls. Repentance is our way of saying, "Doctor, I need your help." If we are to become more like Jesus, repentance is a key part of that process. And his ideas on repentance are perfectly consistent with one of my favorite Old Testament verses:

God says: If my people, who are called by my name, will humble themselves and pray and seek my face and turn from their wicked ways, then will I hear from heaven and will forgive their sin and will heal their land. 2 Chron 7:14 NIV

And we say: Cleanse me from my sin . . . for I know my transgressions . . . blot out my iniquities. Create in me a clean heart, O God. Ps 51:1–3, 9–10

Jesus says: [in his first words of public ministry] The kingdom of God is at hand; repent, and believe in the gospel. Mk 1:15 Mt 4:17 (affirming John the Baptist's earlier statements in Mt 3:2)

Jesus says: It is not the healthy who need a doctor, but the sick. I have not come to call the righteous, but sinners to repentance. Lk 5:31–32 NIV

So they [the disciples] went out and preached that men should repent. And they cast out many demons, and anointed with oil many that were sick and healed them. Mk 6:12–13 Mt 10:7 Lk 9:1–2

Jesus says: Unless you repent (change your mind for the better and heartily amend your ways, with abhorrence of your past sins), you will all likewise perish and be lost eternally. Lk 13:3,5 AMP.

And Jesus told a number of parables about repentance and God's forgiveness. Many of these are in Luke 15, often called the "lost and found" chapter. And in Luke 16:19–31, Jesus told a chilling parable about a man who repented late.

And Jesus says: [speaking in John's vision] Those whom I love, I reprove and discipline; therefore be zealous and repent. Rev 3:19 NASB

Hos 10:12 [12] Sow for yourselves righteousness; reap steadfast love; break up your fallow ground, for it is the time to seek the Lord, that he may come and rain righteousness upon you.

STEP 2. Deny yourself and follow God through Jesus.

Jesus says: If any man would come after me, let him deny himself and take up his cross daily and follow me. Lk 9:23–24 Mt 16:24 Mk 8:34. Also in Mt 10:38–39 and in Lk 14:27

Jesus says: Any of you who does not forsake — renounce, surrender claim to, give up, say 'good-bye' to — all that he has cannot be My disciple. Lk 14:33 AMP

Jesus says: Come to me, all who labor and are heavy-laden, and I will give you rest. Take my yoke upon you, and learn from me; for I am gentle and lowly in heart, and you will find rest for your souls. For my yoke is easy, and my burden is light. Mt 11:28–30 (expanding Jer 6:16)

Jesus says: Don't look for shortcuts to God. The market is flooded with sure-fire, easygoing formulas for a successful life that can be practiced in your spare time. Don't fall for that stuff . . . The way to life — to God! — is vigorous and requires total attention. Mt 7:13–14 MSG

STEP 3. Jesus says: If you love me, keep my commandments. Jn 4: 15 This includes honoring the law and the teachings of the Old Testament.

Jesus told Peter, "Do you love me? . . . Tend my sheep." (Jn 21:16)

Jesus says: Not every one who says to me, "Lord, Lord" shall enter the kingdom of heaven, but he who does the will of my Father who is in heaven. Mt 7:21 Lk 6:46

Jesus says: If you continue in my word, you are truly my disciples, and you will know the truth, and the truth will make you free . . . If the Son makes you free, you are free indeed. Jn 8:31–32, 36

Jesus says: You know these things — now do them! That is the path of blessing. Jn 13:17 NLT

Jesus says: [speaking in John's vision] Those whom I [dearly and tenderly] love, I tell their faults and convict and convince and reprove and chasten [I discipline and instruct them] . . . Rev 3:19 AMP [affirming Prov 3:12 and 12:1, and Heb 12:5–6]

Jesus says: He who has My commandments and keeps them is the one who loves Me; and he who loves Me will be loved by My Father, and I will love him and will disclose myself to him. Jn 14:21 NASB

Jesus says: As my Father has loved me, so have I loved you; abide in my love. If you keep my commandments, you will abide in my love, just as I have kept my Father's commandments and abide in his love. Jn 15:9–10

Jesus expanded and fulfilled the Ten Commandments

(given in Exodus 20:1–17 and in Deuteronomy 5:6–21).

Through Jesus, God fulfilled his promise to establish a new covenant with us, not writing laws on stone tablets, but writing them in our hearts and minds. [See 2 Cor 3:2–3; Heb 8:8–12, and their references to Jer 31:31–34.]

Jesus says: Don't think that I have come to destroy the law of Moses or the teaching of the prophets. I have not come to destroy them but to bring about what they said. I tell you the truth, nothing will disappear from the law until heaven and earth are gone. Not even the smallest letter or the smallest part of a letter will be lost until everything has happened. Whoever refuses to obey any command and teaches other people not to obey that command will be the least important in the kingdom of heaven. But whoever obeys the commands and teaches other people to obey them will be great in the kingdom of heaven. I tell you that if you are no more obedient than the teachers of the law and the Pharisees, you will never enter the kingdom of heaven. Mt 5:17–20 NCV (building on Deut 4:2 and 12:32)

Jesus says: It is the thought-life that defiles you. For from within, out of a person's heart, come evil thoughts, sexual immorality, theft, murder, adultery, greed, wickedness, deceit, eagerness for lustful pleasure, envy, slander, pride, and foolishness. All these vile things . . . are what defile you and make you unacceptable to God. Mk 7:20–23 NLT Mt 15:19

STEP 4. Keep your eyes on Jesus, as he guides you.
Know what he says, and follow every step!

Jesus spoke from the heart on the night before he was crucified – in John 17.
(I discuss John 17 more in chapters 4 and 11. And yes, I confess that I have developed a real passion for Jesus' final words before he died.)

There is great "nourishment we are given in Jesus' high priestly prayer – John 17 . . . The joy set before Jesus, as he prepared to endure the cross (Heb 12:2) included at least two things. Jesus longed to return to the Father, to enjoy the life he shared with him before the world was created. But Jesus also felt great joy in anticipation of redeeming and cherishing his international bride. He now delights in us and rejoices over us, as a bridegroom over his bride" (Isa 62:5; Heb 4:2 AMP) (ESV GTB notes).

Jesus says in excerpts from John 17: [1-3 AMP] . . . You have granted [your Son] power and authority over all flesh (all humankind), [now glorify Him] so that He may give eternal life to all whom You have given Him. And this is eternal life: [it means] to know (to perceive, recognize, become acquainted with, and understand) You, the only true and real God, and [likewise] to know Him, Jesus [as the] Christ (the Anointed One, the Messiah), Whom You have sent. . . . [6-8 NIV] I have revealed you to those whom you gave me out of the world. They were yours; you gave them to me and they have obeyed your word. Now they know that everything you have given me comes from you. For I gave them the words you gave me and they accepted them. They knew with certainty that I came from you, and they believed that you sent me. [Jn 8:26; 12:49; 15:15; and Jn 17:14]

[9-11 NIV] I pray for them . . . for those you have given me, for they are yours. All I have is yours, and all you have is mine. And glory has come to me through them . . . Holy Father, protect them by the power of your name, the name you gave me, so that they may be one as we are one . . .

[17-19 AMP] Sanctify them [purify, consecrate, separate them for Yourself, make them holy] by the Truth; Your Word is Truth. Just as You sent Me into the world, I also have sent them into the world. And so for their sake and on their behalf I sanctify (dedicate, consecrate) Myself, that they also may be sanctified (dedicated, consecrated, made holy) in the Truth . . .

THEN, JESUS WAS CRUCIFIED, DIED, WAS BURIED.
AND ON THE THIRD DAY HE WAS RESURRECTED.

After his resurrection, Jesus appeared to his disciples and to many others before ascending to heaven to be with God. By his resurrection, Jesus conquered death and hell. He lived and died for me and I want to do the same for him. All four Gospels – Matthew, Mark, Luke and John – have information on the life, death, and resurrection of Jesus.

Crucified and Died.
Mt 27:33-54, Mk 15:22-39, Lk 23:33-47, Jn 19:17-30

Buried on Friday, the evening that he died (Mt 27:57-61, Mk 15:42-47, Lk 23:50-56, Jn 19:38-42).

Resurrected —The empty tomb.
Mary Magdalene may have arrived first at the tomb (Jn 20:1–2) ahead of the other women (Lk 24:10).
The other women (Mk 16:1–8, Lk 24:1–10, Mt 28:1–8)
Peter and John at the tomb (Lk 24:12, Jn 20:3–10)

Appeared to the disciples and many others.
Mary Magdalene outside the tomb (Mk 16:9, Jn 20:11–17)
The other women, probably near Jerusalem (Mt 28:9–10)
Cleopas and his companion, on the road to Emmaus (Lk 24:13–32, Mk 16:12)
The disciples w/o Thomas (Mk 16:14, Lk 24:36–43, Jn 20:19–25)
The disciples, including Thomas a week later (Jn 20:26–29)
The disciples, fishing — perhaps several weeks later (Jn 21:1–23)
Disciples receive Great Commission (Mt 28:16–20, Mk 16:15–18,
Lk 24:44–49)
Various appearances over forty days (Jn 20:30-31; Acts 1:3

Ascended into Heaven to be with God.
Mk 16:19–20, Lk 24:50–53, Acts 1:6–11 And demonstrated again his (and our) authority over Satan. See chapter 8 for more.

By his resurrection, Jesus reconciled us to God.
God shows his love for us in that while we were still sinners, Christ died for us . . . We rejoice in God, through whom we now have received reconciliation. (See Rom 5:8–11 and elsewhere)

I love how John Stott explains Jesus' resurrection:
   "Resurrection is not the same as resuscitation. Those whom Jesus raised from death during his earthly ministry were resuscitated. They came back from death, resumed their former way of life, and then later died a second time. Resurrection, however, means the beginning of a new, a different, and immortal life. So our resurrected bodies, though retaining some kind of continuity with our present bodies, will also be changed. They will be as different, Paul says, as the plant is from the seed out of which it grows. They will be set free both from decay and from 'the flesh', the fallen nature

which in some sense belongs to them. They will also have new powers. In fact our resurrection body will be a 'body of glory', like Christ's" (Stott 1984, 400).

JESUS AND THE KINGDOM OF HEAVEN/
THE KINGDOM OF GOD

Jesus says: The kingdom of God is not coming with signs to be observed . . . [it] is in the midst of you. Lk 17:20–21

[13] [God the Father] has delivered us from the domain of darkness, and transferred us to the kingdom of his beloved Son, [14] in whom we have redemption, the forgiveness of sins. Col 1:13–14

The Kingdom of God is the message of Jesus.
Jesus talks about the Kingdom from the beginning of his ministry. [14] Now after John was arrested, Jesus came into Galilee, proclaiming the gospel of God, [15] and saying, 'The time is fulfilled, and the kingdom of God is at hand; Repent and believe in the gospel.' (in Mk 1:14–15)

So, is love the center of Jesus' message? Dr. Mark D Roberts says that, in fact, Jesus did talk quite a bit about love. But "If Jesus had been running around first-century Judea telling people to love each other, he certainly wouldn't have been crucified on a Roman cross. So what exactly was this inspiring, challenging, goading, and apparently subversive message of Jesus all about?

"The core of Jesus' message was the proclamation of the coming of the kingdom of God: The kingdom of God has come near. (Mk 1:14–15) The phrase "kingdom of God" appears 53 times in the New Testament Gospels, almost always on the lips of Jesus. The synonymous phrase, "kingdom of heaven," appears 32 times in the Gospel of Matthew . . . Many of his parables explain something about this kingdom: it is like mustard seed, a treasure, a merchant looking for pearls, and a king who gave a banquet (Mt 13:44–47; 22:2). Jesus even defines his purpose in light of the kingdom: I must proclaim the good news of the kingdom of God to the other cities also; for I was sent for this purpose (Lk 4:43)" (Roberts).

What? Where? and When is the Kingdom of Heaven?
"The kingdom of heaven is not the kingdom that exists in heaven, but the reign of God over both heaven and earth. It is coming now and in the future. It is here, yet it's relatively small and won't reach its full, glorious extent until later.

"Jesus proclaimed the kingdom of God as something present in his ministry and also as something that was still to come in greater fullness and glory. Thus, the kingdom is not either present or future, but both present *and* future . . . The phrase refers not so much to the place where God rules as to the presence and power of God's actual rule. When Jesus proclaims that the kingdom of God has come near, he means that God's own royal authority and power have come on the scene. So, we could paraphrase Mark 1:15, which summarizes Jesus' preaching, as follows: 'God's reign is at hand. God's power is being unleashed. Turn your life around and put your trust in this good news' " (Roberts).

The Kingdom of God is not the kingdom of niceness.
Tim Hansel says, quite rightly, that, "We are not called to mere piety but to genuine morality. We are called to action, not to fancy words. We are members of the kingdom of God, not the kingdom of niceness.

"As Christians we can become addicted to comfort and convenience, the good life, convinced it is somehow related to the truth of Scriptures. Deep down, we want to believe that if we're Christians, we should be good people and good things should happen to us . . . But that's not what Christ calls us to . . . The kingdom of God is a life-changing, life-transforming experience. It's more than just nice. Jesus, to the contrary, was shocking, astonishing, loving, daring, revolutionary, kind, caring, compassionate — but [hardly just] nice" (Hansel 41–42).

The Kingdom of God is not the kingdom of safeness.
Martin Bell, in his intriguing book *Way of the Wolf,* describes what an encounter with Christ must have been like: "To have experienced Christ, to have encountered Jesus of Nazareth, to have run headlong into the person of God in the flesh must have been like stepping into the path of a hurricane. No one would do it intentionally" (Bell, 43).

Along these same lines, Tim Hansel says, "The Bible doesn't give us much reason to believe that being saved is in any way to be equated with being safe. For instance, we often hear that Daniel's faith got him out of the lions' den, but we forget that it also got him into the lions' den. God doesn't promise us safety, but strength . . . So shouldn't we assume, from God's many promises of support, strength, courage and help, that we will meet our fair share of trouble? Jesus promises us at least four things — peace, power, purpose, and trouble. God doesn't promise a carefree life; he promises peace and joy in the midst of trouble (Jn 16:33)" (Hansel, 42).

And who wants to stir up and increase trouble at all turns? Satan and his team! "Despite their overthrow, the powers of darkness have not yet conceded their defeat; they continue to contest every inch of their territory. The kingdom of Satan retreats only as the kingdom of God advances" (Stott 2003).

Jesus says: Seek first God's Kingdom and his righteousness (Mt 6:33)

In the context of the Kingdom of God, Jesus speaks extensively on living a righteous life. Because righteousness isn't a common word these days, here are a few definitions you might find useful, from the Amplified Bible:

* God's way of doing and being right. Mt 6:33 AMP
* Conformity to the divine will in thought, purpose, and action. Rom 6:18 AMP
* What we ought to be, approved and acceptable and in right relationship with Him, by His goodness. 2 Cor 5:21 AMP
* Right standing with God and right doing. Phil 1:11 AMP
* Uprightness, freedom from sin, and right standing with God. 2 Pet 3:13 AMP
* The upright, just and godly living, deeds, and conduct, and right standing with God. Rev 19:8 AMP

This may sound like a tall order. But you aren't walking grim-faced and alone on this journey. You are moving through amazing fields and valleys of God's unconditional love. And you are never alone!

Jesus says: Blessed are those who hunger and thirst for righteousness, for they shall be satisfied. Mt 5:6
Jesus says: Blessed are the pure in heart, for they shall see God. Mt 5:8
Jesus says: Blessed are those who have been persecuted for the sake of righteousness, for theirs is the kingdom of heaven. Mt 5:10 NASB
Jesus says: Unless your righteousness exceeds that of the scribes and Pharisees, you will never enter the kingdom of heaven. Mt 5:20
Jesus says: Grow up. You're kingdom subjects. Now live like it. Live out your God-created identity. Live generously and graciously toward others, the way God lives toward you. Mt 5:48 MSG

Some say Jesus was just a great moral teacher, but C.S. Lewis says that's not an option. "A man who was merely a man and said the sort of things Jesus said would not be a great moral teacher. He would either be a lunatic — on the level with the man who says he is a poached egg — or else he would be the Devil of Hell. You must make your choice. Either this man was, and is, the Son of God, or else a madman or something worse. You can shut him up for a fool, you can spit at him and kill him as a demon or you can fall at his feet and call him Lord and God, but let us not come with any patronizing nonsense about his being a great human teacher. He has not left that open to us. He did not intend to . . . [Therefore] I have to accept the view that He was and is God" (Lewis 1952)

Jesus, help me to live every day praising, as the Doxology does, "Father, Son and Holy Ghost." I trust you to continually encourage the hearts of all your followers, and knit us together in love, to reach all the riches of full assurance of understanding and the know-ledge of your mystery (see Col 1:27), which is Jesus. Please help me remember daily that in you are hidden all the treasures of wisdom and knowledge. Col 2:2–3 [see also Isa 11:2; 45:3; 1 Cor 1:24, 30; 2:6, 7; Lk 11:49; Eph 1:8]

Thank you, Father, for sending Jesus to welcome me personally into your Kingdom. From the beginning, I recognized this as a gift I would never forget or take for granted. And, thank you, Jesus, for coming to me on October 21, 1993, and showing me your love. Help me live my life every single day as a testament to you and to your Spirit, who now resides in my heart and has since I said yes to you. *CGS*

PRAYER AND MEDITATION
FOR CHAPTER 2

CHAPTER 3 OUTLINE: WHEN I BECAME A BELIEVER, GOD EQUIPPED ME WITH THE HOLY SPIRIT, WHO LIVES IN ME

1. In many ways, the Holy Spirit comes from God the Father, as well as from Jesus.
2. The moment we accept Jesus as Lord and Savior, we become a new creation and receive the mind of Christ and his life
    *   The Holy Spirit lives in me, but also acts around, upon, with, and through me.
    *   He gives me everything I need to handle what's ahead.
3. God's Holy Spirit ministers to me. He teaches, guides, and comforts me. He is powerful, but I must continually surrender to Him.
4. If we walk with God, his Holy Spirit will equip and empower us.
    *   When I believe and do things God's way, I become who he wants me to become.
    *   And I have all the strength I need, if I continually surrender to him.
5. The Holy Spirit enriches me in every way, with speech, knowledge, and spiritual gifts. 1 Cor 1:5-7 So, walk daily with the Holy Spirit. Let him fill you up and enjoy the fruit of the spirit in your life.
    *   The Holy Spirit can *fill* all believers, if we follow Christ and continuously ask God's Spirit to take control of us.
    *   Gifts of the Spirit
    *   The Holy Spirit produces fruit in a believer's life

CHAPTER 3

WHEN I BECAME A BELIEVER, GOD EQUIPPED ME WITH THE HOLY SPIRIT, WHO LIVES IN ME

Jesus says: God is sheer being itself — Spirit. Those who worship him must do it out of their very being, their spirits, their true selves, in adoration. Jn 4:24 MSG

Jesus says: [speaking to his disciples on the night before he was arrested]: [15] If you love me, you will obey what I command. [16] and I will ask the Father, and he will give you another Counselor [or Comforter, Advocate, Helper] to be with you forever – [17] the Spirit of truth. The world cannot accept him, because it neither sees him nor knows him. But you know him, for he lives with you, and will be in you. [18] I will not leave you as orphans; I will come to you . . . Because I live, you also will live . . . Jn 14:15–24 NIV

AN OVERVIEW

Sincere Christians from various traditions may understand the Holy Spirit in different ways. That's fine. I'm giving you what I see as the basics here, the bedrock of understanding God's Spirit and what he can do in our lives. And if you stick to the basics, you won't go wrong.

Jesus told his followers to go out into the world, make new disciples, and baptize them in the name of the Father, Son, and Holy Spirit (Mt 18:19). So, new believers receive all of God: Father, Son, and Holy Spirit. That's Jesus' model, and so it is ours as well. Beyond that, there is plenty of room in God's family for honest and loving discussion. But don't be drawn into extended debates or disputes about the Holy Spirit, for that would surely grieve God. Just follow Jesus and ask God daily to fill up more and more of your heart. Ask: "More of you, God, and less of me." If you accept Jesus and follow him, God's Spirit is in you. How you understand that, and how it shows in your life, is between you and God! And don't let anyone tell you differently.

God – Father, Son, and Holy Spirit – continually encourages, guides, teaches, and disciplines us, as we seek his kingdom and his righteousness. There are plenty of spiritual "hugs", but also stern words when we need them. In fact, "If you have never heard the Master say a hard word, I question whether you have heard him say anything" (Chambers Aug 17).

THE HOLY SPIRIT COMES FROM
GOD THE FATHER AND FROM JESUS

"The Holy Spirit is God himself, as he works in the world and our hearts, and as he comes to dwell within us" (Billy Graham).

"The Bible teaches that when we come to Christ, God the Holy Spirit has already been at work in our hearts and lives (Jn 6:44). And when we come to Christ, God the Holy Spirit comes to dwell within us. In other words, if you know Christ, the Holy Spirit already lives within you. But that does not mean he is in control of your life or mine. What we need to do is commit our lives to Christ afresh each day — not so he will save us (for he has already done that and continues to), but so that the Holy Spirit will rule our hearts and draw us closer to God. You do not need to beg for him to come to live within you — but you do need to daily yield your life to him and ask him to guide you. You may not always feel his presence when you do this — but he is still with you!" (Graham 1997). So embrace all that God has for you!

In one of his many remarkable sermons, Charles H. Spurgeon addressed the Special Thanksgiving we owe to God the Father. "God the Spirit comes from God the Father . . . He sends forth the Spirit. And the Spirit is often the instrument with which the Father works . . .

- "It is the Father who says to the dry bones, 'Live' (Ezek 37:5). It is the Spirit who, going forth with the Divine Word, makes them live.
- "It is true that the seal on our hearts is the Holy Spirit. He is the seal, but it is the Eternal Father's hand that stamps the seal. The Father communicates the Spirit to seal our adoption.
- "The works of the Spirit are, many of them . . . attributed to the Father, because He works in, through, and by the Spirit" (Spurgeon 1860).

Here is more scripture on the Holy Spirit:

Jn 15:26 But when the Helper comes, whom I will send to you from the Father, the Spirit of truth, who proceeds from the Father, he will bear witness about me.

Rom 8:15 [15] For you did not receive the spirit of slavery to fall back into fear, but you have received the Spirit of adoption as sons, by whom we cry, "Abba! Father!"

Eph 1: 3,11–14, 30 [3] Blessed be the God and Father of our Lord Jesus Christ . . . [11] In him we have obtained an inheritance, having been predestined according to the purpose of him who works all things according to the counsel of his will, [12] so that we who were the first to hope in Christ might be to the praise of his glory.

[13] In him you also, when you heard the word of truth, the gospel of your salvation, and believed in him, were sealed with the promised Holy Spirit, [14] who is the guarantee of our inheritance until we acquire possession of it, to the praise of his glory . . . [30] And do not grieve the Holy Spirit of God, by whom you were sealed for the day of redemption.

THE MOMENT WE ACCEPT JESUS AS LORD AND SAVIOR, WE BECOME A NEW CREATION AND RECEIVE THE MIND OF CHRIST AND HIS LIFE

[12] But to all who believed him and accepted him, he gave the right to become children of God. [13] They are reborn — not with a physical birth resulting from human passion or plan, but a birth that comes from God. Jn 1:12–13 NLT

When Jesus and others describe the Holy Spirit living *within* all believers, it is God going further than he did in the Old Testament, where he promised to live *among* his people. [See also Ex 29:45–46; Lev 26:11–12; Jer 31:1; Ezek 37:27]

Jesus says: [5] I tell you the truth, unless you are born from water and the Spirit, you cannot enter God's kingdom. [6] Human life comes from human parents, but spiritual life comes from the Spirit. [7] Don't be surprised when I tell you, "You must all be born again." Jn 3:5–7 NCV. Here Jesus builds on Ezekiel 36:25–27, that God will first cleanse us with water and then put a new spirit and a new heart within us. (See 1 Peter 1:23– 2:2)

The Holy Spirit lives in me, but also acts around, upon, with, and through me.

The term "born again", used loosely by so many, causes mixed reactions among believers and nonbelievers alike. Even people with much information and study can see it different ways. Personally, I like how Oswald Chambers describes "born again" as "only when a man is willing to die to everything in his life, including his rights, his virtues, and his religion, and become willing to receive into himself a new life that he has never before experienced (Jn 3:4). This new life exhibits itself in our conscious repentance and through our unconscious holiness. My spiritual history must have as its underlying foundation a personal knowledge of Jesus Christ. To be born again means that I see Jesus" (Chambers Aug 15).

He gives me everything I need to handle what's ahead.

Mt 3:11 [Jesus] will baptize you with the Holy Spirit and with fire.

1 Cor 4:8 Already you are filled! Already you have become rich.

1 Cor 3:12 God gives us his Holy Spirit to help us understand these gifts that God has bestowed upon us.

Col 1:27; 3:11 Christ in you, the hope of glory . . . Christ is all, and in all.

1 Jn 2:20, 27 NLT . . . The Holy Spirit has come upon you, and all of you know the truth . . . He lives within you . . . the Spirit teaches you all things, and what he teaches is true — it is not a lie

1 Jn 4:4b KJV Greater is he that is in you, than he that is in the world.

GOD'S HOLY SPIRIT MINISTERS TO US HE COMFORTS US.
HE TEACHES, DIRECTS, AND OPENS OUR MINDS TO THE MIND OF CHRIST.

Jesus says: If any one thirsts, let him come to me and drink. Whoever believes in me, as the Scripture has said, 'Out of his heart shall flow rivers of living water.' Now this he said about the Spirit, whom those who believed in him were to receive; for as yet the Spirit had not yet been given, because Jesus was not yet glorified. Jn 7:37–39

Jesus says: [26] But the Helper will teach you everything and will cause you to remember all that I told you. This Helper is the Holy Spirit whom the Father will send in my name. Jn 14:26 NCV and in Lk 12:12

Jesus says: When the Spirit of truth comes, he will guide you into all truth; for he will not speak on his own authority, but whatever he hears, he will speak, and he will declare to you the things that are to come. He will glorify me, for he will take what is mine and declare it to you. Jn 16:13–15

And Scripture tells us even more about the Holy Spirit:

* Communicates, intercedes, counsels, guides, directs us. Jn 14:16–26; 16:13; Acts 8:29, 39; 10:19; Rom 8:26
* Sanctifies believers. Rom 15:16; 2 Thess 2:13
* Bears witness of Christ to believers. Jn 15:26; Acts 6:32; Rom 8:16; Heb 10:15
* Comforts believers. Jn 14:16–26
* Gives discernment to believers. 1 Cor 2:10-16; 1 Jn 4:1–6
* Interprets scripture, illuminates the mind. Jn 16:14; 1 Cor 2:12, 13; Eph 1:16, 17
* Instructor. Jn 14:20-21, 23–26
* Reveals the things of God. Isa 40:13, 14; 1 Cor 2:10, 13
* Tells what is yet to come. Jn 16:13; Acts 20:22–23; 21:11
* Spokesman. 1 Jn 2:20, 27

IF WE WALK WITH GOD, HIS HOLY
SPIRIT WILL EQUIP AND EMPOWER US

Father, we waste a lot of time and effort when we live without the power of
the Holy Spirit. He alone can give us the ability to live the holy and meaningful life we so desire (drawn from McDowell, 141). When I believe and
do things God's way, I become who he wants me to become. And I have all
the strength I need, if I continually surrender to him. (For more on this,
see Lk 10:19; Acts 1:8; 1 Cor 2:2–5) [In fact] "There is only one safeguard
[against the enemy] and that is to know Jesus as Savior and for him to be
Lord of your life. It is only through knowing him that the Holy Spirit can
flow through us in power. And it is only through the power of the Holy
Spirit that we have authority over the powers of darkness" (Horrobin 29).

Jesus says: Receive the Holy Spirit (Jn 20:22) . . . [and] You will receive power when the Holy Spirit has come upon you; and you will be my witnesses in
Jerusalem, in all Judea and Samaria, and to the ends of the earth. (Acts 1:8)
    Jesus considered the power of the Holy Spirit essential to the ministry he
was sending his disciples out to do. So important was this power that Jesus told
his disciples they had to wait for the Holy Spirit to come before they could start
their ministry. So "he ordered them not to leave Jerusalem, but to wait there for
the promise of the Father" (Acts 1:4), which was now the promise of the Father
and the promise of the Son. And with this power, Jesus told them to "make disciples of all nations, baptizing them in the name of the Father and of the Son
and of the Holy Spirit" (Mt 28:19).
    Now this is the same Spirit that dwelled in Christ (Rom 8:9), the Spirit of
the Father (Mt 10:20). And this Spirit was to come upon his followers and be
the source of all power in working and witnessing.

[After his resurrection:]
Jesus says: Behold, I am sending forth the promise of My Father upon you
[meaning the Holy Spirit]; but you are to stay in the city until you are clothed
with power from on high. Lk 24:49 NASB
Jesus says: John baptized with water, but not many days from now, you shall be
baptized with (placed in, introduced into) the Holy Spirit. Acts 1:5 AMP . . .

You shall receive power when the Holy Spirit has come upon you; and you shall be my witnesses in Jerusalem and in all Judea and Samaria and to the end of the earth. Acts 1:8

Paul beautifully sums up what God's Holy Spirit can do.
Eph 1:17–19 [We pray] [17] that the God of our Lord Jesus Christ, the Father of glory, may give you the Spirit of wisdom and of revelation in the knowledge of him, [18] having the eyes of your hearts enlightened, that you may know what is the hope to which he has called you, what are the riches of his glorious inheritance in the saints, [19] and what is the immeasurable greatness of his power toward us who believe, according to the working of his great might . . .
Eph 3:14–16 NLT [14] When I think of all this, I fall to my knees and pray to the Father, [15] the Creator of everything in heaven and on earth. [16] I pray that from his glorious, unlimited resources he will empower you with inner strength through his Spirit . . . (see also Mic 3:8)

THE HOLY SPIRIT ENRICHES ME IN EVERY WAY, WITH SPEECH, KNOWLEDGE, AND SPIRITUAL GIFTS. WALK DAILY WITH THE HOLY SPIRIT. LET HIM FILL YOU UP AND ENJOY THE FRUIT OF THE SPIRIT IN YOUR LIFE.

Jesus says: If you then, though you are evil, know how to give good gifts to your children, how much more will your Father in heaven give the Holy Spirit to those who ask him! Lk 11:13 NIV   Mt 7:9–11

[8] For you were once darkness, but now you are light in the Lord. Live as children of light [9] (for the fruit of the light consists in all goodness, righteousness and truth) [10] and find out what pleases the Lord. Eph 5:8–10 NIV

The Holy Spirit can *fill* all believers, if we follow Christ and continuously ask God's Spirit to take control of us.
Jesus was clear about this. And Ephesians 5:18 says, Be filled with the Spirit. The Greek word (*plērousthe*) does not describe a onetime "filling" but a regular pattern of life. So the believer's question is not, "Do I have the Holy Spirit in me?" Ask instead, "Am I willing to surrender to

the Holy Spirit? Will I keep him shut in a small room, or will I continually surrender and give him free run of the house (my heart), to do with
me what he will?"

When we are filled with the Spirit, cooperating with God's ways, we
go from darkness to light. It's a choice we make, and then must renew
daily as we walk with God. Some Christians call this being "baptized" in
the Holy Spirit, and some do not. But don't be distracted by semantics.
If you are John Taylor, and some people call you John, and other people
call you Taylor, they are both correct. Just be glad they call you!

Other Scripture references to being filled with the Spirit:
Exod 31:3; Micah 3:8; Lk 1:15, 41, 67; Acts 2:4; Acts 4:8, 31; Acts 9:17; Acts 13:9,
52;

Gifts of the Spirit.
The gifts described in Scripture are precious and they are a means to
an end. They help us become more Christ-like, fulfill God's plans, and
produce the fruit of the Spirit in us.

1 Cor 12:4-11 NLT [4] There are different kinds of spiritual gifts, but the same
Spirit is the source of them all. [5] There are different kinds of service, but we
serve the same Lord. [6] God works in different ways, but it is the same God who
does the work in all of us. [7] A spiritual gift is given to each of us so we can help
each other. [8] To one person the Spirit gives the ability to give wise advice; to
another the same Spirit gives a message of special knowledge. [9] The same Spirit
gives great faith to another, and to someone else the one Spirit gives the gift
of healing. [10] He gives one person the power to perform miracles, and another
the ability to prophesy. He gives someone else the ability to discern whether a
message is from the Spirit of God or from another spirit. Still another person
is given the ability to speak in unknown languages, while another is given the
ability to interpret what is being said. [11] It is the one and only Spirit who distrib-
utes all these gifts. He alone decides which gift each person should have. 1 Cor
12:4-11 NLT [See also Eph 4:7; 1 Cor 14:26; Rom 12:3].

The Holy Spirit produces fruit in a believer's life.
These are: Love, joy, peace, patience, kindness, goodness, faithfulness, gentleness, and self-control (Gal 5:22–23 NASB).

Here's how it works: We accept Jesus, and the Holy Spirit comes to live in us. We surrender our lives to his guidance, comfort, and teaching. And then we see the results — the fruit — begin in our lives. This fruit of the Spirit is the true evidence of the Holy Spirit's work within a believer. It's the result of living God's way, not ours.

1 Cor 2:10–16 taught by the Spirit . . . we have the mind of Christ.
Eph 1:17–21 NIV . . . the Spirit of wisdom and revelation . . . the hope to which he has called you, the riches of his glorious inheritance in the saints, and his incomparably great power for us who believe.
And Jesus says we are not to turn our back on the Spirit:
There's nothing done or said that can't be forgiven. But if you deliberately persist in your slanders against God's Spirit . . . severing by your own perversity all connection with the One who forgives. Mt 12:31–32 MSG [and in Mk 3:28–29, and Lk 12:10]

Holy Spirit, when you begin to build strengths in our lives, we may be shy about walking in them. That explains why I, for instance, might lean on the strengths I had earlier in my life, and feel comfortable in my feelings of self-sufficiency and familiarity. It takes determination to walk in the new ways and the new strength. But it is well worth the effort, because teaming up with you is a win-win all around! Thank you for loving and living in me – and for being so very patient! *CGS*

PRAYER AND MEDITATION FOR CHAPTER 3

CHAPTER 4 OUTLINE: ONENESS WITH GOD IS LIVING HEART TO HEART WITH HIM AND BECOMING HIS OBEDIENT DISCIPLE THROUGH JESUS.

> Jesus says: If you continue in my word, you are truly my disciples,
> and you will know the truth, and the truth will make you free . . .
> So if the Son makes you free, you will be free indeed. Jn 8:31–36

> Through the incarnation, the divine and the human became
> one. Jesus Christ's claim is that he can manifest his own
> life in any man if he will cooperate with him . . . The goal
> of human life is to be one with God, and in Jesus Christ
> we see what that oneness means. (Chambers 1947)

God asks us to love him for all he is, with all we have and all we are! But "loving" God isn't just some sweet romantic phrase. It's an action verb! So if we truly love God, we will follow him and be his disciple through Jesus. Then we can have oneness with him — Father, Son, and Holy Spirit. That is God's plan.

1. I now understand that God has loved me from my very beginning. So I love him for all he is: our one and only God, loving, fully divine. He is with me as God the Father; God the Son, Jesus; and God's Holy Spirit. And I love him with all I have and with all I am. (Mk 12:28–34, citing Deut 6:4–6 and elsewhere)
2. Loving God means following him and becoming his disciple/his apprentice, through Jesus, day by day. If I truly love, I will obey him.

- Whose disciple are you? Who taught and teaches you?
- Jesus intends that we will follow him so closely that if he stops walking, we bump into his back. Now that's a disciple.
- Obedience to God is very different from the obedience that the world insists on at work, at home, in the military, or even in a slave camp.

3. Oneness – living heart to heart with God – is abiding with — living with — making your home with God. And it is a lifelong process. It's the amazing opportunity God offers to us, through Jesus: his life, his death, and his resurrection.
   - Oneness is God's Great Design.
   - We are one with God in direct proportion to the extent we have allowed the Holy Spirit to have his way with us.
   - Oneness with God affects and is affected by every facet of our spiritual life, including prayer, obedience, and peace with God.
   - Scripture tells us about the Oneness we as believers can have with God the Father, Jesus Christ the Son, and with God's Holy Spirit (with reference to Jn 17).

4. Oneness: The Vine and the Branch
   - Oneness is completeness in Christ, with his life in me.
   - Christian "Fusion"

CHAPTER 4

ONENESS WITH GOD IS LIVING HEART TO HEART WITH HIM AND BECOMING HIS OBEDIENT DISCIPLE THROUGH JESUS.

Jesus says: If you continue in my word, you are truly my disciples, and you will know the truth, and the truth will make you free . . . So if the Son makes you free, you will be free indeed. Jn 8:31–36

Through the incarnation, the divine and the human became one. Jesus Christ's claim is that he can manifest his own life in any man if he will cooperate with him . . . The goal of human life is to be one with God, and in Jesus Christ we see what that oneness means. (Chambers 1947)

[16] I pray that from his glorious, unlimited resources he will empower you with inner strength through his Spirit. [17] Then Christ will make his home in your hearts as you trust in him. Your roots will grow down into God's love and keep you strong. [18]And may you have the power to understand, as all God's people should, how wide, how long, how high, and how deep his love is. [19] May you experience the love of Christ, though it is too great to understand fully . . . [and] be made complete with all the fullness of life and power that comes from God. Eph 3:16–19 NLT

Loving God isn't just some sweet romantic phrase.
It's an action verb! And if I truly love God, I will follow him and be his disciple through Jesus. Then I can have oneness with him: Father, Son, and Holy Spirit. That is God's plan.

One year after I met Jesus, God began giving me songs (music and lyrics). Most of them came to me in their entirety, and definitely *not* from any real musical background. One song told how I'd found God, after years of searching. The lyrics will tell you a lot about me!

> I went searching for God with my head and my mind. And that was a good start. God gave me a good mind and I used it to search. And that was a good start. But once I'd thought and explored and probed all I could, I was no closer to Him. It did me no good. Cause I'd left out my heart — that key unlocks all doors. And without heart, we fail to know God as he is: the true love and the light. WE NEED HEART, NOT JUST HEAD. So just close your eyes, take a deep breath, and reach out. He'll take your hand and guide you. You'll know Him at last. And your life will be sweet with our God in your heart. What a life you will have! What a life, with the Lord. CGS

Of course I often wish I had come to God earlier, but I've found great sweetness and purpose from the way I did meet him. So I have no regrets, except to encourage you to open your heart and embrace him much sooner than I did.

Dallas Willard is an author I enthusiastically recommend! He doesn't dumb things down, but he is so honest and discerning that you will be richly rewarded by everything he says!. He writes, "Discipleship to Jesus is the very heart of the gospel. And the really good news for humanity is that Jesus is now taking students in the master class of life. The eternal life that begins with confidence in Jesus is a life in his present kingdom, now on earth and available to all. So the message of and about him is specifically a gospel for our life now, not just for dying. It is about living now as his apprentice in kingdom living, not just as a consumer of his merit" (Willard xvii). So, God invites us to get off of our comfy seats and follow him: Father, Son, and Holy Spirit. What do you and I say to that?

I LOVE GOD FOR ALL HE IS. AND I WILL LOVE HIM WITH MY HEART, SOUL, MIND AND STRENGTH. MK 12:30 LK 10:27 MT 22:37 DEUT 6:5

God is our one and only God, loving, fully divine, and with me always. I know and love him as:

* **Father.** God is our Father. And even the most wonderful earthly father is but a pale hint of what Father God is like. I love you always, Father. I bow down to your throne and I reach up to your arms.
* **Son.** God gave us Jesus, our brother, our model, our Savior, our Lord. The Father is the Source of Jesus (1 Cor 1:30). God's love for us was the foundation for all of Jesus' life and ministry, which brings us eternal life.
* **Holy Spirit.** God is Spirit, and his Holy Spirit lives in us as believers. So we are never apart from him.

Christians call this idea of Father, Son, and Holy Spirit the Trinity (three in one). But if you think you must understand the Trinity concept fully before you know God, please think again. In fact, if it seems confusing, just set it aside and don't let anyone drag you into the boggy marsh on it. Cherish Father, Son, and Holy Spirit — And move on! Then the God whom you grow to understand will fill in the blanks as needed.

Seek God always.
Both Old and New Testaments confirm this. We are to seek God with our heart, soul, mind, and strength. We follow him, and learn his ways:

Deut 4:29 . . . From there you will seek the LORD your God and you will find him, if you search after him with all your heart and with all your soul.
Ezek 11:19–20 [19] And I will give them one heart, and a new spirit I will put within them. I will remove the heart of stone from their flesh and give them a heart of flesh, [2 Cor 3:3] [20] that they may walk in my statutes and keep my rules

and obey them. And they shall be my people, and I will be their God [and this theme is repeated in many other places, including Ezek 36:26–27].

Jer 29:13–14 You will seek me and find me. When you seek me with all your heart, I will be found by you

2 Cor 3:2–3 . . . ³ And you show that you are a letter from Christ delivered by us, written not with ink but with the Spirit of the living God [Mt 16:16], not on tablets of stone [Ex 24:12] but on tablets of human hearts. [Prov 3:3; 7:3; Jer 17:1]

LOVING GOD MEANS FOLLOWING HIM AND BECOMING HIS DISCIPLE, THROUGH JESUS — AND IF I TRULY LOVE HIM, I WILL OBEY.

"Obedience is a conscious act of the will. Christians in conflict need a tough-minded holiness that is ready for action" (Raymer).

What do you look like when you are loving God with all your heart and soul and mind and strength? . . . "When you are teeming with love for the Lord your God, who are you right then? What is your passion? What are you bursting to do when your heart is flooded with divine affection? That's very likely the stream of your calling. Take a step and get your feet wet. You're supposed to look like the version of you that loves Jesus with every particle. That's the real you!" (Moore 2014, 145)

Whose disciple are you? Who taught — and teaches — you?
We like to think of ourselves as independent people, making up our own mind about things. But throughout our lives, we are all disciples of somebody or several somebodies, whether we know it or not. These people impact how we think, act, and feel, for better or for worse. Their input may be wise and helpful, or not! Either way, they shape us to some extent.

Our parents influence us. Then there are teachers, friends, the media, entertainment channels, pastors, and others. Nearly always they convey to us a strong impression of what life as a whole is all about. And as part of that, they can influence our behavior toward ourselves, others, and God — for good or for bad. "Thankfully, the process is an ongoing one, and to some extent self-correcting . . . And it is one of the major transitions of life to recognize who has taught us, mastered [discipled] us, and then to evaluate the results in us of their teaching. This is a harrowing task, and sometimes we just can't face it. But it can also open the door to choose other masters, possibly better masters, and one Master above all" (Willard 271–272).

Jesus desires – and intends – that we will follow him so closely that if he stops walking, we will bump into his back! *That* **is a disciple!**
"Jesus expected that his people would live their lives as his students and co-laborers . . . They would constantly seek to be in his presence and be guided, instructed, and helped by him in every aspect of their lives. For he is indeed the living head of the community of prayerful love across all time and space. Based on that assumption, his promise to his people was that he would be with them every moment, until this particular 'age' is over and the universe enters a new phase (Mt 28:20; Heb 13:5–6). And the provisions he made for his people during this period (in which we now live) are provisions made for those who are, precisely, apprentices to him in kingdom living" (Willard, 273).

"[But] anyone who is not a continual student [and follower] of Jesus [might] read the great promises of the Bible as if they were for him or her. But that's like someone trying to cash a check on another person's account. At best, it succeeds only sporadically.

"The effect of such continuous apprenticeship/ discipleship under Jesus would naturally be that we learn how to do everything we do 'in the name of the Lord Jesus' (Col 3:17 — that is, on his behalf or in his place, as if he were doing it . . . So, plainly, in the eyes of Jesus, there is no good reason for not doing what he said to do, for he only tells us to do what is best . . . Just try picturing yourself standing before him and explaining why you did not do what he said was best. Certainly we can count on his understanding. But it will not do as a long-term strategy. He has made a way for us into easy and happy obedience — really, into personal fulfillment" (Willard, 273).

Jesus says: If you continue in my word, you are truly my disciples, and you will know the truth, and the truth will make you free . . .
So if the Son makes you free, you will be free indeed. Jn 8:31–36

He does not say we must be perfect apprentices or disciples, because he knows that many of us are either raw recruits or rusty from disuse. And he is not condemning us for our past as Christians. But he does expect us to "show up" now and do what he, the Master, says. It's simple, but not necessarily easy. Being Jesus' disciple is all about love and desire and a willingness/determination to follow him and obey. So, like it or not, true obedience just isn't a once in a while thing.

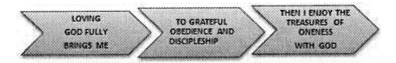

Obedience to God —Father, Son, and Holy Spirit — is very different from the obedience that the world insists on at work, at home, in the military, or even in a slave camp.

"Jesus never says, 'You _will_ submit to me.' He leaves us perfectly free to choose — so free that we can spit in his face or we can put him to death, as others have done . . . Jesus never insists on obedience, but when we truly see him, we will instantly obey him. Then he is easily Lord of our life, and we live in adoration of him from morning till night. . . .

"This kind of obedience is only possible between people who are equals in their relationship to each other, like the relationship between father and son, not that between master and servant. Jesus showed this relationship by saying, 'I and my Father are one.' (Jn 10:30) . . . 'Though he was a Son, yet he learned obedience by the things which he suffered.' (Heb 5:8) The Son was obedient as our Redeemer, *because he was the Son*, not in order to become God's Son" (Chambers, July 19).

There is ample support scripturally for what we've said so far about discipleship. But I think that obedience and discipleship are things too many Christians today take lightly. So let's have a heart checkup. How much have you been taught about this before — this very clear expectation that Jesus is our Master and we are his apprentices? That our lives are to be drenched with him as we follow in his footsteps? How do obedience and discipleship fit into your life? Is there something — or several "somethings" — you want to change? I certainly do!

ONENESS — LIVING HEART TO HEART
WITH GOD — IS A LIFE-LONG PROCESS

"Sanctification makes me one with Jesus Christ, and in Him one
with God. And it is done only through the superb atonement of Christ.
Jesus and the Father are the cause. The response in me is obedience
and service and prayer, and is the outcome of speechless thanks and
adoration for their work on our behalf" (Chambers Oct 20 entry).

Let me begin with a personal note.
In late February 2015, I considered this book to be almost 90 percent
complete (ah, youth and hope). But the hustle towards the finish made
me a bit jittery! I went to my friend, Shelley, who has a gift of prayer. She
immediately sensed God saying I should take a four-week break from
the book. I was astonished, but agreed it was from God. (How do I know
this? Because on my own, I would never in a million years have taken a
break from this book at that stage of completion!)

For many years, I have treasured my closeness with Jesus Christ and
with the Father. But during my "book break" which began on March 3,
2015, I actually pondered (for the first time) my opportunity to experience "oneness with God" –a phrase I hadn't really considered before.
And over several days of scripture meditation, I realized the absolute
significance and desirability of that oneness with our God, Father and
Son and Holy Spirit. So this section on oneness is one of the many gifts
God gave me and — through this book, he gave you — during that time
of prayer and scripture meditation. And lest you think I was focused on
God 24/7, living in some retreat center, I was not. But when you spend a
substantial amount of time with God, I promise you that God is on your
speed dial the rest of the time as well.

Oneness: God's Great Design
"God and Jesus cooperated with God's Holy Spirit to make known to us
the mystery of their sovereign will, and their method of redemption and
salvation. Together, they used his written word, preached gospel, and
Spirit of truth to heal the separation between God and man. Through

God's graces of faith and love, we are made one with God and among ourselves. The sanctifying and comforting influences of the Holy Spirit seal believers as the children of God, and heirs of heaven. These are the first-fruits of holy happiness. For this we were made, and for this we were redeemed. This is the great design of God in all that he has done for us" (Henry 1706 – yes! 1706).

Jesus wants us to live in love and harmony with other believers. And that makes perfect sense, because when the world sees that love, it shows them our God. But Jesus goes beyond that, and speaks of us making our home in him and in the Father — and them in us. "The goal of the in-dwelling Holy Spirit is not just to unite us with God, but to do it in such a way that we will be one with the Father in exactly the same way Jesus was. And he had such a oneness that he was obedient when his Father sent him down here to be poured out for us" (See Jn 20:21) (Chambers, March 3).

I visualize a oneness so tight with God that it's like clasping your two hands in front of you, fingers intertwined, so you can hardly tell one hand from the other. "Jesus himself taught this perfect oneness be-tween himself and those who believe in him [in John 17]. This language, though often described as mystical, also has clear overtones of a physical *and* spiritual union . . . [In fact] The complete and permanent oneness between husband and wife is a powerful pointer to the relationship, for time and for eternity, between Christ and his church" (Prior 1985).

It's natural to wonder what on earth it would be like to make your home with God. Would it be one "shalt not" after the other, with time outs and shouting if you mess up? Happily, no! Instead, Jesus says it brings him joy to contemplate our cohabitation. We share that joy when we follow God, through Jesus, with heart, soul, mind and strength, each in his/her own unique way.

We are one with God in direct proportion to the extent we have allowed the Holy Spirit to have his way with us.
"The fruit of the Spirit is fruit of a totally new disposition. Now, instead of self-realization, self-consciousness, and sin, there is sanctity and spiritual reality, bringing forth fruit unto holiness" Rom 6:22 KJV (Chambers 1947).

"We are magnificently interconnected with our Lord . . . From eternity, the Father loved the Son, and the Son enjoyed equal glory with the Father. The two were (and are) essentially and inherently one" (Carpenter and Comfort 2000).

This oneness is an amazing opportunity God offers to us, through Jesus: his life, his death, and his resurrection.
It affects, and is affected by, every facet of our spiritual life. Consider these great scripture references:

God is dwelling with us. Leviticus 1–3; Jn 1:14
In Leviticus times . . . holiness rituals were required for God to interact with His people — a temporary way for people to reach Him. And in the Gospel of John, Jesus' life is cast as an offering to make all people one with God again . . . Not only do these ancient rituals show the need to appreciate the entire created order, they also show how much we should appreciate a faith that doesn't require all these rituals. . . . Just as God camped in the middle of his people in the wilderness, today he wants to set up his tent in the middle of our lives. Are there areas of your life you don't want God to dwell in? What could you change to invite Him in?" (Barry & Van Noord Feb 18 entry)

Jesus abides in believers who acknowledge him before men.
Mt 10:32–33 AMP [32] Therefore, everyone who acknowledges Me before men and confesses Me [out of a state of oneness with Me], I will also acknowledge him before My Father Who is in heaven and confess [that I am abiding in] him. [33] But whoever denies and disowns Me before men, I also will deny and disown him before My Father Who is in heaven.

We are united with the Lord in spirit and through the Spirit.
1 Cor 6:14–20 NIV [14] By his power God raised the Lord from the dead, and he will raise us also. (See Rom 6:5; Eph 1:19, 20; 1 Thess 4:16). [15] Do you not know that your bodies are members of Christ himself? (Rom 12:5) . . . [17] But whoever is united with the Lord is one with him in spirit. (Jn 17:21–23; Rom 8:9–11; Gal 2:20) . . . [19] Do you not know that your bodies are temples of the Holy Spirit (see Jn 2:21), who is in you, whom you have received from God? You are not your

own (Rom 14:7–8). ²⁰ You were bought at a price. (Ps 74:2; See Mt 20:28; Acts 20:28; 1 Cor 7:23; Rev 5:9; 14:4)

Eph 4:3–6 AMP ³ Be eager and strive earnestly to guard and keep the harmony and oneness of [and produced by] the Spirit in the binding power of peace. ⁴ [There is] one body and one Spirit — just as there is also one hope [that belongs] to the calling you received — ⁵ [There is] one Lord, one faith, one baptism, One God and Father of [us] all, Who is above all [Sovereign over all], pervading all and [living] in [us] all.

Followers of Jesus are now part of God's family.
And Christ rejoices in the household of God. Now we can all share in Christ, "if indeed we hold our original confidence firm to the end" (Brown, 1988).

Heb 2: 10–13 NLT ¹⁰ God, for whom and through whom everything was made, chose to bring many children into glory. And it was only right that he should make Jesus, through his suffering, a perfect leader, fit to bring them into their salvation. ¹¹ . . . Jesus is not ashamed to call them his brothers and sisters . . . ¹³ He also said, 'I will put my trust in him, that is, I and the children God has given me (citing Ps 22:22).

Heb 3:6 NIV ⁶ᴺᴵⱽ But Christ is faithful as the Son over God's house. And we are his house, if indeed we hold firmly to our confidence and the hope in which we glory. (For more, see 1 Cor 15:2; Heb 3:14; 10:23.)

Now we come again to John 17, which is rightly called a view into the innermost Sanctuary (Edersheim p 528).
Jesus is praying to his Father on the night before his crucifixion. "Because the disciples were given permission to eavesdrop on this prayer, we know what Jesus thinks of us and what he is now praying for us. Jesus counts us as a love gift to him from the Father (Jn 17:6 and 24). He treasures and cherishes us as a bridegroom treasures his bride, for that is what we are (Eph 5:22–33). Should anyone ask, 'Who gives these sinners to this Savior?' the Father responds enthusiastically, 'I do!'

"Jesus prays for the increase of our joy, the same joy that fills his own heart. He also prays for our protection in the world, a battlefield that is also our mission field. Jesus also prays for our sanctification by the truth of the Father's words. And the Father's words will always point us to Jesus — who is our wisdom from God, our righteousness and sanctification and redemption (1 Cor 1:30). All saving benefits come from our union with Christ" (ESV-GTB).

Here are some excerpts from John 17:

Jesus says: . . . [6-8 NLT 6] I have revealed you to the ones you gave me from this world. They were always yours. You gave them to me, and they have kept your word . . . [13 AMP] . . . I say these things while I am still in the world, so that my joy may be made full and complete and perfect in them [that they may experience my delight fulfilled in them, that my enjoyment may be perfected in their own souls, that they may have my gladness within them, filling their hearts] . . .

[20 AMP] . . . I pray for all those who will ever come to believe in (trust in, cling to, rely on) me through their word and teaching, [21 NIV] that all of them may be one, Father, just as you are in me and I am in you. May they also be in us so that the world may believe that you have sent me.

[22 NLT] I have given them the glory you gave me, so they may be one as we are one . . . [23 NLT] I am in them and you are in me (Jn 14:20; Rom. 8:10; 2 Cor. 13:5). May they experience such perfect unity that the world will know that you sent me and that you love them (Jn 16:27) as much as you love me (See Jn 5:20).

[24-26 MSG] Father, I want those you gave me [[AMP] as your gift to me] to be with me, right where I am, so they can see my glory, the splendor you gave me, having loved me long before there ever was a world . . . [On this mission] I have made your very being known to them — who you are and what you do . . . so that your love for me might be in them, exactly as I am in them.

ONENESS: THE VINE AND THE BRANCH

Jesus says: [1] I am the true vine, and my Father is the vinedresser. [2] Every branch in me that does not bear fruit he takes away, and every branch that does bear fruit he prunes, that it may bear more fruit. [3] Already you are clean because of the word that I have spoken to you. Jn 15:1–3.

[4] Remain in me, and I will remain in you. A branch cannot produce fruit alone but must remain in the vine. In the same way, you cannot produce fruit alone but must remain in me. [5] "I am the vine, and you are the branches. If any

remain in me and I remain in them, they produce much fruit. But without me they can do nothing. (reflecting Hosea 14:8b) [6] If any do not remain in me, they are like a branch that is thrown away and then dies . . . [8] You should produce much fruit and show that you are my followers, which brings glory to my Father. Jn 15:4–8 NCV

"Jesus Christ's claim is that he can manifest his own life in any man if he will cooperate with him.
Oneness is completeness in Christ (Col 2:9–10 NKJV). With Christ's life in me, "through the incarnation, the divine and the human became one.. . . The goal of human life is to be one with God, and in Jesus Christ we see what that oneness means" (Chambers 1947).

Charles Spurgeon compares this oneness, this union, to the eternal union of Father, Son, and Holy Spirit, "a doctrine of undoubted truth and unmingled comfort. The Church is so allied with her Lord that she is positively one with him. She is the bride, and He the bridegroom. She is the branch, and He the stem. She is the body, and He the glorious Head. So also is every individual believer united to Christ . . . and blessed with all spiritual blessings in heavenly places in him . . . It is from oneness with Christ . . . that we receive all our mercies" (Spurgeon 1858).

Considering all of this, I ask myself: "Is God having His wonderful way with me? Is God's will being fulfilled, so that *his* Son has been formed in me? (Gal 4:19) Or have I carefully pushed him to one side?" (Chambers Aug 8 entry)

Fusion Jesus-style.
Fusion combines separate elements into a unified, entirely new whole, and it can be achieved by heating and/or mixing things together. When Jesus came to Earth, divine *and* human, God created a supercharged third element, Jesus, who was "God and man." By that same act, Jesus the Christ offered to merge with us, sanctifying us by making us one with him. And this amazing "fusion" — our oneness with God — keeps on growing as we become his disciples and are being changed, day after day.

John 3:16–17 NIV (with extensive cross references)
¹⁶ **For God so loved the world** (Rom 5:8; Eph 2:4; 2 Thess 2:16; 1 Jn 3:1 and 4:9-19), Jn 1:29 **that he gave his one and only Son** (Gen 22:12; Jn 1:18; Rom 8:32), **that whoever believes in him shall not perish but have eternal life** (Jn 3: 36; Jn 6:29,40; Jn 11:25, 26).
¹⁷ **For God did not send his Son into the world** (Jn 5:36, 38; Jn 6:29, 57; Jn 7:29; 8:42; 10:36; 11:42; Jn 17:3; 20:21); Rom 8:3; 1 Jn 4:9-10,14) **to condemn the world, but to save the world through him.** (Isa 53:11; See Mt 1:21; Lk 2:11; 19:10; Jn 1:29; 5:45; 8:15; 12:47; Rom 11:14; 1 Tim 2:5, 6; 1 Jn 2:2; 3:5)
Rom 1: 16–17 NIV ¹⁶ For I am not ashamed of the gospel, because it is the power of God that brings salvation to everyone who believes: first to the Jew, then to the Gentile. ¹⁷For in the gospel the righteousness of God is revealed (Rom 3:21; Phil 3:9). This righteousness is by faith from first to last, just as it is written: 'The righteous will live by faith'."

Father, help us to remember that the goal of human life is to be one with you. And in Jesus Christ, we see what that oneness means. I am beyond grateful for your love, your patience, and your faithfulness to me. Somehow, from my first day of loving you, I understood that YOU were the prize. Not some treat or shiny toy you could give me. Not some slot machine to play with a guaranteed outcome. Not some Santa, giving me everything on my selfish little wish list. I now see this as a true miracle of sorts!

Jesus, your life brought me this prize, this treasure. And the fact that you showed this to me in the very beginning was, I know now, a gift beyond price. Following you is everything to me now. I want to be your true disciple, and nothing less! "If I am going to nourish the pure Divine in my human life, I must first of all let you deal drastically with my sin. By my own willing agreement I must let you put [the Father's] axe to the root of sin, and then when your life has come into me, I must obey it" (Chambers 1947). CGS

PRAYER AND MEDITATION FOR CHAPTER 4

CHAPTER 5 OUTLINE: GOD'S PRESENCE IS DELICIOUS, SO TREASURE ALL YOUR TIME WITH HIM: IN CONVERSATION, IN HIS WORD, IN MEDITATION, IN PRAYER, AND ANYWHERE ELSE YOU CAN GET TOGETHER

Because of Christ and our faith in him, we can now come boldly and confidently into God's presence Eph 3:12 NLT. Because I accept Jesus as my King — not just my Savior — my heart, soul, mind and strength are joined forever to: God the Father; God the Son Jesus; and God the Holy Spirit. I am never alone!

OVERVIEW: QUALITY TIME WITH GOD. God wants to spend quality time with me, so I can live abundantly and continually in his presence.

1. Go first, last, and always to God.
2. Spend time daily in his word, so I can experience his knowledge, understanding, and wisdom.
3. Be a bible meditator, marinating and meditating in God's word (includes a reference in Jn 17).
4. Conversations with God: God talks to me, and I listen. And I talk to God, and he listens. In all of this, he reveals himself, his purposes, and his ways.
5. Prayer is part of our conversation with God! Pray. Align yourself with God's will. Speak and listen. Ask and listen
   * The purpose of prayer is to get hold of God, not the answer. Wade out to the deep: pray, ask, listen. (And check out three short, true descriptions of prayer that help us keep our eye on the ball.)

- We need to examine our hearts before God – about our prayer-life or any other issue.
- Please take me higher, Father. And direct my prayers.
- True prayer versus a habit or a performance
- Answered prayer: Our way or God's way?

6. Intercessory Prayer is praying for others whom we may or may not know or ever meet.
   - Prayer is called for at all times, but there are also certain well-timed times to pray.
   - Healing and prayer

7. Prayers can be simple, short or long, and filled with gratitude
   - Short prayers are long enough.
   - God's words to me – in or out of a prayer setting – can be general or very specific.

8. Other ways God gets our attention.

9. God's truth comes by listening to him and reading his word. It will set me free, in all ways. Only with his truth can I have a correct and truthful view of myself, not one that is skewed one way or the other. (For more on this, see chapter 6.)

10. God wants me to spend enough time in his word that I can gain his knowledge, understanding, and wisdom. So I am a student of God's word.

11. Hearing God's word isn't enough; then we must do it! The hard stuff, as well as the easy stuff!

12. Follow — and keep consulting — your leader/God

CHAPTER 5

GOD'S PRESENCE IS DELICIOUS, SO TREASURE ALL YOUR TIME WITH HIM: IN CONVERSATION, IN HIS WORD, IN MEDITATION, IN PRAYER, AND ANYWHERE ELSE YOU CAN GET TOGETHER

Because of Christ and our faith in him, we can now come boldly
and confidently into God's presence.   Eph 3:12 NLT

I accept Jesus as my King, not just as my Savior. So my heart, soul,
mind, and strength are joined forever to God the Father; God the
Son, Jesus; and God the Holy Spirit. I am never alone!

"Form a habit of conversing with God continually, and referring all we
do to him. The shortest way to go straight to God is by a continual exercise of love and doing all things for his sake" (Brother Lawrence,18,
21). Then we can pray for God's grace with a perfect confidence.

OVERVIEW: QUALITY TIME WITH GOD

The notion of God talking and listening to us may seem easy or it may
be quite foreign to you. I used to think that God only talked to us from
a burning bush, and that was long ago. I certainly never considered that
he might talk to us today. But in 1993, I discovered that I was absolutely
wrong – and that God speaks to each one of his people, and often! Does
this mean he is chattering along to you all day, every day? Not in my experience. But he does speak to us a lot, and all we have to do is tune our
minds and our ears to his "channel". How this happens is different with
each one of us, but there are certain basic truths which we can consider

now. Does God really want quality time with us? If so, what does that
look like? Is God interested in regular people like us, or do we have to
be a scholar or famous preacher to hear from God? (I think you'll be
able to guess the answer to that last one right off!)

In a sense, spending time with God is like spending time with a
good friend. You don't have to dress up to visit each other. The venue
doesn't matter, and there is no printed agenda! Some moments with
our friend are perfectly ordinary, while others are really mountaintop
experiences. But either way, we are glad to be together, yes? That's
just like being with God, although there are, of course, a few differences. My friend, no matter how special she is, is not the Creator of the
universe, the power and mind behind all existence. She is not full of
divine wisdom and power and goodness. She cannot dispense so much
grace that it never runs out. And she definitely did not send her Son
to live and die for me.

Oh, and one more thing: don't get all bent about how to meet with
God. And don't let others make you think it's an elaborate dance that
must be done just right. It's not like that with your good friend, and it is
not that way with our Father. Just think of him, listen to him, and bare
your heart and soul to him. *That* is quality time with God, no matter how
you slice it!

GO FIRST, LAST, AND ALWAYS TO GOD

God wants me to live abundantly and continually in his presence.
We have been set free to experience our rightful heritage . . . fully
adopted as his own children . . . [with] that privilege of intimate
conversation with God . . . [as] an heir, with complete access to the
inheritance. Gal 4:4–7 MSG

**"At any moment, and in any circumstance, the soul that seeks God can
find him and practice the presence of God.**
In order to form a habit of conversing with God continually, and referring all we do to him, we must first apply to him with some diligence.

Then, after a little care, we should find his love inwardly excites us to it without any difficulty" (Brother Lawrence, 13,16,18).

[Brother Lawrence was a humble monk living in a French monastery in the late 1600s. His job as a cook wasn't fancy. But some of his words were so profound that they have survived until now.]

There is no bad time to go to God!
If you are delighted, tell God. When you have a question, need direction, are in a pinch, or just want to cry about something, go to God first thing. But if you don't think of him at first, then go to him when it occurs to you. And if not then, when you are absolutely at the end of your rope and have exhausted the food or beer or friends or whatever other crutch you favor, then go to God. I repeat: there is no bad time to go to God!

"Get into the habit of dealing with God about everything. Unless you learn to open the door of your life completely and let God in from your first waking moment of each new day, you will be working on the wrong level throughout the day. But if you will swing the door of your life fully open and 'pray to your Father who is in the secret place'(Mt 6:6), every public thing in your life will be marked with the lasting imprint of the presence of God" (Chambers Aug 23).

SPEND TIME DAILY IN HIS WORD, AND EXPERIENCE HIS KNOWLEDGE, UNDERSTANDING, AND WISDOM.

- God's word is life -giving! The world was created by the word of God. (Gen 1; Heb 11:3; 2 Pet 3:5–7) And Jesus tells us that man does not live by bread alone, but by every word that proceeds from the mouth of God. (Mt 4:4 quoting Deut 8:3) And in John 6:63, Jesus says: the words that I've spoken to you are spirit and life.
- Bearing fruit. When we spend time in God's word, we are like trees planted by streams of water, bearing much fruit. Ps 1:1–3
- God's word is a delight. Ps 119:14–16, 24, 143
- God's word is perfect, sure, right, pure, true, and righteous. He is more precious than gold and sweeter than honey. Ps 19:7–9

* God's word is a light to our feet, showing us the right way to go. Ps 119:105, 130
* God's word sustains us and gives us endurance. We are to focus on God: – keep our eyes on Him and His word — even when times are hard. Ps 119:15, 23
* God can provide wisdom — knowledge — understanding.
* *Ask* to be filled with the knowledge of God's will in all spiritual wisdom and understanding Col 1:9–10. *Ask* to have all the riches of assured understanding and knowledge of God's mystery, of Christ, in whom are hid all the treasures of wisdom and knowledge. Col 2:2–3. *Ask* to use Scripture inspired by God to teach, reprove, correct, and train in righteousness. Ps 119:98–100   And *ask* that it brings knowledge and understanding. 2 Tim 3:16

BECOME A BIBLE MEDITATOR:
MARINATING AND SOAKING IN GOD'S WORD

. . . [2 MSG] Thrill to God's Word . . . chew on Scripture day and night.
[3 ESV] . . . like a tree planted by streams of water that yields its fruit in
its season, and its leaf does not wither. Ps 1:1–3

God told Joshua (and us) that we should meditate on His word
day and night, – and do all that it tells us to do. Josh 1:7–8

"Come to the Bible and meditate. Then faith grows . . . I challenge
you to try it for a month and see how it works" (Tozer, 56–57).

God's Word isn't just any. It is the power, wisdom, and love of God at work in our lives, and every line is saturated with God's living breath. In fact, it's a lot like CPR, but less violent! I've found it quite satisfying to spend at least fifteen to thirty minutes or more daily, communing shoulder-to-shoulder with the One God. I can promise you it doesn't take a theologian to do it, because I have been meditating regularly (or sometimes just off and on) since God changed our lives with the concept.

In the Fall of 1993, my husband and I were blessed to hear Dr. Ron Smith teach for a week on the topic of Bible meditation. Of all the many things I learned during those months, Ron's lessons were right at the top! So I was glad when his book *Hooked on the Word* was published the following year. My profound thanks to a great teacher, his great teaching, and the great God behind it all! I've never forgotten what he said. And the treasure that came from his teaching, increased intimacy with God, was beyond description.

Over the years, I've come to see Bible meditation as my way of putting my feet onto the playing field for the big game, engaging in a personal and intimate dialogue between Father and daughter (or son). So picture yourself sitting in a large arena. You get up, walk down to the field, and put your feet on that special ground. Now you are ready to go, to enter into God's activity and mind, and let him guide you. My husband and I didn't know anything about that field before we discovered Jesus, but we stepped out onto it anyway. And nothing's been the same since. Thank you, Jesus!

Smith writes: "Unfortunately, we have become preoccupied in the church with doing things, getting caught up with activities, rather than with being quiet before God and delighting in His Word. Somehow we have lost sight of the fact that God places His highest value on the character and depth of our relationship with Him and not on the sheer volume of things we can accomplish for His kingdom. We have grown accustomed to measuring spiritual success in terms of doing and accomplishing. [So] sitting in prayer or silently contemplating the Word of God, for many, is akin to wasting time.

"Another problem is that the word 'meditation' has taken on negative connotations in the language of today's Christians. The mere mention of the word evokes pictures of saffron-robed gurus sitting cross-legged on the floor, babbling mantras and drifting into trances. The idea, though, of meditating on the Word of God is firmly rooted in the Bible and is central to the lives of many of the people whose stories are recounted within its pages . . . There is a pure, holy, good and edifying form of meditation which the Bible sets forth and which today we call "Bible meditation". . . It is time for us once again to become a people who delight in the Word of God and meditate on it day and night (Ps 1:2)" (Smith 13–16).

Select one or two verses to wrap your mind and heart around, as you sit quietly. You can start any place: Psalms, the book of John, Jesus' Sermon on the Mount, anywhere really. You aren't studying the verse, but considering it. Often, if the verse is long, I pick the first phrase and meditate on it. Then the next day, I consider the next phrase. And I like to make a note on my calendar, to keep track and hold me accountable to myself at least.

Oh, and one funny note: When Dr. Smith told us we could start any place with meditation, I heard him suggest Psalm 1 as one possibility. So that's where I started. A few weeks into it, someone told me he'd said Psalm 119, *not* Psalm 1. And others I checked all agreed. But *I heard* (or God shouted to me) Psalm 1. So I stuck with that and I spent the next two years meditating through the Psalms. And it was one of the richest times in my faith life, for which I'll always be grateful. (PS: I skipped the parts where David wanted to crunch his enemies' bones. I figured I had enough of that in me already.)

My soul magnifies the Lord.
In Luke 1, Mary, the mother of Jesus, praises God and her soul magnifies the Lord. Charles Spurgeon wrote, "Often, the word "magnify" means to make great or to make to appear great, as in using a microscope. But when we are praising God and meditating on Scripture, we cannot make God greater than he is. Nor can we have any conception of his actual greatness . . . We are, instead, magnifying our Lord by having higher, larger, truer conceptions of Him . . .

"It is no idle occupation to get alone, and in your own heart, to magnify the Lord: to make Him great to your mind, to your affections; great in your memory, great in your expectations. It is one of the grandest exercises of the renewed nature (Spurgeon 1891).

So meditation isn't just reading. It's more like taking one delicious candy, and then slowly savoring it while it sits on your tongue. It's not a sprint; it's a happening! In fact, Ron Smith compares Bible meditation to a cow chewing its cud. You take small passages of Scripture and turn them over and over in your mind until you begin to unlock the truths God has stored in it for you. And like cows, we may not all work on the same schedule or have the same approach to Bible meditation. The object isn't to make little robots, all doing the same thing. The object is to meet and commune with God.

When you sit quietly and savor a particular verse, or part of a verse, distractions *will* poke their little heads into your space. Just move back to the verse and resume. There are no "distraction police" writing tickets on you, and no penalty points either! David Ross, in *The Church's Lost Treasure*, writes, "When we meditate, we allow the Holy Spirit to direct our spirits, like a rudder guides a boat, to the goal of the Word we are meditating on . . . It sets our minds on the Word, on God's truth, to concentrate on Him and what He desires to say, to fix our gaze upon Him and concentrate with our minds and hearts" (quoted in Smith, 88–89).

I'll give you a recent example. I was quietly reading and re-reading John 17, for another section of this book. And I was so taken by it, that I did the same thing for days on end. Eventually, I expanded to John 13, 14, 15, and 16. And God began to show me how important these last words were to Jesus and to his disciples. So for the first time in all the years I've followed Jesus, I understood how powerful these words were, especially since Jesus knew it was his last night before dying. The more I read, the more I soaked up Jesus' heart for his disciples — and for us — on that last night. That is the power of scriptural meditation, spending time with your Bible, with God, and with Jesus. You will be affected in ways that I cannot even adequately describe. And you will never be sorry! In fact, I find that when I regularly spend time with God, considering a line or two of his Word each morning, it sets a tone for the whole day that is rich and satisfying. If I do not — if I'm "out of the groove" for days or even weeks on end —everything begins to slowly grind down and my peace with God is somehow less.

CONVERSATIONS WITH GOD

God speaks to everyone who loves him and follows Jesus. And he often speaks to others. So we need to listen. And we talk to God, and he listens. We pray, ask, thank, and sing praises, with the Spirit and with the mind. In all of this, he reveals himself, his purposes, and his ways.

On this topic, I owe so much to Henry Blackaby, the author of *Experiencing God.* If you want to learn more on this topic (and who wouldn't?), I recommend that you buy his workbook (of the same title) and start through it, either on your own or with a small group. I've done it several times over the years, each time with a fresh workbook, and I've always learned something new!

We establish ourselves in a sense of God's presence by staying in touch with him. Like a good friend, God may have some serious things to discuss, but we can trust him to do it lovingly! And we want to hear him! God "gets us"! He understands when my child stumbles into the same old ditch at school. Or when your brother is sent into harm's way in a remote part of the world. God understands your fear when your family hovers on the edge of bankruptcy. And he knows your thrill when someone you love comes home, safe and sound, and maybe even thriving!

God will not be put in a box by us.
You may hear people say, "God only speaks this way" or "God does not speak this way". But he is *so* much bigger than human categories or thoughts, and he speaks to us in *many* different ways. Blackaby mentions four, including the Bible, prayer, circumstances, and the church. But my own experience is that there are many times when God just talks to me in my head, completely out of the blue. The bottom line is that I must watch and listen to see (and hear) how God communicates uniquely.

Don't get caught up on which "hat" God is wearing when he speaks with you. That's only a distraction. For instance, God spoke to our forefathers through the prophets at many times and in various ways. Then God spoke to his people through Jesus, his Son (Heb 1:1). Now, God also speaks through the Holy Spirit. The Holy Spirit will teach you all things, call to your memory the things Jesus said (Jn 14:26), guide you into all truth, speak what he hears from the Father, tell you what is yet to come, and glorify Christ as he reveals Christ to you. (Jn 16:13–14)

We can all have conversations with God, although some of you will insist he doesn't talk to you at all. But please challenge yourself on this topic. God *is* speaking to us. We just need to tune our ears to hear him. Give it a try, *please!* Bible characters through whom God worked had three similarities, and I want my walk with God — and yours — to be like theirs. "When God spoke, they *knew* who it was. They knew *what* God was saying. And they knew what they were *to do* in response" (Blackaby, 22).

Examples from a *very* ordinary Christian.
On occasion, I have a strong, persistent sense that I should do something. And often, the topic or words are way outside my usual activities or skills. For the most part, I have learned to go with it, even though I don't fully understand why— because I realize it is from God. On other occasions, I experience what I've come to call "two-fers" (or two-for-ones) from God. I may read a verse during my Bible time that really hits me. Then later in the week, someone will mention the same verse. Then the sermon a week or so later focuses on the same verse. Then I know that is God speaking to me. Or God will put a phrase in my head and it persists, day after day and week after week. In early 1995, God gave me this phrase: "refugee children from the war". How did I know this was from God? Well, the words came out of nowhere and made no "practical" sense. I was not a kid person. I had never met a refugee, and I was thousands of miles from any war. But, over a period of weeks and then months, this phrase echoed in my head, not as an audible voice, but as a persistently recurring phrase.

For months, my husband and I scrambled in every direction, trying to figure out what God had in mind. But nothing surfaced. Finally, August 1 came, and we saw an ad for cheap tickets to London. We figured that refugee children from the war were probably somewhere east of London. But because we were still unsure what to do, we called our friends, John and Joy Raney. They assured us that there had been times in their lives when they had traveled as far as God told them, and then waited for further directions. That *immediately* resonated with us — proving once again it was all God! — so we bought the cheap tickets to London and waited (and wondered, I must admit).

Still nothing happened. But then an inquiry we had faxed to Croatia was delivered "by mistake" into the hands of a Texan who was ministering to blind children and refugees from the Bosnian War. And he was happy to have us come and help. We had received our destination, all in God's due time! So on November 1, we flew using the tickets we'd bought three months earlier in blind faith. We flew to London and then on to Croatia, just as the Bosnian-Serbian-Croatian war was beginning to wind down. In fact, the day we flew out of the United States was the day formal peace talks began. (Do you see what I mean by no sense in a practical way?)

Another time, God prompted me with the phrase "women in desperate circumstances." Again, this went on for months until we understood that we were to buy a house for women coming out of prison. Was it delightful? No, not really. But we did what God asked us to do, and for that we were hugely grateful. And women who might not have been taken care of before received housing, food, and some spiritual care. Now isn't God just plain clever?

Then there are smaller examples of God putting an idea into my head. For example, in February 2015, I sensed that I should go to West Texas and spend time with Rich, my daughter-in-law's dad, who had been in the hospital for more than a week with pneumonia. I had no clear idea of what I would do when I got there (a recurring theme, by the way, with God and me). But I was certain I should go.

So you can see this isn't exactly rocket science. It's just God reaching out and tapping me on the shoulder. Then many times, I turn my head and say, "I hear you!" No burning bushes, but *lots* of communication between us. How I love that! And if I can do it, anyone can!

PRAYER IS PART OF OUR CONVERSATION WITH GOD. SO PRAY. ALIGN YOURSELF WITH GOD'S WILL. SPEAK AND LISTEN. ASK AND LISTEN

Let petitions and praises shape your worries into prayers, letting God know your concerns. Before you know it, a sense of God's wholeness, everything coming together for good, will come and settle you down. It's wonderful what happens when Christ displaces worry at the center of your life. Phil 4:6–7 MSG

The purpose of prayer is to get hold of God, not the answer.
At one time or another, most of us may wonder why we need to pray. Can't God do it on his own? What if God doesn't answer? And so on. It's easy to get lost in the weeds on the topic of prayer, and to wander between two extremes: (1) God doesn't care about us, or listen to our cries, and (2) God will give us whatever we ask, no matter how materialistic and selfish our request. So I have decided to stay out of the weeds as much as possible. Here, instead, are three short, true descriptions of prayer, which help me keep my eye on the ball. I pray they will help you, too.

* Oswald Chambers wisely writes: "The purpose of prayer is to get hold of God, not the answer" (Feb 7 entry). Too often we miss the fact that God himself is the center of everything, not our requests. He is the source, and our connection to him is everything. If we forget that — and get full of ourselves — we are apt to see things in a distorted way. That's when we find ourselves demanding an immediate answer from God or giving him conditions.
* "Prayer is coming into perfect fellowship and oneness with God, not simply getting things from God" (Chambers Sept 16). This comes naturally when we follow 1 Corinthians 14:15, which says, I will pray in the spirit, and I will pray with the mind, also. I will sing with the spirit, and I will sing with the mind, also. And we have to ask things of God that are in sync with him and his Son, Jesus.
* "Prayer is essentially a partnership of the redeemed child of God working hand in hand with God toward the realization of his redemptive purposes on earth" (Hayford, 92).

When we examine our hearts before God – about our prayer-life or any other issue – we need to be honest about our strengths *and* our short-comings.
And we need to listen carefully to whatever God has to say. He knows it all and can help us throughout our life-long faith – and prayer – journey.

I will be perfectly straight with you. There have been many times when I didn't pray as I should have. And other wonderful times when I was burning with prayer for someone God put on my mind. God knows all that. What he wants from me now is to stop saying "I don't pray as much as I should" and step out of that boat and into the beautifully deep waters of heart to heart prayer with God. Further, he wants to direct my prayers as well as hear them. God can help any of us learn to listen, pray as he directs, and then sit back and watch! And here's good news: beginners can do this as well as "experts".

Remember, God's voice can be very direct and specific. At other times, though it is a gentle, loving nudge into your consciousness. Then you will find people or issues coming into your mind and – hurrah – you have your prayer "list" for the day. Enjoy any spiritual fireworks during your time with God, but remember, they are not required!

Please take me higher, Father. And direct my prayers.
My friend Ginger Rogers says that sometimes it seems there is just too much to pray for. She says to God, "When I try to pray, all this stuff is just crowding in on me and I feel like I will never get through addressing the issues, much less hear your response." So God directed her to the old story of Zacchaeus, the fellow who climbed a tree so he could see Jesus (Lk 19). And showed her something vital. "Zacchaeus could not see Jesus because of the crowd. In the same way, I could not see Him in my prayers, because my thoughts were crowded with worries and fears and issues. But his desire to see Jesus was greater than any self-image issues, Zacchaeus found a solution. He climbed a tree! And Jesus spied him up there and said, "Come down, Zacchaeus. Today I will visit you in your house." (Rogers 2015)

"Wow", Ginger continues. "Who of us wouldn't want to hear that from the Lord?! But what does the story have to do with us? The point is, because of the press of the crowd, Zacchaeus went higher. He got above the crowd to find Jesus. And that is what Jesus is saying to us. Come up higher. Get above the threats of terrorism and stock market crashes and foolish people winning the presidency; above all the sicknesses among our church friends and deaths in the community and children running amok." (Rogers)

Father, please take us all higher! Direct our prayers. Let us follow *your* steps in our prayers today. Help us pray what is on *your* heart. [2 ESV] Take me to the rock that is higher than I . . .

[2 NLT] Lead me to the towering rock of safety . . . [and] [4 ESV] Let me dwell in your tent forever . . . [4 NLT] Let me live forever in your sanctuary. (Psalm 61:1-4).

True prayer versus a habit or a performance.
E. M. Bounds says that "prayer, as a mere habit, as a performance gone through by routine or in a professional way, is a dead and rotten thing . . . [Instead] We are stressing true praying, which engages and sets on fire every high element of the preacher's [and every Christian's] being. [This is] prayer which is born of vital oneness with Christ and the fullness of the Holy Ghost, which springs from:

- "the deep, overflowing fountains of tender compassion, death-less solicitude for man's eternal good;
- "a consuming zeal for the glory of God;
- "a thorough conviction of the preacher's difficult and delicate work and of the imperative need of God's mightiest help." (Bounds

"Praying grounded on these solemn and profound convictions is the only true praying. Preaching backed by such praying is the only preaching which sows the seeds of eternal life in human hearts and builds men up for heaven" (Bounds).

God yearns for all to be close to him, and prayer is a great way to do this. Even the lost can call out to God, and he can hear their yearning and desire for him. [But too often], "we talk about prayer as if God hears us regardless of what our relationship is to Him (see Mt 5:45). And we mistake defiance for devotion, arguing with God instead of surrendering . . . Then prayer can become some trivial religious expression . . . producing [only] spiritual fog" (Chambers Aug 24).

Answered prayer: Our way or God's way?

Remember, God is *not* Santa Claus or a genie in a bottle. And he is not our butler, existing merely to serve us goodies that we "pray" for. Yes, prayer is answered — God's way, but not always our way. And really, aren't we glad that God is wise enough not to always give us our desires? Just think: If answered prayer amounted to God just tossing candy willy-nilly from a festive sleigh throughout the Earth, where would that get us? How would we be better for it?

Edersheim writes that even the "unlimitedness" of prayer is actually limited, or, rather, conditioned, by our abiding in Christ and his Words in us, and our fellowship with him. "It is entirely opposed to the teaching of Christ, to imagine that the promise of Christ implies such absolute power — as if prayer were magic — that a person might ask for anything, no matter what it was, in the assurance of obtaining his request . . . Our relation to Christ and His Word in us, union and communion with Him, and the obedience of love, all are the indispensable conditions of our privileges" (Edersheim p 521).

For more, see Matthew 7:7–8 (one who seeks and knocks); John 14:12–14 (asking in Jesus'name, character, and teaching); and John 15:-8, 16 (regarding our unlimited liberty of prayer being connected with our bearing much fruit, because thereby the Father is glorified and our discipleship evidenced).

INTERCESSORY PRAYER IS PRAYING FOR OTHERS
WHOM WE MAY OR MAY NOT KNOW OR EVER MEET

In the very beginning, Adam was given responsibility for (not ownership of) the Earth. Since that time, God has chosen to work through humans to accomplish many of his goals and plans. Is he limited to that? No, but it could explain why God needs us to pray. Dutch Sheets suggests that "our prayers do more than just petition the Father. I've become convinced that in some situations they actually release cumulative amounts of God's power until enough has been released to accomplish his will. . . . Indeed, I can't help wondering how many promises from God have gone unfulfilled because he can't find the human involvement he needs" (Sheets 1996, p 31).

So working with and through humans definitely appears to be God's preference. And I suspect that this arrangement is probably more for our good than for his! In fact, God's watching us fumble around with prayer must feel a lot like a parent's frustration while watching a child learn to sweep his own room! And can you imagine what our characters would be like if God gave us literally anything we asked for?

When we are drawn into prayer, we talk to God simply, sharing our heart and listening to his. That is the way to grow close to God. So praying is asking, sure, but it's also a whole lot more! Remember, praying isn't always about you or those close to you. God loves people all over this troubled world, and he wants his people to join him in that concern. Prayer is one major way we can do that. We need to learn that when others are in trouble, we should lift them in prayer, and let *God* do the moving.

Oswald Chambers said that the real business of a saved soul is intercessory prayer — praying for others. Of course, God wants us to pray for ourselves and for our friends. But he equally desires that we pray for those people whom we may never meet. The hungry, the angry, those who don't know the love of Jesus — all of these need our prayers. We don't need to know their names. In fact, we may only know their country or their circumstance (earthquake, drought, famine). And sometimes we know even less than that. Maybe all you will know is that they live in a country or region where the Christian faith is completely suppressed and where touching the Bible is a criminal/prison offense.

You can find excellent prayer guides that help you pray for the world. And you can sit quietly and ask God, "Show me who I should pray for this morning." Then listen and follow what you sense he is saying to you. If you don't hear something specific after a time, head to your "Go To" list: those who do not know God and have not accepted Jesus, his Son. You don't have to be an expert to stand with God in concern for others. And even the simplest Christian can have intercessory prayer experiences that are absolutely amazing and surprising to boot!

Well-timed times to pray
Prayer can be strategic, coming against temptation and persecution.
The Bible speaks of well-timed (*kairos*) temptations (see Lk 4:13; 8:13)
And it also informs us of strategically-placed persecution (see Acts 12:1;
19:23). "Is it possible that such attacks could be stopped or rendered unfruitful if we were alert and interceded against it? Ephesians 6:18, in the
context of spiritual warfare, says 'we are to be on the alert . . . for all the
saints' and 'pray at all (*kairos* — strategic or right) times in the Spirit'. If
we are alert, we can create a boundary of protection by praying (Sheets
83-84).

God wants us to have a prayer life in the secret place, but "it's not
automatic for believers. Although we are promised protection from our
enemy, we have a definite part to play in the securing of it for ourselves
and for others. The intercessor knows this and leaves nothing to chance,
posting signs for all the forces of hell to see: 'Under the shadow of the
Most High. Keep out!' " (Sheets 90)

Healing and Prayer
There is all kind of healing of course: physical, mental, emotional,
and so on. And there are many different approaches to healing in the
Christian faith today. Some think there is no such thing, and others
think that prayer does affect physical and emotional healing. But Jesus
had a big interest in healing. So, for that reason if no other, I propose
that we keep our minds open on the topic. Like other things we've discussed so far, I take the position that only God knows the whole truth.
And we will not debate this or engage in "I know it all and you don't" jabs
that are sadly all too common these days.

Ellel, an international prayer and healing ministry, says: "We believe
healing is God's supernatural work of bringing order into a person's life
where there has been disorder! It includes looking at the root problems
that may be the cause of a person's struggle — dealing with any unforgiveness, sin, wounding, or hold of the enemy. As we help a person do their
business with God in forgiving, repenting and making godly choices, we
then pray for the Lord to bring His healing. It's not the weird or wacky picture of healing that some people have - just basic discipleship" (Ellel 2015).

I have often said that God parting the Red Sea is like a parlor trick compared to his changing my heart. So I understand fully that "many Christians feel that there is no real answer to the problems they face on a daily basis – problems such as fear and anxiety, addictions and anger outbursts, long-term consequences of trauma or abuse and relationship dysfunction . . . to name but a few. The list is endless! The wonderful fact, however, is that God is willing, able and longing to restore His people and equip them to fulfill all the plans He has for them! No one is excluded and we have seen thousands of lives healed and transformed since the work began" (Ellel 2015).

Personally I have witnessed – and participated in – several dramatic and miraculous physical healings in my life. But it isn't something I've been called to very often. Still, I learned to do what God said, even though I was green as grass in the area of healing! In each case, God specifically told me to go and pray for the individual. But he didn't say how I should proceed or what I should pray — just pray. Still, he knew that my first concern is always whether someone knows Jesus, rather than their physical condition. (I guess that tends to happen when you come to Jesus as late as I did.) I may not be God's go-to girl for physical healing prayer, but there are still times when he sends me.

My first experience was one year after we'd met Jesus at YWAM. God told me to go to the hospital to pray for a young woman who was comatose and had no real prospects of recovery. I was so new at all this that I couldn't visualize me walking into the hospital room and asking to pray in the name of Jesus (the woman was part of a large Jewish family). So I didn't do what God said, but did pray for the woman faithfully. A month or so later, I learned that she had completely recovered. And I knew that God had taught me something I would never forget.

My next God assignment was Barbara, who in 1999 was unconscious after a surgical procedure produced an infection. *All* of her doctors had said she had no prospect of waking up or recovering. When I first saw her in the nursing home, she was completely comatose and lying flat in bed. I came to her two or three times a week. I told her that God loved her, I sang hymns, and I read Bible verses. But I didn't ask God to heal her physically. (I wasn't being stubborn. I was just so focused on the fact that she didn't know God, which I considered far more disastrous.) Eventually she opened her eyes and could converse a bit. After several weeks of this, I told my husband Stayton: "You know, I think Barbara is getting better." His answer? "No duh!" Eventually Barbara was *completely* healed physically, and it was *all* because of God!

PRAYERS CAN BE SIMPLE, SHORT OR LONG, AND FILLED WITH GRATITUDE.

Here are some simple prayers that feel right to me.
Because God's love for me is so real, it's easy to be grateful for it and for him. And as I've said before, I am not perfect in pursuing a hair-on-fire prayer life. But over time, I have experienced some simple prayers that feel right:

- "Father, show me who needs prayer today."
- Then open your mind as God prepares his answer, because the answer might surprise you.
- "Father, let me stand with you in this particular matter. Align me with your will and tell me how to pray and how to help."
- "Jesus, please speak to me about how you want to use me. It's easy to get enthusiastic and run off in some direction that you haven't chosen. Better to ask first!"

If an area makes you shake, tell God, and ask for his strength and guidance. I know for a fact that God answers our honest and even desperate pleas for wisdom. And I can tell you of a time when I didn't ask, but just cowered under my bed in absolute dread, way out of logical boundaries! (I'm guessing you can imagine how that went, right?)

"Short prayers are long enough."
Spurgeon also says, "There were but three words in the petition which Peter gasped out as he began to sink — 'Lord, save me' (Mt 14:30) — but they were sufficient for his purpose. Not length but strength is desirable . . .

When we can do nothing, Jesus can do all things. So let us enlist his powerful aid upon our side, and all will be well" (Spurgeon 2010, Jan 14).

God's words to me – in or outside of a prayer setting – may point me in a general direction, or on rare occasions, to a very specific, detailed plan.

In the past, I've heard a general mission statement such as "refugee children from the war" or "women in desperate circumstances" (as I discussed earlier). And they don't usually include a carefully designed schedule with dates and destinations all tied up with a bow. I've always figured that's because God knows me so well and figures that if he gave me too many details up front, I would go charging off, not hearing anything else he said!

But I can remember an assignment that was clearly spelled out to me in detail from Day 1. My dear friend and Bible teacher, Candi Seely, was dying of ovarian cancer. On Sunday, April 6, 2014, I was sitting quietly before God, and I asked him: "How can I pray for Candi? I really have *no* idea. And what can I do?" His response was quick — less than six to eight minutes — and clear (although *not* in a booming external voice kind of way and *not* something I came up with on my own!) He said I should gather letters from Candi's friends, put them in a book, and take them to her. And I was to be quick about it. (Ah, he knows me well, and how long I can take in my pursuit of perfection!) So — no surprise here — I did just what he said.

I took his message that same day, passed it on to friends who knew and loved Candi, and gave everyone a deadline of Tuesday at noon. And it was all done by then! When I took her the book on Tuesday, April 8, she was surprised and so very pleased. And I made it clear to her that I was just following God's idea; I had *not* come up with it on my own. Candi was loved by all — seriously — and you might think she'd know that she was loved so well and so widely. Yet she was still blown away by the book and the love it conveyed from her many friends. Delighted, I'd say.

Every day from April 8 until April 18, when Candi went home to heaven, I thanked God for the opportunity to delight this wonderful woman and show her how very much God loved her. In many ways, the situation, for

Candi and her husband Greg, reminded me of my own long, satisfying, and at times crazy-making time with my darling Stayton. So it was wonderful to see God give her and Greg (and me) a kiss on the cheek with the book!

Prayer as Jesus taught it.
"If we think of prayer as the breath in our lungs and the blood from our hearts, we think rightly. Our blood flows, and our breathing continues without ceasing; we are not conscious of it, but it never stops. *We are not always conscious of Jesus keeping us in perfect oneness with God, but if we are obeying Him, He always is.* Prayer is not an exercise; it is the life [of a believer]. So beware of anything that stops the offering up of prayer. 'Pray without ceasing' (1 Thess 5:17). Maintain the childlike habit of offering up prayer in your heart to God all the time. And remember, Jesus never mentioned unanswered prayer. He had the unlimited certainty that prayer is always answered. Jesus says, 'Every one that asks receives' (Mt 7:8). And yet we say, 'But God, what about . . . ?' *God answers prayer in the best way, not sometimes, but every time*" [Italics mine] (Chambers May 26).

What Jesus says about prayer:
Jesus says: If you abide [live] in me, and my words abide in you, ask whatever you will and it shall be done for you. Jn 15:7
Jesus says: When you pray, don't be like the hypocrites who love to pray publicly on street corners and in the synagogues where everyone can see them. I assure you, that is all the reward they will ever get. Mt 6:5 NLT [And he says the same thing about fasting in Mt 6:16–18.]
Jesus says: Find a quiet, secluded place so you won't be tempted to role-play before God. Just be there as simply and honestly as you can manage. The focus will shift from you to God, and you will begin to sense his grace. Mt 6:6 MSG
Jesus says: The world is full of so-called prayer warriors who are prayer-ignorant. They're full of formulas and programs and advice, peddling techniques for getting what you want from God. Don't fall for that nonsense. This is your Father you are dealing with, and he knows better than you what you need. Mt 6:7–8 MSG
Jesus says: In this manner, therefore, pray: Our Father who is in heaven, Hallowed by your name. Your kingdom come. Your will be done, on earth as it is in heaven. Give us this day our daily bread. And forgive us our debts, as we

also have forgiven our debtors. And do not lead us into temptation, but deliver
us from evil. For Yours is the kingdom and the power and the glory forever.
Amen. Mt 6:9–13 NASB   Lk 11:2–4

Jesus says: Ask and it will be given to you; seek, and you will find; knock, and it
will be opened to you. Lk 11:9   Mt 7:7–8

Jesus spoke often about praying in his name. But he wasn't saying, "Use my
name as some sort of magic formula." Instead, when we pray, we should be one
with him *and* in him — praying with *his* heart, *his* character, *his* will, and *his*
purposes. (Check out the section on oneness in chapter 4 for more.)

Jesus says: This is what I want you to do: Ask the Father for whatever is in keeping with the things I've revealed to you. Ask in my name, according to my will,
and he'll most certainly give it to you. Your joy will be a river overflowing its
banks! Jn 16:23–24 MSG

Jesus says: On that day you will ask in my name. I do not say to you that I will
ask the Father on your behalf; for the Father himself loves you, because you
have loved me and have believed that I came from God. Jn 16:26–27 NRSV

Many people try to bargain with God in prayer. I don't suggest it!
I have heard people say that they could command God or demand
something from him. In fact, I was in a Bible study where the author (a
famous pastor) boasted about threatening God. "If you don't heal my
mother, I will no longer follow you." It made me shudder.

Or we might say to God, "Lord, I will purify my heart if you will answer my prayer." Or, "I will walk rightly before you if you will help me"
in some other area (Chambers June 20). But that's an odd way to have a
conversation with someone, isn't it? Imagine your best friend saying to
you, "I will be a loyal friend to you *if* you give me what I want." Is that
what *you* would want to hear?

OTHER WAYS GOD GETS OUR ATTENTION

"When we follow God, our spiritual antennae alert to him, we hear
what he is saying to us as a natural part of our spiritual walk. This is
the Christian life, being keenly responsive to the voice of God however
he may choose to speak to us. We can have our attention focused on a

person, a chore, or an idea, but at the same time, we are so tuned to God's voice that if he speaks to us, we immediately turn our attention to Him" (Stanley 1996).

Here's a little example: In May (2015), I was in a coffee shop and saw Julie, a woman I adore but don't see often. I said hi, and then impulsively went back to her table, hugged her, and said, "Have you told these people how very much I love you?" Later, as she was leaving, Julie stopped by and said, "I've just been in the bathroom and was a little teary, asking God, 'Why does Claudia love me like this? What have I done?'" And God showed her: "It isn't about you. She's spending so much time on this book — which is all about me — that the love is just flowing out of her." I was stunned by this. God is infinitely, massively huge and yet he takes the time to hug both of us and say, "I love you. I *am* here! I am paying attention." As we parted, I told her, "This is great, but my affection for you is *also* about you!" And she smiled, because she *must* know it's true.

Sadly, of course, there are times when we go our own way, instead of God's. And we find ourselves headed in a dangerous direction. Maybe we think God doesn't speak to us, or maybe we just don't want to listen. In these times, Dr. Stanley says, God can use unusual means to get our attention, including: "A restless spirit; an unsolicited word from another person; unusual circumstances (both bad and good); and unanswered prayers. Although God uses these methods to get our attention, they don't necessarily have a meaning in and of themselves. In other words, we should not conclude that because we have a restless spirit, we are on the right track or the wrong track.

"God's voice brings about a deep calmness in the spirit. Although we may be challenged by what God says for us to do, we will not have a sense of inner conflict, worry, or a troubled heart . . . This inner peace is not shaken, regardless of circumstances. When that sort of peace comes to us, we know we've heard from God, and we feel confident it is His voice: 'Let the peace of God rule in your hearts' (Col 3:15) . . . Pay attention to this feeling that flows from your innermost being. It is a confirming sign to you that you have or have not heard from God.

Finally, "If your heart is touched by a matter, or if you can't seem to shake the message that you have heard, take the matter before the Lord . . . Weigh the message and the messenger . . . Stop and ask the Lord what He is trying to say. Spend even more time in the Word and in prayer. Don't attempt to outrun this feeling or to throw yourself into some activity just to keep busy and to keep your mind occupied. Quiet yourself before the Lord so you can hear from Him clearly" (Stanley 1996). Get back in your "you and me, God" mode.

GOD'S TRUTH COMES BY LISTENING TO GOD AND READING HIS WORD, THEN DOING WHAT HE WANTS

Only with God's truth can I have a correct and truthful view of myself and the situation, not one that is skewed one way or the other. James 1:21–25 tells us it's not enough to *hear* the truth. We must *do* what we know to be true. And not delay! Brother Lawrence was a good model for this. He was very aware of his faults, but not discouraged by them. He confessed them to God, but did not obsess on them. When he had confessed, he peaceably resumed his usual practice of love and adoration. Like Brother Lawrence, whether I fail or succeed, I must admit God's role — or my refusal to include God. When I fail in my duty, I should readily acknowledge it, and say it's not surprising, since I was acting without God's presence. If I succeed, then I give God thanks, acknowledging that the strength comes from him. (Brother Lawrence, 20–22)

Some truth can be hard to hear.
The Bible tells the story of a rich young man/ruler who encounters Jesus and asks him what he must do to be saved. Jesus' hard words to the man are famous. First, Jesus told him to obey the commandments. Then, [21] Jesus, looking at him, loved him, and said to him, "You lack one thing: go, sell all that you have and give to the poor, and you will have treasure in heaven; and come, follow me." [22] When the young man heard this he went away sorrowful, for he had great possessions. (Mk 10:17–30; also

Mt 19:16–29; Lk 18:18–30) [Note: I'd never noticed that Jesus, looking at him, loved him. This is only in the Mark account, but it is striking.]

"Has God ever said something very difficult to you? This man understood what Jesus said. He heard it clearly, realizing the full impact of its meaning, and it broke his heart. He did not go away as a defiant person, but as one who was sorrowful and discouraged. He had come to Jesus on fire with zeal and determination, but the words of Jesus simply froze him. And Jesus did not go after him, but let him go" (Chambers Aug 17).

"Have you ever been there? Has God's Word ever come to you, pointing out an area of your life, requiring you to yield to him? Maybe he has pointed out certain personal qualities, desires, and interests, or possibly relationships of your heart and mind. If so, then you have often been speechless with sorrow. The Lord will not go after you and he will not plead with you . . . But this is where the battle is truly fought — in the realm of your will before God . . . What Jesus says is difficult — it is only easy when it is heard by those (believers) who have his nature in them. Beware of allowing anything to soften the hard words of Jesus Christ" (Chambers Aug 18).

ALWAYS FOLLOW THE LEADER
AND CONSULT HIM AS YOU MOVE FORWARD

So far, we've seen that God is loving, all-powerful, wise, and perfectly capable of mounting any kind of operation he desires. Our job is to learn how to listen and follow, rather than try to grab his reins and take over. It's a steep learning curve for some of us (she said smiling), but practice makes perfect. And I promise, you will be astonished at how well things work out! I'll illustrate with a very recent project, and how it went when I was grabbing the reins and when I was not. (Spoiler alert: this is a recurring "lesson" I have to learn!)

In November 2014, I was thinking about short-term missions. And that set me thinking about my grandson Christian, who wanted to learn more about God and experience him in a closer way. So we were strictly in God's ballpark here. And all was well. But then I grabbed the reins (can you relate?) and charged off in one direction. The idea was so appealing that I immediately got busy, getting applications, writing e-mails, and so on. Looking back, I can imagine God shaking his head just a little and saying with a smile, "Well, there she goes again." After a week or two of this, I began to wear down. Some doors were opening, but many were not. Did I instantly recognize this? You know I didn't, because I can be a *very* focused and determined woman when I have a goal in sight. I began to push harder, with fewer and fewer results. Then one morning, I woke up and recognized an important lesson: Don't try to drag God up or down the hill. HE is the leader!

. So God's lesson for me – one of many – is to continually consult with and listen to him even when I think I have the plan all figured out. In my case, I got the initial idea from God, but I tweaked that into something else. Not something bad or wicked. Just an add-on that was coming out of me rather than from God. So I need to get better at paying attention to all God's signals, and keep checking in with him. Then I can correct my course as he suggests.

So how did it turn out? Christian is listening to me as I write (and talk) my way through this book. He is reading parts of it, and our conversations are quite rich. So God's objective is being met, just not in the way I first imagined.

HEARING THE TRAIN: SOME CLOSING THOUGHTS

I live several miles from the closest train track and almost never hear the trains passing. But every once in a while, when I am outside and it is still, I can hear the whistle blowing. And it usually comes as a surprise to me. I will hear the whistle and then I think about trains.

In January 2013, as I heard the train, I realized that my experience with trains is a lot like our experience with God. Some of us have never heard the "whistle", and may even doubt there is such a thing as hearing God. Others have heard the whistle once or twice, but no longer listen for it. And even those of us who love "trains" and have heard the "whistle" often in our lives can still drift far from the tracks and experience long, silent times! Oswald Chambers often says that whether I hear God's call or not depends on the condition of my ears. And exactly what

I hear depends upon my spiritual attitude. In other words, am I listening? Am I close enough to the tracks? And do I believe the train will be there and that I can hear it?

Dearest Father, I thank you with all my heart for your continual help in staying close enough to you to hear your whistle. I delight in your Word, your instruction, and encouragement. I want to meditate daily on you and what you have to say to me — in the Bible and in the air! Because you sent your Son Jesus for me and I embrace him, I am like a tree planted by streams of water. And under your care, I yield fruit in my season, and my leaf does not wither (drawn from Ps 1:2–3).

Jesus, you know I struggle with several of the things we've talked about so far in this book: consistently spending lots of time with you, following faithfully instead of grabbing the reins and running, and on and on. But I never get a sense from you that you are disgusted with me, or "done with me". And that is a great gift from you to me, and I thank you. And it spurs me on, with love!

Help me to remember that the point of prayer is not to get answers from you, Father, but to have perfect and complete oneness with you . . . As believers, we are not here to prove that you answer prayer, but to be living trophies of your love and grace. . . . Finally, remind me daily that the only thing that can account for my prayer life is that it has become one with the prayer life of Jesus Christ. (drawn from Chambers, August 6). *cgs*

PRAYER AND MEDITATION FOR CHAPTER 5

CHAPTER 6 OUTLINE: GOD, WHO DO *YOU* SAY I AM? AND WHAT IS MY RELATIONSHIP TO YOU?

Jesus asks his disciples, "Who do you say I am?" And I believe
he continues to ask it of us. What does your life say to him?

Introduction: No matter what you think, God's crazy about you! And we can choose to bring God joy with our lives.

1. I am defined by God. I am who *God* says I am, not who I say I am, not who my circumstances say I am, not who my enemies or even my friends say I am.
    *   Scripture indicates that human beings are special to God in a number of ways.
    *   A healthy self-image is seeing yourself as God sees you, no more and no less.
2. If Jesus says I am valuable, who am I to disagree?
    *   Self-worth is interwoven into God's redemptive process.
    *   Self-worth is not the same as pride
3. In our close personal relationship with God, through Jesus, God leads and we follow. That's the plan.
4. My life in a car — or whose hands are really on the wheel? When I become a believer, God "installs" all sorts of "equipment" in me. I need to understand that and fully utilize everything he has given me. And I should ask him for whatever I need as I follow him.
    *   Everything we need for our spiritual walk is given to us.
    *   God has built each car/person for great things

- But do we know we have help at hand?
- If you don't know God and haven't met Jesus, I suggest you seriously take steps to do so. It isn't complicated!
- Some of the equipment and supplies God gives me are permanent and self-renewing. Others can be depleted and must be restocked often, even daily in some cases.

5. God also gives me courage and confidence in him so I can move forward. (More on this in chapter 9)
6. As a disciple of Jesus, I am God's partner in his great plans and work, not a passive onlooker. Together we produce "Holy Sweat".
7. Is God my Number 1? Does my life show it?

CHAPTER 6

GOD, WHO DO *YOU* SAY I AM? AND WHAT IS MY RELATIONSHIP TO YOU?

Jesus asks his disciples, "Who do you say I am?" And I believe
he continues to ask it of us. What does your life say to him?

Before you start this chapter, I'd like to suggest a little personal exercise. Sit quietly *by yourself*, with a pad and pen. Then ask God to show you what he has placed in you: character strengths, strong interests, talents, etc. I believe this is a key question for all Christians to consider.

I first did this with my daughter-in-law Kristi, during a 2014 Beth Moore conference. And neither of us found it easy. (Who am I kidding? We couldn't even do it at first!) Then in March 2015, I was sitting quietly, probably meditating in Scripture, and spontaneously God started reminding me of all he has put in me. I was surprised, but more than willing to play! The process took quite a while, because neither of us was in a big rush. And I listed items as he showed them to me — seeing each one for the grace-filled gift it was. It was a great experience, so try it, please. Find a "buddy" who will also do it, in his or her own private space, and you can keep each other accountable.

PS – Now it's September 2015 and I can't find the list I made after my session with God. But I'm thinking that *maybe* it's a question I should ask God periodically, rather than a one-time and then enshrined kind of deal

AN INTRODUCTION: "NO MATTER WHAT YOU THINK, GOD'S CRAZY ABOUT YOU!"

Years ago, I read an article with this title that blew me away, and I've never forgotten it. It was written by a Youth With A Mission (YWAM) leader Jim Stier, who begins by asking:

"Do you know that God loves you? God's love is such a foundational part of our faith that we probably don't think about it enough. But knowing that God loves us and understanding the true nature of that love are two different things. [As I was growing up] I heard a lot of sermons that went something like this: 'God is love, but he's also holy. He's pristine purity in an absolute sense. He dwells in unapproachable light. And us? We're just like worms! Before him even our acts of righteousness are like filthy rags. But in spite of everything that you are, God still loves you.

"Unfortunately, with the sort of background we have of being loved imperfectly [in the natural world], messages like this end up twisting our concept of God's love. I get the picture in my head of God reaching down with one hand to pull me to himself, yet with the other he's plugging his nose so he won't smell the stench. We're not taught that God is enthusiastic about us. We're taught instead that because he is such a noble God, he overcomes his natural repugnance and loves us since, after all, he's God, and God is love" (Stier, 3).

Stier remembers when he and his wife Pam were married and wrote their own vows to each other. "Now, suppose during the ceremony, she turned to me and said, 'Jim, I'm a very noble and compassionate woman, and you desperately need someone to love you. God knows it's not going to be easy to find anyone. So, I'm ready to offer my life on the altar of this sacrifice, and in a great act of pity and compassion, I will marry you today.' If she had done that, I would have left there as quickly as possible. None of us wants to be loved that way. In the same way, we're not attracted to God if we think that we're just another point on his list of divine obligations. But, thank God, the Bible doesn't reveal his love that way" (Stier 3).

Isaiah 62:4–5 tell us that as a bridegroom rejoices over his bride, so will God rejoice over you. So Stier asks, "Does this scripture reveal a God in heaven who is revolted by us but forces himself to do His duty and love us anyway? Of course not! It shows us a God who is actually emotional about us. He likes us. He has a desire for us. He wants to be close to us. Did you know that you're delightful? The Devil doesn't want you to find this out. [Because] If you discover how much God likes you, you'll want to hang around with him all the time and hear him tell you how much he delights in you. We usually call this a prayer life" (Stier 3).

We can choose to bring God joy!
Stier concludes with this astonishing thought: "God continually risks deep emotional pain by offering us his love. As a result, the greatest victim of all the sin in the world, all the evil, all the rejection of God and his law hasn't been any of the sinners. It's been God himself. The most amazing revelation in all of scripture is that after thousands of years of almost continual rejection by the vast majority of the human race, God still keeps Himself vulnerable to us.

"The central issue of your life, then, is that you have the potential to bring infinite joy or infinite sorrow to the heart of God. This is not because you're infinite but because he is and because the results of your choices here on earth will last forever. If I look into Jesus' eyes on that final day and see sadness because the sum of my life has been a source of disappointment and pain to him, it's not going to make any difference to me whether I had any money, or achieved any position, or was famous. None of that stuff will make any difference. Success for me and for you will be knowing that we have brought joy to the heart of God by returning the intimate love He has offered us" (Stier 6).

Thank you, Jim, for these wise words that echo even now in my mind, years after reading them. I am delighted to pass them on, now! And that leads me to our first key point in this chapter.

I AM DEFINED BY GOD. I AM WHO GOD SAYS I AM.

God says he loves us. Even before we accepted Jesus, God loved us. So, I am not who I say I am. I am not who my circumstances say I am, or who my enemies say I am. And I'm not even who my friends say I am. I have misunderstood this for many years, and since I'm probably not the only one, I've decided to address it here in this book.

In June 2001, I wrote in my journal: "It's easier to travel around the world, tramp on foreign soil, and engage in challenging ministry, than it is to submit my personality to God for his reshaping." And I'm guessing this is true for many of us. So, as a true-life example for you, I am facing my own serious flaw here in this book: a persistent and life-long distorted – and negative – view of myself. Even when I began my relationship with Jesus, I carried over my old self-image into my new life. So seeing myself as substantially less than God says I am has been something very difficult to shake. For way too long, I've heard that dog (a hound of hell?) nipping at my heels. This may not be your particular wound or personality glitch, but whatever yours is, I'm hoping this conversation will help us both!

Thirteen years after my journal entry, God finally said enough! And he said it so loud in my head, I couldn't miss it. In September 2014, I was having lunch with Tanya and Shelley, my two sisters from other mothers! And I was telling them for the tenth time (at least) about this problem of my tattered self-image. For several years, they've heard this, tried to encourage me, and show me that my view of myself is nowhere near the facts. But on *this* day, they both faced me down and said, "Make no mistake! This is Satan messing with you. He's been at it a long time, and you've let him have his way." So, over good Texas BBQ, we talked. And when I left that day, I knew clearly that God has had enough of this! It was time for me to acknowledge how serious this was. Time to start believing God and time for me to kick Satan to the curb — along with my determination to see myself as less than I am! Do you have anything like this dogging you? Let's see if what God says can bring some light!

Scripture tells us that human beings who faithfully follow him are special to God in a number of ways:

* He has redeemed me, called me by name; I am his. Isa 43:1
* Precious in God's eyes . . . Honored by God . . . Loved by God. Isa 43:4 . . . The apex of God's creation
* Called by his name, created for God's glory, made by God. His witness and his chosen servant. Isa 43:7, 10

- Branch of his planting, the work of his hands, to glorify God. Isa 60:21 A tree known by its fruit. Mt 12:33
- Oaks of righteousness that glorify the LORD. Isa 61:3
- A crown of beauty in the hand of the LORD and a royal diadem in the hand of my God. Isa 62:3
- Like a tree planted by water, that sends out its roots by the stream, doesn't fear the heat, and is fruitful even in drought. Ps 1:3; Jer 17:8 Rooted and grounded in love. Eph 3:17
- He rejoices over me . . . Isa 62:5 He rejoices over me with gladness. He quiets me by his love. He exults over me with loud singing. Zeph 3:17
- His treasured possession. Malachi 3:17
- A servant of Christ and a steward of the mysteries of God. 1 Cor 4:1

"A healthy self-image is seeing yourself as God sees you – no more and no less.
Having a healthy self-esteem is not our ultimate goal. Knowing Christ in all his fullness is. Some people have an inflated view of themselves (pride), while others have a self-deprecating view of themselves (false humility). Sometimes this is a result of pride and other times a result of the lack of knowledge. What we need is a realistic and biblical view."
(McDowell, 35)

IF GOD THE FATHER AND HIS SON JESUS SAY
I AM VALUABLE, WHO AM I TO DISAGREE?

Don't you see that you can't live however you please,
squandering what God paid such a high price for? The physical
part of you is not some piece of property belonging to the
spiritual part of you. God owns the whole works. So let people
see God in and through your body.   1 Cor 6:19–20 MSG

Paul described Jesus as the image of the invisible God, the firstborn of all creation (Col 1:15-20). This connection is no accident but part of God's plan.   Paul mentions seven unique characteristics of Christ, which fittingly qualify him to have the supremacy (v 18+). So, if Jesus *is* indisputably supreme, according to God's plan, why would I refuse to accept his view of me?

"The feeling of being important to Christ and to each other was intended to be the normal experience of our lives. It's a wonderful experience to be able to appraise yourself honestly and still feel good about who you are. And we should look at ourselves and our God-given abilities — not as an individual competition — but as a basis for serving others. Christians who believe we should negate self and put ourselves down fail to stress that humankind also has great worth to God. This worth is not from what we have made of ourselves, but from what God has done for us and in us. We are fallen sinners, yet we still were created in God's image. We were, in fact, the crown of his creation, which gives all humankind intrinsic worth. As Francis Schaeffer says, 'Man is sinful and wonderful' " (McDowell 37).

Self-worth is interwoven into God's redemptive process.
"The One who bought us with a price knows our true worth. The price God paid for you and me is Jesus (1 Cor 6:20; 1 Pet 1:18–19)

. . . His death on the cross was the payment for our sins . . . That is his statement of your value. And God's view of you and your worth is the true one. Ephesians 1:18 (LB) confirms this: 'I want you to realize that God has been made rich because we who are Christ's have been given to him.'

"God's grace is shown in that, even though people are sinners in their fallen state, God considers them valuable enough to be 'purchased back', even when the price is something truly precious, the blood of Jesus (see Lk 15) . . . Only through a loving God's intervention can humankind's two natures be reconciled. That reconciliation is a divine solution, foreign to human intellect and understanding" (McDowell 38–39).

But self-worth is not the same as pride.
"It is a conviction that you have fundamental value because you were created by God in his image and because Jesus died for your sins . . . Pride [by contrast] points to self . . . [and] is an attitude of superiority,

a puffed-up mentality, that manifests itself in an arrogant, unrealistic estimation of oneself in relation to others." See 1 Cor 4:6–7, 18–19; 5:2; 8:1–2; 13:4. (McDowell 38–39).

God opposes pride and a haughty spirit (Prov 16:18; 1 Pet 5:5; Jas 4:6). But sometimes Christians fall into the trap of wanting people to glorify or praise them, not God, for what he has done in their lives. But our success comes through Christ only. Elizabeth Skoglund writes: "The problem is not . . . the Scriptures but rather that the words pride and humility are not correctly understood in the total light of Scripture. Pride in the biblical sense involves a not-honest estimate of oneself. Real humility is simply an absence of concentration upon oneself. It means that while I accept myself, I don't need to prove my worth excessively either to myself or to others" (Skoglund quoted by McDowell 39–40).

IN OUR CLOSE PERSONAL RELATIONSHIP WITH GOD THROUGH JESUS, GOD LEADS AND WE FOLLOW. THAT'S THE PLAN.

"Living a life of faith means never knowing where you are being
led. It also means loving and knowing the One who is leading.
It is literally a life of faith, not of understanding and reason — a life
of knowing Him who calls us to go . . . A life of faith is not a life of
one glorious mountaintop experience after another, like soaring on
eagles' wings, but is a life of day-in and day-out consistency — a life
of walking
without fainting (see Isa 40:31)." Chambers Mar 19

In Jesus, the whole fullness of deity dwells bodily. And I have been
filled in him, who is the head of all rule and authority. Col 2:9–10

Psalm 139 beautifully pictures how intimately we are related to God.
¹ O Lord, you have searched me and known me!   ² You know when I sit down and when I rise up; you discern my thoughts from afar. ³You search out my path and my lying down and are acquainted with all my ways. . . . ¹³ For you formed my inward parts; you knitted me together in my mother's womb. ¹⁴ I praise you, for I am fearfully and wonderfully made. Wonderful are your

works; my soul knows it very well . . .[17] How precious to me are your thoughts, o God! . . . [23] Search me, o God, and know my heart! Try me and know my thoughts! [24] . . . and lead me in the way everlasting.
Heb 13:20–21 AMP [20] Now may the God of peace [Who is the Author and the Giver of peace] . . . [21]Strengthen (complete, perfect) and make you what you ought to be and equip you with everything good that you may carry out His will; [while He Himself] works in you and accomplishes that which is pleasing in His sight, through Jesus Christ (the Messiah); to Whom be the glory forever and ever (to the ages of the ages). Amen.

MY LIFE IN A "CAR" — WHOSE HAND IS REALLY ON THE WHEEL?

When you become a believer, God installs all sorts of "equipment" in you. We need to understand that and fully utilize everything he has given us. And we should ask him for whatever we need as we follow him, including wisdom, peace, grace, strength, and patience.

My grandson Jacob (age 16 at the time), and I were talking about God in June 2011. He told me that in English class that spring, they had somehow gotten onto the topic of God (you've *got* to love West Texas, seriously). And a girl said that God's hand was on the "steering wheel" of our lives. But Jacob disagreed, saying, instead, that God has firmly put our hands on the wheel.

We call that "free will" and many of us (if we're honest) have wondered why on earth God gave it to us, considering how flawed we all are! And many of us, having no idea of God or his character, muddle on without him, trying to live life in our own strength, and falling constantly.

This conversation with Jacob led to a series of talks over several weeks, leading us to a very unconventional picture of us as both car and driver. God created each one of us (nonbelievers and believers alike) unique, sitting in our own "car"— body, mind, and emotions. We each have basic equipment, and we come in all shapes, sizes, and colors. God likes it that way! Before we know God, we are headed on a lifelong journey with no map, no Driver's Education, no GPS, and no one in the car with us to guide, encourage, and teach us. We have no special provisions other than our natural talents.

But God has planned and built in very special equipment that must be "activated" or poured in from above. After we accept Jesus, God activates that equipment and places even more things into our car to help us on the journey. Under the hood and in the back seat you'll find a full supply of provisions.

Everything we need is given to us:

- A comprehensive "manual" (the Bible) telling how the car works and how to maintain it properly
- The Holy Spirit in the front seat with us, guiding, correcting, encouraging, and teaching
- An engine with two compartments: a hybrid system that switches between two forms of combustion: the "regular" engine, *and* the second engine powered by God, not us!
- A state-of-the-art GPS system, with God's voice speaking to us
- Refreshments and treats for the long journey (along with one or two bitter pills when we need them)
- Lots of maps
- An unlimited "gas" card, which, when activated, pro-vides all the "power" we'll need (Think of God's Word and the time you spend with God as a gas station, refilling your spirit.)

God has built each car/person for great things.
He created us — the car, the driver, and our talents — but we have a choice. Do we turn to him for the rest? Do we activate the optional features? Or do we go it alone? Life changes radically (or should) when we meet the Father, Jesus his Son, and the Holy Spirit. God offers us Driver's Education, with a great manual (the Bible) and an instructor by our side every step (the Holy Spirit). And like Driver's Ed, there is a "book learning" component *and* a practical course. Just reading the book won't make you a good driver. We have to get out on that road

and do what we've learned. Just like regular Driver's Ed, instructors can cover the material, but they cannot force us to drive well.

But do we know we have help at hand? And do we use it?
God has placed many provisions within our reach. But do we know they are there? Do we act like we do? I am a believer and follower of Jesus. And I see the wonderful provisions under the hood, on the dash, in the passenger seat, and in the back seat — at least intellectually. But I've found that in many areas, I still push forward at times, using only my own will and knowledge for fuel. Foolishly, I don't activate the second engine, out of pride, ignorance, feeling defeated when I'm not, etc. Too many times, I leave the gas card untouched. I don't even hear the GPS talk to me. And I don't turn to the other person in the car, the Holy Spirit, and confess, "I can't do this alone. I won't go another mile without your help."

I'll admit this is a fairly "out of the box" picture of our lives before and after God. But I'm hoping it has served as a sort of spiritual brain teaser for you and me. And maybe now we can consider our own lives. What does the road ahead look like for *you?* Is it rocky? Smooth? Both? What's your destination? Have you taken a wrong turn? And are you using the equipment God gave you for the trip?

If you don't know God and haven't met Jesus at this point, I suggest you seriously take steps to do so. Is it complicated? Absolutely not! Just say to God:

- "I don't know you, really. I've heard about you, but I haven't really talked to you, or taken advantage of all the special 'equipment' you've laid out for me."
- "I want to know you, not just for what you can do for me, but for who you really are: the great Creator, the ultimate loving Father, the Savior who has given everything to bring me closer to you, and the Holy Spirit who will guide, comfort, and teach me."

- "I want you, God, however that works! And I know from Jesus' life that you want me too!"
- I fully accept you and your Son Jesus. I know he was – and is – your plan to bring me to you, Father. Thank you for sending him to save me!

If you do know God and have met and accepted Jesus, be super grateful. But ask yourself, am I using the special equipment God has laid out before me? Or am I one of those Christians who knows about the equipment and the provisions, but won't pick them up and use them! Then ask God: "If I am that person, Father, let me start today to hear you and do what you ask. Help me fully use all the equipment and provisions you have given me — in my own life and in the lives of others around me. Work on me from the inside out, and I promise to rely on all the wonders that were mine the day I accepted your love and your sacrifice for me."

Some of the equipment and supplies God gives me are permanent and self-renewing. Others can be depleted and must be restocked often, even daily in some cases.
God wants me to access these gifts and equipment, and to ask him for whatever I need to accomplish his plans and purposes. If I need a peaceful spirit – and do I ever! – I need to ask him. If I need to rein in my temper or tap into God's wisdom, I need to ask him for help. And so on. Because the truth is this: Only God can give me the equipment, the power, and the grace to do whatever he wants me to do, and to become everything he plans for me to become! Without him, it's impossible.

"In a very real sense, not one of us is qualified, but it seems that God continually chooses the most unqualified to do his work, to bear his glory. If we are qualified, we tend to think that we have done the job ourselves. If we are forced to accept our evident lack of qualification, then there's no danger that we will confuse God's work with our own, or God's glory with our own" (L'Engle 1980).

GOD GIVES ME COURAGE AND CONFIDENCE
IN HIM, SO I CAN MOVE FORWARD

This may be a completely new idea for you. But take a deep breath and consider this: We are all bound to fear something, or several "somethings". But the truth is that God can and does give us courage and wisdom in those times. Even when we seem to be drowning, he can feel our splashing and crazy attempts to stay above water and will join us in our struggle. Now whether we experience this will depend in large part on how we connect with God. For instance, if I'm God and I'm standing on your porch with an armload of courage for you — but you refuse to open the door — what do you think will happen next?

In his sermon on May 3, 2015, Pastor Ray Still spoke about an older couple whom he had known from childhood. Years before, they had suffered the terrible loss of a son. And yet they had moved gracefully through that loss, and had even supported Ray in his own later sorrows. One day he asked them how on earth they had done it. And they said that each morning they prayed, "God, just help me put one foot in front of another today." Doesn't that hit you right in the heart? Every day, this precious couple lifted their arms to God and asked him for strength, wisdom, and grace for the day – a wonderful example of how God, despite their tragedy, clearly worked in and through them to grow and perfect his new creation within their hearts.

Josh 1:6–9 NRSV . . . Be strong and courageous; do not be frightened or dismayed, for the LORD your God is with you wherever you go.
2 Chron 20:15b, 17b . . . Fear not, the battle is not yours but God's.
Eph 3:20 . . . [20] I trust God, who is able to do immeasurably more than all we ask or imagine, according to his power that is at work within us.
Heb 10:35–36 AMP [35] Do not, therefore, fling away your fearless confidence, for it carries a great and glorious compensation of reward.
[36] For you have need of steadfast patience and endurance, so that you may perform and fully accomplish the will of God, and thus receive and carry away [and enjoy to the full] what is promised.

AS A DISCIPLE OF JESUS, I AM GOD'S PARTNER IN HIS GREAT PLANS AND WORK, NOT A PASSIVE ONLOOKER. TOGETHER WE PRODUCE "HOLY SWEAT"

When I am in the groove spiritually, together God and I produce *"Holy Sweat"*, a wonderful term created by author Tim Hansel in his book of the same title. He says the phrase is designed "to shock us in a joyful way and provoke us to a new level of thought", and it certainly does that for me!

"Holy sweat is a paradox. The word holy is to remind us of our highest calling and our common bond. And the word 'sweat' is something we must do on our own . . . *Holy Sweat* reveals that the holy is here within us, waiting to pour out of us, and that it's much more accessible than we ever would have thought. It's grace with blisters; it's redemption in overdrive" (Hansel 12).

Tim Hansel has tapped into an essential and lasting truth, of course. And throughout our pages here, you will read scripture and comments that bolster this notion of a partnership with God. It may be old news to you, but for me, it's a daily reminder that while God has his marvelous part to play, so do I!

Long before this holy sweat phrase was born (and before *any* of us was born, for that matter), Oswald Chambers and others were hammering away at the same theme. "God formed His Son in me through sanctification, setting me apart from sin and making me holy in his sight (see Gal 4:19). But I must begin to transform my natural life into spiritual life by obedience to him . . . I also have a responsibility to keep my spirit in agreement with His Spirit. And when I do, Jesus gradually lifts me up to the level where he lived, a level of perfect submission to his Father's will" (Chambers Mar 18).

IS GOD *REALLY* MY NUMBER 1?

If so, does my life show that? Daily we can learn to love and follow God more and more, with all that we have and all that we are. God has equipped us to do this through his Spirit.

We've established that loving God with all you have is vital (Lk 10:27; Mk 12:29–30; Mt 22:37–38). It is the absolute *foundation* for all of Jesus' life and ministry. And God has equipped me through his Spirit so that I can do it! So this message is woven throughout the Bible and throughout this book. Jesus was *always* pointing us toward the Father, urging us to love him, believe in him, and to serve him. We need God's help to do it. For more, see chapter 4.

Oswald Chambers says, unflinchingly as usual, that when I look at my priorities, "The first thing I must be willing to admit – when I begin to examine what controls and dominates me – is that *I am the one responsible* for having yielded myself to whatever it may be" (Oswald Mar 14).

Father, once I have settled in my mind and heart that I love you, I need to make my life agree with that. If I place all sorts of things, people, and ideas ahead of you, I need to revisit those decisions often and make my love for you more than lip service.

PRAYER AND MEDITATION FOR CHAPTER 6

CHAPTER 7 OUTLINE: STRAIGHT TALK ABOUT GRIEF, SORROW, AND GOD'S PEACE AND COMFORT — WHEN YOUR OX IS *REALLY* IN A DITCH

God is ever-present and active, even when my ox is in a ditch and life is hard. But surprisingly, there are little gifts — hard to spot, I'll admit — in the cart, even when the ox and the cart are in the ditch with me!

OVERVIEW: Following God, in good times and bad.

1. God is always present with us and working in our lives. We need to stop, look, and listen, and then join him.
2. God permits trials and painful circumstances, and even discipline when we need it. But God is not about fixing my every problem.
3. Grief and sorrow are not one-size-fits-all. Each of us has our individual experiences and ways of coping. But in all cases, we can share our sorrow and grief with God. He is a great comfort and source of wisdom and peace during our times of trouble and grief, whether we caused the difficulty or not; even when our suffering and grief seems too horrible to bear; and even in those times of discipline and pruning, which we richly deserve because of our own mistakes and bad choices.
    *   You have every right to grieve.
    *   My own grief story
    *   Happy Anniversary, dear boy
4. God's peace and comfort can invade the deepest grief and suffering. God is our comforter, always! And his peace is amazing.

* The God of peace will crush Satan as he tries to exploit our grief and suffering.
* God's peace and comfort can be extended to come through fellow travelers, friends new and old, small prayer and study groups, pastors and other counselors. Scripture is rich with words of comfort, including Jesus' words, Isaiah 40, and Jeremiah 31, among others.

5. We are still the people God says we are, in good times and in bad. As believers, we know he will never leave us. And he forgives us. *But* we also know that any vice or sin takes its toll on us, even when God forgives.

6. Cherish God's help as we endure and cope with our struggles.

7. A major part of God's help during our tough times is his faith-building gym – which is always open — in good times and in bad. The elements are:
* The foundation
* The wood
* The nails
* And my life depends absolutely on whether I spend enough time in the 'gym'.

8. And finally, let's talk about some of the surprising "gifts" tucked into our cart, even while we, the ox, and the cart are still deep in that ditch.

CHAPTER 7

STRAIGHT TALK ABOUT GRIEF, SORROW, AND GOD'S PEACE AND COMFORT — WHEN YOUR OX IS *REALLY* IN A DITCH

Jesus says (just before he is arrested and crucified): I have told you these things, so that in me you may have peace. In this world you will have trouble. But take heart! I have overcome the world. Jn 16:33

"A typical view of the Christian life is that it means being delivered from all adversity. But it actually means being delivered in and through adversity and hard times, which is something very different. (Chambers August 2).

OVERVIEW: FOLLOWING GOD
IN GOOD TIMES AND BAD

God is ever-present and active even when my ox is in a ditch, and life is very hard. And surprisingly, there are even little gifts (hard to spot, I'll admit) in the cart, even when the ox, the cart, and I are all in the ditch!

You will find that I am very focused on how God comes into play during our difficult and tragic times. And you may correctly assume that one reason for this focus is my own years-long journey with my husband through the horrific sea that is Alzheimer's disease. But we are not alone in what we've gone through. It is replayed throughout the world, even though the details and intensity may differ. So it's a valid field of inquiry: Where does God fit in when things aren't all ponies and merry-go-rounds?

As I've said before, I didn't know God until later in my life. Naturally, that had its downsides. But one upside is that we met Jesus

person-to-person in the midst of an exciting and faithful mission orga-
nization. And there, the focus of all teaching and projects was twofold: a
close and personal relationship with God, and a heart for telling people
about God and how they too could have that relationship. So, we never
heard messages like this: If things are trouble-free in your life, you are
doing something right and you have God on a string, doing what you
want. On the other hand, if things are bad, God is bashing you for some
reason, and you either deserve it, or you don't.

In this new and exciting environment, no one presented God as a
disinterested old man in the sky, a watchmaker who had finished his
work and now just sat with arms folded, watching us. And he was not
portrayed as a a whimsical puppet master or as a slot machine rigged to
guarantee me success or wealth. So, from the beginning of my walk with
God, I've known that life is not a guaranteed recess period for faithful
believers. There is great joy in life, and there may indeed be times of
great difficulty. During these tough times, it is fair for solid believers to
cry and ask God, "Why me, God?" But it's not a question I ask.

I will be as straight with you as I can, sharing what I know are truths
from God's own Word and from my own life. So relax. No need to put
on your "pumps and pearls" for this conversation. Shoot, you don't even
need to put on your shoes. Just come with me, and let's examine God's
role as a power and a comfort in our dark days.

Ditches can be small and scary or large and almost hopeless.
What looks easy to one of us may be quite disturbing to someone else.
And we can find ourselves in a ditch – small or large – when we never
even saw it coming! So we won't be comparing ditches here, but looking
at how to survive them – by fully clinging to God for help and comfort.
For he is our God of hope!

God is working inside and outside the ditch!
As we've seen so far, God is always in there pitching, wooing, loving,
teaching, building our faith, and (when we need it) disciplining us. And
all that he does can happen in and out of the ditch! So, I want us to look
at life *during* the trouble, in the fire, and how we can connect with God

in a life-affirming and faith-building way. And I want us to look at the time *before* the trial or trouble. What are we doing now (with God's help) to strengthen our faith, to change our hearts and minds, so we become more Christ-like? What can we do now to build our faith, for a better life today and to sustain us in later, more difficult times?

Everything we've learned so far will help. But in this chapter, we'll go a bit further, to address the inevitable times when we find ourselves in difficulty, either by our own design or at the hands of someone (or something) else. One thing I will not be doing is shining you on! There are enough religious platitudes and gloss-overs in this world to last us for all eternity. Instead, we will be dealing with truth, not wishful thinking. And believe me, *the truth of God is big enough and good enough to handle it all!*

You will meet critics and cheerleaders near the ditch.
Stand firm when someone starts to tell you that your presence in a "ditch" is always your own fault or God's way of disciplining you. Or that you just didn't pray enough. I was once in a Bible study where the study's author used the word "discipline" over and over to describe times of sorrow. I flinched whenever I read his assertions, because while God may indeed discipline me (and rightfully so), all trouble is *not* — I repeat, *not* — God's discipline on my life. So please feel free to reject that particular cup of poison whenever someone offers it to you. (Obviously, I will not be citing that author in this book!)

As we move along this path of discovery and determination, let's consider these words from Charles H. Spurgeon, a preacher who lived *many* years ago and *still* speaks truth to us today. "I walked last week through the long galleries which vanity has dedicated to all the glories of France. You pass through room after room where especially you see the triumphs of Napoleon in writhing bodies and in the blood and vapor and smoke . . . In another place in Paris there stands a column made with the cannons taken by the Emperor in battle.

"O Jesus! You have better than this—a trophy made of forgiven souls—of eyes which wept but whose tears have been wiped away — of broken hearts that have been healed and of saved souls that forever more rejoice! What trophies Christ has to make him glorious, both now and forever: trophies of living hearts that love him. Trophies of immortal spirits who find their Heaven in gazing upon His beauties" (Spurgeon 1862).

GOD IS ALWAYS PRESENT AND WORKING IN OUR LIVES, IN GOOD TIMES AND BAD. WE NEED TO STOP, LOOK, AND LISTEN, AND THEN JOIN HIM!

Jesus says: [17] . . . "My Father is working until now, and I am working . . . [19] . . . the Son can do nothing of his own accord, but only what he sees the Father doing. For whatever the Father does, that the Son does likewise.
[20] For the Father loves the Son and shows him all that he himself is doing. And greater works than these will he show him . . . Jn 5:17, 19–20

God is always working on, around, through, and in me.
Henry Blackaby's *Experiencing God* Bible study is priceless. One reason is its emphasis on God's continual presence and activity. Blackaby calls it "watching God work and then joining him", just as Jesus watched to see where his Father was working and joined him. God accomplishes his work through his people. And this is the way he works with you and with me. God reveals what he is about to do and that becomes an invitation to join him. Then I come to know God by experience as I obey him and he accomplishes his work through me" (Blackaby 16,19, 24).

"Jesus' purpose is to make a person exactly like himself, and the Son of God is characterized by self-expenditure.
If we believe Jesus, it is not what we gain, but what he pours through us that really counts . . . Our spiritual life cannot be measured by success as the world measures it, but only by what God pours through us — and we cannot measure that at all . . . God poured out the life of His Son 'that the world through him might be saved' (Jn 3:17). Are we prepared to pour out our lives for him? . . . Now is the time for us to break 'the flask' of our lives, to stop seeking our own satisfaction, and to pour out our lives before him. Our Lord is asking who of us will do it for him" (Chambers Sept 2).

GOD PERMITS TRIALS AND PAINFUL CIRCUMSTANCES
IN OUR LIVES, AND DISCIPLINE WHEN WE NEED IT

Some say that God actually causes *all* of our trials and difficulties, and that they show his concern for us. That may be true if we are on a dangerous path, and God sticks a giant speed bump in our way to discipline us and set us straight. But there are *many* other trials and troubles that don't fit in that category at all. God certainly does permit these terrible things, and uses them to work in our lives for good. And if you see every downturn or disaster as God's punishment or God's active hand, that is certainly your right. But I do not. Some enjoy debating this, but since God is the only one who knows it *all*, I am more than happy to leave all of that to debate team members, and move on.

Our difficult times may come because we have made mistakes, stepped off the right path, and turned our back on God and what we know is right. Then hard times come, as a consequence of our screw up. If we have done wrong things, we can confess them, repent or turn our back on them, and run back to God and his way! But there are other times, when we do our very best to live a wise and just life, only to have our ox fall in the ditch anyway! A painful, even devastating circumstance or trial arises, and we have done nothing to deserve it. Trust me, I've experienced both kinds of grief and suffering. And I know the difference. (Remember, you are talking to a woman whose darling and faithful husband suffered for years with Alzheimer's.)

Finally, there are those faithful and heroic Christians who experience trials as they stand up for Jesus in a doubting and fallen world. Their suffering may be great but their behavior is honorable and glorifies God. So, however I end up in the ditch — whether I drove my ox straight into it, or I was sideswiped and ended up there — my life is still hard! And God is still concerned and willing to help, guide, and comfort me.

But God is not about fixing my every problem.
We know that for those who love God and follow Jesus daily, all things work together for good, for those who are called according to his

purpose (Rom 8:28). And no matter what problem I am facing, God's grace is sufficient for me (2 Cor 12:7-10). In fact, he can use my problems as part of his sanctifying process in my life (See Job 23:10). All the while, God is keeping his eye on the ball, fulfilling his eternal purpose in the midst of my problems (Rom 5:3-4; Jas 1:2-4). So even though on the outside it may look like our life is falling apart, on the inside, where God is making new life, not a day goes by without his unfolding grace (2 Cor 4:16-18 MSG). Remember, God is in this for the long game, and it's a good perspective for us to have as well. Look at David's life if you want an example. The Bible shows us that David was in and out of life's school of hard knocks throughout his entire lifetime, and we are no different. And as he did with David, God can teach us much during these times. And along with some hard lessons, there are also showers of grace, refreshing streams, and green pastures. So we can agree that life is an unending sequence of good times and hard times. If we can accept that, then perhaps we can begin to understand that building our character in the easy times will reap rewards when (not *if*) we hit the wall!

Jesus certainly knows what a deep ditch – and fear – looks like!

And he knew what to do! Go first to God. Max Lucado describes it in his book *3:16: . . . The Numbers of Hope:*

"Jesus anguished? Cheeks streaked with tears? Face flooded with sweat? . . . You remember the night. Jesus . . . kneeled down and prayed, 'Father, if you are willing, take away this cup of suffering. But do what you want, not what I want' . . . His sweat was like drops of blood falling to the ground" (Lk 22:41–44 NCV).

"Jesus was more than anxious; he was afraid. How remarkable that Jesus felt such fear. But how kind that he told us about it. We tend to do the opposite. Gloss over our fears. Cover them up. . . . Not so with Jesus. We see no mask of strength, but we do hear a request for strength. 'Father, if you are willing, take away this cup of suffering'. *The first one to hear his fear is his Father.* He could have gone to his mother. He could have confided in his disciples. He could have assembled a prayer meeting. All would have been appropriate, but none was his priority.

"How did Jesus endure the terror of the crucifixion? He went first to the Father with his fears. He modeled the words of Psalm 56:3 NLT: 'When I am afraid, I put my trust in you'. Do the same with yours. Don't avoid life's Gardens of Gethsemane. Enter them. Just don't enter them alone. And while there, be honest. Pounding the ground is permitted. Tears are allowed. And if you sweat blood, you won't be the first. Do what Jesus did; open your heart" (Lucado 2007, 185-186).

And what do we *really* fear?

Of course there are many things we fear, too long a list to itemize here. But Oswald Chambers suggests some other things that frankly shocked me, because most of them are not on our conscious radar, but they were so on target. Oswald suggests that we have a fear of letting go. And we fear that somehow Jesus Christ will be defeated. We fear that the very things our Lord stood for – love, justice, forgiveness and kindness among men – will not win out in the end and will represent an unattainable goal for us. He says that God doesn't just call us to hang on by our fingernails and do nothing. Instead, he calls us to work deliberately, knowing with certainty that God will never be defeated" Chambers Feb 22).

These hit me like a brick – or really, a load of bricks. And I thank God that he showed this to Oswald, so he could show it to me almost one hundred years later!

GRIEF AND SORROW ARE NOT ONE-SIZE-FITS-ALL

We each have our individual experiences and ways of coping. But in every situation, we can share our sorrow and grief with God. He is a great comfort and source of wisdom and peace during our times of trouble and grief,

- whether we caused the difficulty or not;
- even when our suffering and grief seems too horrible to bear;
- and even in those times of discipline and pruning, which we richly deserve because of our own mistakes and bad choices.

Most of us have known suffering, sorrow, and grief. Some soldier on, while others hide under the bed. But whether or not I can see your grief, inside you it is painfully alive and real! And sadly, whether we intend to or not, we may sometimes judge how someone else copes with sorrow. I was in a group once when several people were praising a woman (not in attendance) who was handling her husband's out-of-the-blue death with great serenity (at least in public). They said it was clear that God was with her. I agreed in principle, of course. But I contend, and said so then, that if, instead, this woman had been in her bed sobbing for a week or three, God was *still* there with her.

I have a dear friend Pat, whom I've loved since 2005, when we first met! Her adult son died some years ago. He was her youngest, a wonderful companion, and of course she loved him mightily. Now, Pat doesn't walk around today shrieking with grief, but I promise you, Kevin is still as strong in her heart as he ever was. She will never forget him and she will never "get over it" in the sense that people (who are not mothers) think grieving mothers "should" behave. Her sorrow is on the inside, and she doesn't commit her life to it. But still, her darling boy is there, with her, always. And I *so* get it, because of my time and loss of Stayton!

We may not understand all the dimensions of someone else's grief, but we *can* remember that it is real and difficult for them. And we need to treat them accordingly, with the love and compassion God calls for. The very last thing we need is for someone to judge us from the shadows, and somehow measure our closeness to God by how politely and calmly we seem to handle our grief and sorrow.

You have *every* right to grieve!

My concept of loss and grief has expanded while writing this section. I am grieving the loss of my husband, but others are grieving the loss of a child, or a stable financial life, or the slow deterioration of their body or their mind. Whatever the source, grieving people can be frustrated by the lack of understanding from those around them. On-lookers (children, friends and others) can be baffled by the level of grief in their dad or friend, because he or she had been so strong before the loss. Some even try to talk the mourner out of it by saying, "Hey, you've known for several years that he/she was failing. Surely his death is no surprise."

Fortunately, as I talk with people about this, I am able to be calm (now *that* is God, I promise you). I assure them that their friends and family probably aren't trying to be deliberately cruel. But if the griever can somehow get back in the saddle, so to speak, then others won't have to worry about him/her any more. And then I share with them one of my precious "gifts" from the cart: You have every right to grieve. Your husband (or wife or son) was a wonderful person. *No one* truly knows all that you are going through. There is no timetable or schedule. You must be true to yourself in this. God is with you and will be no matter how long it takes.

My own grief story.
As I write this particular section on grief, my husband has been gone two years. When Stayton was diagnosed, I started crying (never in his sight of course), and I couldn't seem to stop. It wasn't giant sobs, but what I called "leaking", water just oozing out of my eyes much of the time. Many months into this, I had a checkup with my internist so I could get a refill on my cholesterol meds. He asked me how Stayton was, and of course I started "leaking". After a while, he suggested that I should try an antidepressant to help deal with this struggle. I rejected the idea, considering it weak and almost cliché for a middle-aged woman. But he said, wisely, "What if it helps you quit crying?" Now *that* got my attention!

So he prescribed the medicine, and after seeking "permission" from several friends for such a weak approach, I started taking the pills. And I did so off and on for several years. It didn't make me numb or high or blind to the loss. I just was able to stop "leaking", which was a *very* good deal! I tell you this because if you are drowning in grief, it is easy to somehow worry about what other people will think of you. And that includes your taking the "easy way", medication. Please, I beg you, don't be influenced by what you imagine are the opinions of friends and family. Do what is prudent and wise, consulting with your doctor. And accept that medication does *not* mean you don't trust God, although some may try to sell that slop to you at some point!

Because we loved each other so intensely, I always figured that I wouldn't really survive my husband's death. You may say that's a bit melodramatic *and* a lapse in faith, but it's true anyway. But when the time came for him to move to heaven after years of illness, God miraculously wrapped me in a sort of divine cotton. And I remained upright, to my continuing astonishment! But if God had allowed another route, and I had clung to my mattress for weeks (or longer), he would have still been my companion and my support, loving me and not judging me as I lay there bereft.

Whether I was vertical or prone, I loved, and still love. my husband as fiercely and passionately as I did when he was alive. That kind of amazing love never dies! And eventually, I surrendered to that truth, no matter how it looked to those around me. So, I feel free to talk about him. I have pictures of him all around. To me he is alive in heaven. But I miss him terribly, because we really were joined at the hip. And that does not change as time passes. I am sure that some of you have experienced that same feeling in your own lives. My advice? Embrace it! Don't surrender your life to it, but continue to love your lost one. And be grateful to God every day that you were blessed enough to have him or her in your life as long as you did.

Happy Anniversary, dear boy.
As I write this bit, it's mid-May 2015, and as usual, I've been happily working on this book. But today is also the anniversary of the day I met Stayton thirty-seven years ago! From the very beginning, it's been our most important anniversary, because that day changed our lives forever and gave us a love neither of us ever suspected was possible. In fact, when we'd known each other three months, Stayton made me a little "award" commemorating the date, with a quarter (for a quarter of a year) smack in the middle. Then, when we'd known each other six months, he made a larger "award" with a half dollar in the center. And of course on our one-year anniversary, I had a dollar bill on the "award".

That was our life together, so it's no surprise that I've been thinking about this day for weeks. I thought I should celebrate it, but just didn't know how. Instead, this afternoon I sat in my living room chair and cried and cried. Now, does that mean God wasn't with me? Absolutely not! But as Evy, my dear friend in Greece, told me when I called her and cried some more, we can try to manage how we deal with our grief, but every now and then, the pain just wells up and we have to take it! So I write this with tears, but with such gratitude for all the days I had with my husband, and all the days we both still have with God!

GOD'S PEACE AND COMFORT CAN INVADE THE DEEPEST GRIEF AND SUFFERING. HE IS OUR COMFORTER, ALWAYS, AND HIS PEACE IS AMAZING!

Greater is He [God] who is in me than he who is
in the world [Satan, the enemy]   1 Jn 4:4 KJV

Peace with God is the fruit of oneness with God, and purity
blossoms from the same healthy stock (Stanley 2005).

The God of Peace will crush Satan (Rom 16:20) as he tries to exploit our grief and suffering.
Whether Satan comes in with a jackhammer, or a tiny sharp dagger, you can rely on God and God's peace to reign. Do we have to struggle at times to call on God's peace and believe in it? Sure! And will there be times when we hug the carpet in despair? Yes, indeed. But the fact is this: God is fully capable of bringing his peace to bear in your life, no matter how much grief and suffering you are experiencing.

Pastor and author Francis Frangipane has such wisdom in this area. "Our peace does not come from extreme indifference, nor is it from becoming so 'spiritual' that you fail to notice a problem. It is being so confident in God's love, regardless of the battle and the difficulties in your circumstances. When you have spiritual authority, you have established God's peace in an area that once was full of conflict and oppression. [So] to truly be able to move in authority, we must first have peace. When we maintain peace during warfare, it is a crushing death blow to satanic oppression and fear. Our victory never comes from our emotions or our intellect. Our victory comes by refusing to judge by what our eyes see or our ears hear, and by trusting that which God has promised will come to pass.

"Your peace is the proof of your victory . . . Peace is Spirit power . . . In the battles of life, your peace is actually a weapon . . . The first step toward having spiritual authority over the adversary is having peace in spite of circumstance. The focal point of all victory comes from seeking God until you find Him, and having found Him, allowing His Presence to fill your spirit with His peace" (Frangipane, 50–54).

My own experience is that God drenches some people with such compassion for a particular situation that they can bring blankets of comfort and love to any grieving person. This may be continuous or just momentary, but either way, it's all good! I could give you many personal examples, but I'll give you two so you get the idea.

One example is women friends from my small group Bible study on Thursday mornings. Some of us have been together for several years. And we have new members as well, whom we cherish! These women loved and sustained me throughout the worst times in Stayton's illness. I say they kept me alive, but they — and I — know that it was God funneling his immense love and comfort through them. They listened to God, they comforted me, and they also told me the truth when I needed it. I tell everyone now: surround yourself with friends like this, and *be* a friend like this yourself!

I also have friends in Houston, Tennessee, England and Greece, who love and support me. These friends knew my darling Stayton before he became terribly ill. So while it may be years between visits, our hearts are still knit together. For instance, Evy's home outside Athens was my unquestioned destination a couple of months after Stayton died. When friends asked me what I was going to do there, I told them honestly, "I am going to fall into the arms of people who love me *and love Stayton* down to our toes!" That's just what I did for about four weeks. And it was every bit as good as I imagined!

Every one of these women friends is precious to me, each in a different way. Some are soft, gentle, and truly sweet, like my friend and book soul mate Ginger Rogers. Priceless! Others, like Tanya and Shelley, are fun and yet so tough and strong that they will stand by me with unlimited determination. Also priceless! And some, who are too numerous to name, will hug and encourage and talk turkey. Priceless! So let your tortured soul loose and wrap yourselves in love! Trust me, it's the best!

A second example of God's extended peace and comfort can be a pastor like Brett Mosher. One reason I cherish him is that he knew and enjoyed my darling Stayton when he was alive and well (or mostly well). This is something I don't have with most of my women friends in town, and it is a real treasure. Also, Brett and I are "equally yoked" in loving to explore and learn more about our Father and his Son. He has recommended some great books, and we delight in the back and forth of conversation about God! We don't see each other a lot, but I remember special times when he came and sat with me, and listened, and cared, and loved us to the end. Brett conducted Stayton's memorial service, and infused it with his own love for Stayton and me, as well as God's love for us. In a terribly sad situation, he made it uplifting and glorious! And he is still my friend, valuable beyond belief!

SCRIPTURE IS RICH WITH WORDS OF COMFORT.

God's message to us in trouble, promising comfort, winds its way throughout the Bible. Thanks to God, the Bible is full of places to look for His words of comfort. For instance, the words "comfort," "comforted," and "comforts" appear thirteen times in chapters 40–66 of Isaiah.

Jeremiah 31 is also rich in comfort. And Jesus had many words of comfort for those in distress, scattered throughout this collection. Here are several examples:

Psalm 4:8 tells us: [8] In peace I will both lie down and sleep [Ps3:5] for you alone, O LORD, make me dwell in safety [Ps 16:9; Lev 25:18, 19; 26:5; Deut 33:28].
Isaiah 40+ is a great example of the majesty and comfort of God. It begins with God reassuring his people that their time of trial — their seventy-year captivity — is seen as almost over. They have sinned and they have paid for it. Despite their sinful past, they are still his people, and God speaks tenderly to them. He offers deliverance, reminds them of his majesty and might, and at the same time promises to watch over them like a gentle shepherd.
For instance, in Isaiah 43:19, God says: Behold, I am doing a new thing; now it springs forth, do you not perceive it? I will make a way in the wilderness and rivers in the desert.

Jesus says: Blessed are the poor in spirit . . . they who mourn, for they shall be comforted . . . the meek . . . those who hunger and thirst for righteousness . . . the . . . the pure in heart . . . the peacemakers . . . those who are persecuted because of righteousness' sake . . . [and] you when others revile and persecute you . . . on my account. [All of you] Rejoice and be glad, for your reward is great in heaven, for so they persecuted the prophets who were before you. Mt 5:3–12 (also in Lk 6:20–23)

Jesus says: Come to me, all who labor and are heavy laden, and I will give you rest. [29] Take my yoke upon you, and learn from me, for I am gentle and lowly in heart, and you will find rest for your souls. [30] For my yoke is easy, and my burden is light. Mt 11:28–30 (expanding Jer 6:16)

Jesus says: Peace I leave with you; My [own] peace I now give and bequeath to you. Not as the world gives do I give to you. Do not let your hearts be troubled, neither let them be afraid. [Stop allowing yourselves to be agitated and disturbed; and do not permit yourselves to be fearful and intimidated and cowardly and unsettled.] Jn 14:27 AMP

And finally this, about Christ, in Rom 8:35–39

[35]Who shall separate us from the love of Christ? Shall trouble or hardship or persecution or famine or nakedness or danger or sword? . . . In all these things we are more than conquerors through him who loved us. [38]For I am convinced that neither death nor life, neither angels nor demons, neither the present nor the future, nor any powers, [39]neither height nor depth, nor anything else in all creation, will be able to separate us from the love of God that is in Christ Jesus our Lord.

WE ARE STILL THE PEOPLE *GOD* SAYS WE ARE,
WHETHER WE ARE IN GOOD TIMES OR IN BAD

God says over and over that he loves us. And Scripture is clear that we are his cherished children, whom he loves without fail. (Remember chapter 6?) So, God will never abandon us, no matter how deep our ditch is. Father, Son, and Holy Spirit are ready with open arms to accept us, comfort us, and guide us throughout our difficulty. And he does forgive us. But we also know that any vice or sin takes its toll on us, even when God has forgiven us. So keep that in mind!

But often, the ditch we find ourselves in is not of our own making. We are innocents crushed in a lost and fallen world. Other times, of course, we have taken our lives in our own hands and made a real mess of it. Either way, God is with us throughout. Here is a great example from the Old Testament. Deuteronomy 4:27–31 says that even when the people have been scattered and disciplined because they were unfaithful, God reassures them. No matter how deep their particular ditch was, God promised: "From there you will seek the LORD your God and you will find him, if you search after him with all your heart and with all your soul." Deut 4:29

Like many of you, I've had personal experience with a ditch that was so long and wide that I felt overwhelmed much of the time. You could fairly describe such a ditch as being of epic proportions! But there was more truth to it than that, because I would not have abandoned my post for anything. At some point, God showed me that it was an "honor" (God's word exactly) to serve there in the ditch beside my husband, the love of my life. And even when I was crazy, we had a God who loved both of us inside the ditch and out. And that is the absolute truth!

There are also smaller ditches in our lives, and they can be troubling as well. Competing demands, endless tiny jobs, emotional conflicts, people trying to avoid their own responsibilities and foist them on you — maybe none of these are epic, but they can grind on you anyway. Maybe you aren't being gored by an ox, but you are being nibbled to death by ducks! (an old phrase but a goodie!) And I can tell you, even in a small ditch, I still need God!

CHERISH GOD'S HELP, AS WE
ENDURE AND COPE WITH OUR STRUGGLES

In March 2011, almost five years into Stayton's Alzheimer's diagnosis, I began to see that this disease is a lot like the North Sea: cold, dangerous, and deadly. A lot of good people have been devastated by Alzheimer's. Some have stood on the shore, watching others drowning, and felt helpless to intervene. Others have heard stories about the forbidding disease and grieved alongside those getting wet. And many have been drenched as they watched mothers or sisters or dads flail in the deep water, as they, their loving relatives, tried to reach them with lifeboats and protective gear.

All of these are legitimate experiences with the deadly Alzheimer's. But there are also those who stay as far away as they can, for their own comfort (but I don't have to tell you what I think of them, do I?) But regardless of their reactions, no one is untouched by a tragedy, even those hiding at what they hope is a safe distance.

I believe that those of us who are married to the love of our life may face an even sharper level of wet and cold. We are those blessed souls who have shared a life of physical and emotional connection, marvelous conversations, mutual discoveries, and many shared ups and downs. So in one way we are better prepared than some others, because we know our lover so intimately and so completely. But in another way (and this is pretty obvious, I know), our loss is uniquely huge! When our time together is over, we find ourselves without our greatest supporter and our most ardent fan. And believe me, that loss is really beyond imagination.

When my son Christian worked in the North Sea and had periodic sea safety training, one of the instructors darkly advised that if thrown overboard, they should just swim to the bottom. That would shorten their misery. At the time that seemed awful to me, but now, after these years of Alzheimer's, I fully understand the advice.

Yes, it's easy to focus on the loss. You simply can't escape it, day in and day out, literally moment by moment. But I'll tell you this, as a woman who was able to celebrate thirty-two years of marriage with the love of her life, that amazing ride was worth *anything* that the world could throw at us! And for us there was an extra bonus, besides the wonderful journey we shared all these years. The bonus was — and is — God, and knowing he was with us *both*, not just with every step, but with every stroke in that wet, scary, scary deep. Even when the mighty dark waves close over my head, or yours, God is still, and always will be, with us.

Finally, if I may repeat, when we are feeling particularly weak or lacking, we need good friends we can trust with our feelings. And we need to check ourselves carefully— and often — to make sure we are as connected to God as we should be. If something has happened to disconnect us, there is one person who knows the answer, so run to him and throw your arms around him! I promise, He will help!

A MAJOR PART OF GOD'S HELP DURING OUR TOUGH TIMES IS HIS FAITH-BUILDING GYM – WHICH IS ALWAYS OPEN – IN GOOD TIMES AND IN BAD

Father, Son, and Holy Spirit are always engaged in training and teaching their children. And here's a picture that helps me understand how God's plan for faith-building works. Imagine a gleaming, tricked–out gym with all sorts of machines and sweaty bodies. If I asked you to describe the gym, you could probably go on and on, naming the various machines, pointing out where the showers are, waving at yourself in the giant mirrors, and so on. But instead of peering into each sprocket and pedal, let's look *first* at the floor.

The Foundation/The Floor is God Himself.
The floor? That wasn't included in your description, was it? But where would all the rest of the gym be if the floor weren't there? Silly question? Not really. Sadly, in the "faith-building gym", it's easy to disregard the floor, the base for it all. And that foundation for our faith is in two parts, like a hardwood floor with nails.

The wood — the wonderful solid material that spans the entire building — is God!
Without that solid foundation of God and his steadfast love for us, nothing else in the gym works. The wheels jam, the showers don't drain properly, the machines are unsteady. And may I say that eventually, the whole place gets a bit stinky!

The nails represent Jesus Christ, bringing us into personal relationship with God the Father himself.
We have discussed God: the solid wood, our foundation, his character and his overflowing love for us. And now we'll focus on Jesus. The nails — those sharp little spears that hold things together — are our intimate relationship with God made possible by his Son Jesus. "Only one

thing will bear the ordinary and the extraordinary strains and pains of life, and that is a personal relationship with God himself, through Jesus Christ. When my personal relationship with God has been examined, purified and tested, only one purpose remains and I can truly say, 'I am here for God, to do whatever he wills'" (drawn from Chambers Sept 25).

My life depends absolutely on whether I spend enough time in God's "gym", building my faith, and receiving all of the wisdom and guidance the "trainer" provides.
If, instead, I take another approach, and make excuses and dodge the required time and effort, my life will show it.

"Jesus prayed that you and I may be one with the Father as he is (John 17). Are you helping God to answer that prayer, or do you have some other goal from your life? . . . God reveals in John 17 that his purpose is not just to answer our prayers, but that through prayer we might come to discern his mind . . . God allows these [troubling and sad times] . . . for his own purposes. The things we are going through are either making us sweeter, better, and nobler men and women, or they are making us more critical, fault-finding, and insistent on our own way. And it depends entirely on our relationship with God and its level of intimacy.

"If we pray, regarding our own lives, 'Your will be done' (Mt 26:42), then we will be encouraged and comforted by John 17, knowing that our Father is working according to his own wisdom, accomplishing what is best. [As we learned in chapter 4], Jesus prayed nothing less for us than absolute oneness with him, just as he was one with the Father. Some of us are far from this oneness, yet God will not leave us alone until we are one with him" (Chambers May 22).

AND LET'S TALK ABOUT SOME OF THE SURPRISING "GIFTS" TUCKED INTO OUR CART, EVEN WHILE WE — AND THE CART — ARE DEEP IN THAT DITCH

My husband had been gone for months when I realized that as deep as the ditch was that we had occupied for years — Alzheimer's and the downward spiral it brings — there were some surprising "gifts" that came from that long, sad time. And I'm beginning to suspect that many other bad times have some good tucked in with the terrible. Let me give you an example from my own life.

In August 2013, I lost the love and companionship of the finest man and the best friend I've ever known or ever will know. As I've said many times before, Stayton Roehm was my husband, my best friend, the love and passion of my life, and my life partner in loving and serving God. He loved me unconditionally, and I him! There is no good side to losing that kind of love. But the experience of caring for another in trouble, of giving your all for the good of another, the long and increasingly close walk with God, two sons who loved me throughout — all of these bear a different kind of fruit that has a certain sweetness.

For instance, I can now talk honestly and lovingly with spouses whose husbands or wives are going through this same decline. I can share hard lessons that will help and sustain them rather than bring them down in defeat. I have also learned the priceless value of dear women friends, who loved and sustained me throughout. As I've said before, find some godly men or women (not prissy, but followers of God) and build new relationships with them. You will not regret it, *ever.*

Another bit of advice I'm passing on is to *lean, lean, lean* on God, at every opportunity, and every day! And learn how to listen to your own heart and trust it in caring for your loved one. Those around you may mean well, but they do not have your answer. Still, they can contribute helpful ideas and loving arms around your poor beat-up mind and body.

And finally, I've learned that when you are in a very dark situation, you must rely on people who've been there before. In our case, I leaned on the hospice nurses and aides who were life-giving to me and to my darling Stayton. (Thank you, Dawn, Babette, and Alma.) And I leaned on the caregivers whom I hired for thirty or so hours a week toward the end. (I will always love you, George and Linda!) And for you others whose names escape me, thank you for *everything* you did for us! I have told many other spouses to do the same thing, rather than struggling along, and alone, as if there were some sort of nobility in stubbornness. As my friend Deanna told me after we'd talked for several hours, "Well, this hasn't exactly been fun, but it has been very good!" And I knew just what she meant.

God has showed me that all of these difficult lessons are indeed gifts I can share with other suffering men and women. And there is some sweet sense that this is what God wants us to be, a blessing to those in need. So, consult God. Look inside yourself, and then around you to see if you have a precious gift, small or huge, that someone else desperately needs from you today.

I will not forget, dear Father, that you and Jesus were with me in our deepest and darkest ditch ever. Your love carried us both, and I am beyond grateful. You have proved that you will be with us always, no matter how desperate the situation. And I thank you for that.

At times, you've disciplined me and I've deserved it — like a calf that needs training for the yoke (Jer 31:17–19 NLT). But even when you are teaching and disciplining me, I understand your loving reasons. You never come at me with a scary, abusive stick, and I thank you for that!

Jesus, when things are hard, help me remember your many reassuring words of comfort. I know that you under-stand our grief and sorrow. And I know that covering up that grief or pretending it isn't there is foolish, and *not* what you want for us. Just help me, moment by moment in my despair, to remember you are right there with me in the ditch. You are not just on a throne, disinterested and uninvolved. Your love, guidance, and comfort mean everything to me. And I pray that everyone reading this book can feel the same way! cgs

PRAYER AND MEDITATION FOR CHAPTER 7

CHAPTER 8 OUTLINE: THE BATTLEGROUND OF THE MIND

Always be alert to the inevitable obstacles and
stumbling blocks to a life with God.

Introduction

We'll begin with a recap of two big "S" words: – Sin and Satan. We will keep it as simple as we can. Then we move on.

1. It is critical to see ourselves with clear eyes, as God sees us. Earlier, in chapter 6, we said: if my view of myself is not aligned with God's view of me, I am in trouble, and usually big trouble! Now we are going to learn exactly why that is true! As a believer, the very good news is that God has given me power and authority to see things his way and overcome evil. I am not a helpless pawn in Satan's or anyone else's game!

2. We can deceive and ruin ourselves, giving in to barriers and obstacles of our own making. But we must also remember that evil is at work in this world, and we must never underestimate the enemy.

   * How do I know if I'm hearing from God or Satan?
   * Influences on our mind

3. Pulling down demonic strongholds.
   Be alert, for Satan feeds on our sin.

4. The godly also have strongholds, based on their solid faith in God: Father, Son, and Holy Spirit.
   * The stronghold of Christ's likeness is God's highest purpose for us.
   * The goal is Christ-likeness, not warfare.
5. Some common stumbling blocks to a life with God.
   * Pride: being self-centered vs. God-centered.
   * Playing God: taking the reins when I should be letting God lead. This can lead you into a swamp of self-centeredness, hypocrisy, pride, and other smelly things!
   * Majoring on the minor: lacking proper focus.
   * Overreliance on feelings – like fear – instead of God's truth, which is fact.
   * Lack of restraint and self-discipline
   * A judgmental and critical spirit.
   * Hypocrisy and self-righteousness.
   * It's all or nothing.
6. No matter what the obstacles, including my own stress, sorrow, and pain, Jesus can provide "living water" and draw us into a life of freedom and following God.
7. When God helps you gain new spiritual ground, he will help you to defend that new ground!

THE BATTLEGROUND OF THE MIND

[8] Stay alert! Watch out for your great enemy, the devil. He prowls
around like a roaring lion, looking for someone to devour.
[9] Stand firm against him, and be strong in your faith . . . 1 Pet 5:8–9
NLT (with imagery from Ezek 22:25)

"Every battle we face in life is over the Word and whether or not we
can build our lives upon the faithfulness and
integrity of God" (Frangipane 43–44).

"Allow God to have complete liberty in our lives. Before
God's message can liberate other people, his liberation
must first be real in me" (Chambers Mar 10).

INTRODUCTION

"What men call 'salvation' is simply the first stage of God's plan for our
lives, which is to conform us in character and power to the image of
Jesus Christ. What comes after is equally important" (Frangipane, 23).

We need to always be alert to the inevitable obstacles and stumbling
blocks in our path to a life with God. They may be of our own making
or come from the forces of evil, the enemy. Either way, be confident in
God's power to help you overcome them.

We'll begin with a recap of two big "S" words — Sin and Satan. And
don't worry; this is important but we will keep it simple.

Sin.
In chapter 2, I shared how I see sin – as not just turning your back on God, but as dropping your trousers and mooning him. And I gave you my favorite definition of sin, from Oswald Chambers: "red-handed mutiny against God" (Chambers June 23).

Satan a.k.a. the Enemy or the Devil
To defeat Satan's efforts to mess with our lives, we must be renewed in the spirit of our minds and fully aware of God's purposes and resources for our lives! For more on this, I heartily recommend a book by Francis Frangipane called *The Three Battlegrounds*.

"Satan's domain is the realm of darkness. Wherever there is spiritual darkness, there he will be. The areas we hide in darkness are the very areas of our future defeat. Victory will not be consummated until the nature of Jesus is in your heart. Our rebellion toward God gives a place for the devil in our lives. He feeds upon our sin. *Remember, when our thought-life is in agreement with unbelief, fear, or habitual sin, the enemy has rest*" (Frangipane 11, 14,16, 25, 27, 32).

"The only way Satan can affect God's work through me is when I believe Satan and disbelieve God" (Blackaby,194).
Henry Blackaby says that he has determined not to focus on Satan. "Satan is defeated. Yes, Satan will always try to deceive me, but ultimately, he cannot thwart what God purposes to do. So how should you approach spiritual warfare with Satan? Know the ways of God so thoroughly that if something doesn't measure up to God's ways, you will recognize it is not from Him and turn away from it. Jesus never debated with Satan or focused on him. He just kept doing the last thing his Father told him to do until the Father told him what to do next. *So, our greatest weapon in spiritual warfare is obedience to God's Word*" (Blackaby, 194–195).
    "If we're in Christ, the Devil cannot have our souls . . . For us, eternity is settled. Satan can, however, wreak havoc with our indecisive, prideful earthly lives and sift us like shredded wheat" (Moore 2011, 142). "This world is dark and shadowed at times. If we naively step

out unprotected, we'll be susceptible to the evil influences of darkness around us. But if we wisely follow the map God has given us in His Word (and don't wander aimlessly), it will guide and protect us, making each step of our walk intentional. Then we too can say [as 1 Cor 9:26 does] that I run straight to the goal with purpose in every step" (Rothschild 15).

Be strong in the Lord. Ephesians 6:10–17 NLT

[10] Be strong in the Lord and in his mighty power. [11] Put on all of God's armor so that you will be able to stand firm against all strategies of the devil. [12] For we are not fighting against flesh-and-blood enemies, but against evil rulers and authorities of the unseen world, against mighty powers in this dark world, and against evil spirits in the heavenly places. [13] Therefore, put on every piece of God's armor so you will be able to resist the enemy in the time of evil. Then after the battle you will still be standing firm. [14] Stand your ground, putting on the belt of truth and the body armor of God's righteousness. [15] For shoes, put on the peace that comes from the Good News so that you will be fully prepared. [16] In addition to all of these, hold up the shield of faith to stop the fiery arrows of the devil. [17] Put on salvation as your helmet, and take the sword of the Spirit, which is the word of God. (For more on Eph 6:10–18, see Additional References page)

We have two choices spiritually: Life or Death. Jas 1:12–15

But the Bible tells us repeatedly that God and Satan are not equally matched opponents. One is our Creator. And the other is merely a creature.

[Life] [12] Blessed is the man who remains steadfast under trial, for when he has stood the test he will receive the crown of life, which God has promised to those who love him.

[Death] [14] But each person is tempted when he is lured and enticed by his own desire. [15] Then desire when it has conceived gives birth to sin, and sin when it is fully grown brings forth death. Jas 1: 12–15

Later, James describes the route to Life (Jas 4:7–8):

[First] [7] Submit yourselves therefore to God. Resist the devil, and he will flee from you. [Then] [8] Draw near to God, and he will draw near to you. Cleanse your hands, you sinners, and purify your hearts, you double-minded.

Jesus says this about evil and Satan:

Jesus says: [Pray] lead us not into temptation, but deliver us from evil. Mt 6:13 KJV Lk 11:4

Jesus says: I send you out as sheep in the midst of wolves; so be wise as serpents and innocent as doves. Mt 10:16 (as he sent out the twelve disciples to preach) and also later, in Luke 10:3 (when he sent out seventy others)

Jesus says: . . . I saw Satan fall like lightning from heaven. Behold, I have given you authority to tread on serpents and scorpions, and over all the power of the enemy, and nothing shall hurt you . . .

Do not rejoice in this, that the spirits are subject to you, but rejoice that your names are written in heaven. Lk 10:18–20 ESV

Jesus says: If I am casting out demons by the power of God, then the Kingdom of God has arrived among you. For when Satan, who is completely armed, guards his palace, it is safe — until someone who is stronger attacks and over-powers him, strips him of his weapons, and carries off his belongings. Lk 11: 20–22 NLT

[Jesus speaking on his last night before dying] Watch and pray so that you will not fall into temptation. The spirit is willing, but the body is weak. Mt 26:41 NIV Mk 14:38   Lk 22:40, 46

Jesus says: [to God] My prayer is not that you take them out of the world, but that you protect them from the evil one. Jn 17:15 NIV

IT IS CRITICAL TO SEE OURSELVES
WITH CLEAR EYES, AS GOD SEES US.

In chapter 6, we said that part of seeing ourselves with clear eyes is know-ing that God has given us – believers – power and authority to see things his way and overcome evil. (See Lk 10:19; Acts 1:8; Eph 1:17–19) So we are *not* helpless pawns in Satan's (or anyone else's) game! Yes, my heart has potential for evil and sin, but it also has great strength from God for great good. "It is only through knowing Jesus, and making him Lord of our lives, that the Holy Spirit can flow through us in power. And it is only with the power of the Holy Spirit that we have authority over the powers of darkness" (Horrobin 29). Now this is the same Spirit that dwelled in Christ (Rom 8:9) — the Spirit of the Father (Mt 10:20). And this Spirit was to come upon his followers and be the source of all power in working and witnessing.

Jesus demonstrated at Calvary that he had the authority to give his disciples (and us) the power and the authority to cast out demons. And because we are "in Christ", we no longer have to be subject to the spiritual powers of this world (Gal 4:3–5 NLT). "No spiritual power under Satan's control, be it demon, evil spirit or fallen angel, can ultimately stand against the power of the name of Jesus. Whatever opposition they put up, they have to submit to the authority Jesus has given to his church. Christ is in us (Col 1:27), so we are beneficiaries of his victory and have a rightful share in the glory to come" (Horrobin, 83, 84).

WE CAN DECEIVE AND RUIN OURSELVES, GIVING IN TO BARRIERS AND OBSTACLES OF OUR OWN MAKING

1 Jn 3:3–10 [7] . . . let no one deceive you. Whoever practices righteousness is righteous, as he is righteous. [8] Whoever makes a practice of sinning is of the devil, for the devil has been sinning from the beginning. The reason the Son of God appeared was to destroy the works of the devil. [9] No one born of God makes a practice of sinning, for God's seed abides in him, and he cannot go on sinning because he has been born of God . . .

But we must also remember that evil is at work in this world, and we must never underestimate the enemy. Satan has great power and he works to deceive and ruin us, separating us from God. But we can destroy arguments and every lofty opinion raised against the knowledge of God, and take every thought captive to obey Christ. 2 Cor 10:5.

"Satan's intention, from the beginning, has been to change our thinking about God and his ways, and to drive a wedge between God and his creatures. His tools are deception, lies, manipulation, and half-truths. Instead, we need to learn and believe God's Truth. Believing and acting on this truth is our only way to freedom, not mere survival, not escape, but true, glorious freedom, in the midst of this fallen, corrupt, and hurting world" (DeMoss, 20).

Am I hearing from God or from Satan?
Satan will try many tricks to convince us to listen to him instead of to God (See Mt 4:1–11). The devil is always on the prowl, seeking to get in a roar that instills fear or confusion (See 1 Pet 5:8).

Pastor Charles Stanley says, "The Bible assures us that there is a way to tell Satan's voice from that of our Lord. Satan says: Do your own thing. Do what you want to do. Live for the moment. Don't concern yourself with what others say. You're as mature as you ever need to be. You're a grown-up. But Jesus says: Consider the effects of your behavior on others. Live a selfless, self-giving life. Receive godly counsel. Continue to grow and mature and to become more and more like me.

"The outcomes are different too. Satan's path leads to loss, destruction, and death. The Lord's way always leads to abundant life and eternal life with God (See Jn 10:10) . . . Rebellious teens often say to their elders, 'Don't tell me what to do! I'm a grown-up, too!' That is the attitude of many people toward the voice of God. It is an attitude of pride, based on an assumption that we know as much about any given situation as God knows. Nothing could be farther from the truth" (Stanley 1996).

Influences on our mind
As children and adults, many things influence us: how and where we grew up, our physical and mental traits, our life experiences, and what we've been taught. To keep your mind true to God, examine your heart. And if you see dejection and hopelessness, ask God for help. The Bible tells us God has provided for us a new heart, a new mind, a new spirit, a new nature, and ultimately, even a new name (Heb 8:10; 1 Cor 2:16; 2 Cor 5:16–17; Rev 2:17). And Christ is always with you. So we are not just our past!

"New faith and hope should be growing in you daily . . . and in terms of what you are being taught, humbly ask the Lord to confirm any questionable doctrines. If what we're being taught doesn't lead us into Christ's love, his holiness, or his power — if we are not being prepared in these spiritual dimensions for Jesus and, through him, for others — that [teaching or doctrine] is a strong-hold which is limiting and oppressing us" (Frangipane 41, 43).

PULLING DOWN DEMONIC STRONGHOLDS

[4] For the weapons of our warfare are not of the flesh but have divine
power to destroy strongholds. [5] We destroy arguments and every lofty
opinion raised against the knowledge of God, and take every thought
captive to obey Christ, [6] being ready to punish every disobedience,
when your obedience is complete. 2 Cor 10:4–6

Satan feeds on our sin

"A demonic stronghold is any type of thinking that exalts itself above the
knowledge of God, thereby giving the devil a secure place of influence
in an individual's thought-life . . . Your rebellion toward God provides
a place for the devil in your life. Wherever there is a habit of sin in a
believer's life, expect to find demonic activity in that area. The sin habit
often becomes the dwelling place for a spirit that is robbing a believer of
power and joy, and that habitation (or habit) is a stronghold.

"You may not agree that evil spirits can frequent and occupy atti-
tudes in a believer's life, but you must certainly agree that each of us
has a carnal mind which is a source of vain imaginations and thoughts
that exalt themselves above God (2 Cor 10:3–5). We deal with the devil
by dealing with the carnal thought systems, the strongholds that protect
the enemy. Pulling down strongholds is the demolition and removal of
these old ways of thinking, so that the actual Presence of Jesus Christ can
be manifested through us. And it begins with repentance" (Frangipane
23–27).

Defeating the strongholds of failure, fear, unbelief (and others)
involves this process:

* "Repent — change, not merely feel sorry or remorseful.
* "Capture the thought. Arrest it. 2 Cor 10:5
* "Renew your mind (Eph 4:23) — speak God's truth, not the lies
  you've been telling yourself.
* "Forgive and release those who hurt you.

- "Don't be discouraged by the strongholds you discover or the occasional setback . . . God does not want you in bondage" (Frangipane 21, 35–37).
- Then Christ must enter and be allowed to build His house of righteousness in the very area where Satan once dwelt (see Mt 12:45; 2 Pet 2:20).

THE GODLY ALSO HAVE STRONGHOLDS, BASED ON THEIR SOLID FAITH IN GOD

Believers must rest on the truth that they are headed to heaven, the final destination of their spiritual rebirth. Our confidence in our present life and our eternal life with God is firm (1 Peter 1:2–7). The stronghold of the godly is humility. (Heb 4:16; Eph 4:24)   And we are taking every thought captive to Christ. (2 Cor 10:5)

The stronghold of Christ's likeness is God's highest purpose for us

- "We are delivered out of sin, not that we might live for ourselves, but that we might come into Christlikeness. Many of our spiritual conflicts simply are not going to cease until the character of the Lord Jesus is formed in our hearts. (See Rom 8:29)
- "When our spirits are fully saturated with the Living Presence of the Lord Jesus, it produces an indestructible defense, a fortress within which we are hidden from evil. 1 Jn 4:17; 1 Jn 5:18
- "It is not Satan who defeats us; it is our openness to him. To perfectly subdue the devil we must walk in the 'shelter of the Most High' (Ps 91:1). Satan is tolerated for one purpose: the warfare between the devil and God's saints thrusts us into Christlikeness, where the nature of Christ becomes our only place of rest and security" Gen 1:26 (Frangipane, 46).

The Goal is Christ-likeness, Not Warfare
"The Father is more concerned with the coming forth of His Son in our lives than He is in defeating Satan. Who is the devil, that he can

defy the Living God? Indeed, it is of the greatest truth that, once the devil recognizes his assault against your life has not pulled you *from* God, but *toward* Him, once he perceives that his temptations are actually forcing you to appropriate the virtue of Christ, the enemy will withdraw.

"There are occasions when your battle against the devil is actually a digression from the higher purpose God has for you . . . Listen very carefully: we are not called to focus on the battle or the devil, except where that battle hinders our immediate transformation into Christ's likeness. Our calling is to focus on Jesus_. . . . It is better to develop godly virtues than to spend our day praying against the devil. Indeed, it is the joy of the Lord that casts out spirits of depression. It is our living faith which destroys spirits of unbelief; it is aggressive love which casts out fear" (Frangipane 45-49).

HERE ARE SOME COMMON STUMBLING BLOCKS OR OBSTACLES TO A LIFE WITH GOD

"As we walk by faith, the Holy Spirit helps us fix our eyes on the source of our help instead of the sting of our problems" (Rothschild, 16).

We're going to talk now about some things that can seriously get between you and God. Some of them may have no real hold on you. Others may have been strangling you for years. They've burrowed into your life and you now think of them as "just how I am". Satan *loves* that! The trick is to identify the obstacles and then beg God to help you obliterate them. Without God's help, your own efforts will be like taking a nail file to a coal mine and trying to excavate the stuff. They cannot be overcome without God's wisdom and power. Even if a barrier or stumbling block is completely your own doing, you will see that the enemy is more than happy to make it worse whenever and wherever he can! And the same goes for barriers that you had no hand in creating or feeding! Be careful but be encouraged and remember that God knows *all* about this! You are not alone on your journey.

Obstacle 1: Pride
Pride is the first major obstacle to living God's way. This is being self-centered vs. God-centered, and it really drives a wedge between me and God. So I must humble myself before God and others. But don't confuse this with false humility, because that is really just pride in a chump suit!

There are many Old and New Testament references on pride and humility, with some included below. But several of them make me think of our world today. Check out Isaiah 2:5-22 (in Additional Scriptures) and just substitute our brand of stuff and obsession for the ancient fixation on chariots, warhorses, and gold and silver idols.

Read this warning from Jer 13:15–17: [15] Hear and give ear; be not proud, for the Lord has spoken. [16] Give glory to the Lord your God before he brings darkness, before your feet stumble on the twilight mountains, and while you look for light he turns it into gloom and makes it deep darkness. [17] But if you will not listen, my soul will weep in secret for your pride; my eyes will weep bitterly and run down with tears, because the Lord's flock has been taken captive.

What Jesus says about pride and humility:
Jesus says: . . . All who exalt themselves will be humbled, and those who humble themselves will be exalted. Lk 14:10–11 and 18:14b NRSV   Mt 23:11b-12 (reflecting idea in Prov 25:6–7)
Jesus says: [Repeatedly, Jesus says] Whoever would be great among you must be your servant . . . For the Son of man also came not to be served but to serve, and to give his life as a ransom for many. Mk 10:43–45 Also in Mk 9:35 Mt 20:26 and again in Mt 23:1–12 and in Lk 22:26–27
Jesus says: Beware of these teachers of religious law! For they love to parade in flowing robes and to have everyone bow to them as they walk in the marketplaces. And how they love the seats of honor in the synagogues and at banquets. But they shamelessly cheat widows out of their property, and then, to cover up the kind of people they really are, they make long prayers in public. Because of this, their punishment will be the greater.
Mk 12:38–40 NLT, Lk 20:46–47 and again in Mt 23:5–7, 13–14

Other Scripture on pride and humility:
Mic 6:8 . . . And what does the LORD require of you but to do justice, and to love kindness, and to walk humbly with your God.
1 Pet 5:5 (and also in Jas 4:6) . . . God opposes the proud but gives grace to the humble . . . (both echoing Prov 3:34)
1 Pet 5:6–7 (and also in Jas 4:10) Humble yourselves, therefore, under the mighty hand of God so that at the proper time he may exalt you, casting all your anxieties on him, because he cares for you.

Obstacle 2: Playing God
This is the opposite of living God's way, and probably is an ugly first cousin of pride. It's another major barrier which can lead you into a swamp full of self-centeredness, hypocrisy, pride, and other smelly dark things!

I began to see "playing God" differently in August 2012. We all know people who play God, who elevate themselves above others and fake it on every level, if they can't make it. But then I discovered it can have a second, and key, definition. I began to see that I have played God in a different sense, and was completely unaware of doing it. As my beloved husband slid downhill with Alzheimer's, my life, as most of you can imagine, was sad and stressful. I hit the wall from time to time, and on bad days I hit it over and over. Sound familiar at all? But a year before my husband died, I gained more insight, and that only with the help of friends and God!

I've loved God throughout this journey and sensed him with me, but there were still times when I hurled myself against a few unnecessary walls, all alone. Now if this were an Olympic sport, I would have medaled in it months before. But it is *not* an Olympic sport. It is an exercise in *playing God*. It is gathering up the reins in my own hands and too often missing the truth that Jesus wants to pull along with me, in the same yoke. He offers over and over to help, but when I am playing God, I don't ask for help. I just go thud, thud, thud against that wall and then fall into a depressed heap on the floor.

Is this what God has in mind for me? Or for you? Of course not. So if the urge creeps in, I pray that God will give me — and you — an unmistakable tap on the head and say, *"Stop it! I am here. I can help!"* Will my life then change into butterflies and lollipops? No! God didn't promise me – or anyone – that it would. But he did promise me love, comfort, direction, wisdom, and help. I just had to put down my little "'God baton'" and reach out for all that he had for my wonderful husband and me.

Obstacle 3: Losing focus and majoring on the minor.
Here is one example. When I long for and pursue the love, approval, and favor of others, while taking my eyes off God, I'm looking in the wrong direction! And I'm taking my eyes off the spiritual ball. That's why Jesus says this:

Jesus says: [1] I do not receive glory from people . . . [Mt 6:1, 2; 1 Thess 2:6]
Jesus says: [44] How can you believe since you accept glory from one another but do not seek the glory that comes from the only God? Jn 5:44 NIV

Another example of losing focus is majoring on material things:
Jesus says: . . . Be on the lookout for the disease of wanting. A person's life is not to be measured by the amount of things that a person has secured. Lk 12:15 WMF
Jesus says: It is written, 'Man shall not live by bread alone, but by every word that proceeds from the mouth of God.' Mt 4:4 NKJV Lk 4:4 (citing Deut 8:3)
Jesus says: Don't store up treasures here on earth . . . Store your treasures in heaven. Wherever your treasure is, there your heart and thoughts will also be. Mt 6:19–21 NLT Lk 12:33–34
Jesus says: No one can serve two masters. For you will hate one and love the other, or be devoted to one and despise the other. Mt 6:24a NLT
Jas 5:1–6 NLT Look here, you rich people: Weep and groan with anguish because of all the terrible troubles ahead of you. [2] Your wealth is rotting away, and your fine clothes are moth-eaten rags. [3] Your gold and silver have become worthless. The very wealth you were counting on will eat away your flesh like fire. This treasure you have accumulated will stand as evidence against you on the day of judgment. [4] For listen! Hear the cries of the field workers whom you have cheated of their pay. The wages you held back cry out against you.

The cries of those who harvest your fields have reached the ears of the Lord of Heaven's Armies . . .

Obstacle 4: Over-reliance on feelings – like fear – instead of God's truth, which is fact.

"The only test we should use to determine whether or not to allow a particular emotion to run its course in our lives is to examine what the final outcome of that emotion will be. Think it through to the logical conclusion, and if the outcome is something that God would condemn, put a stop to it immediately. But if it is an emotion that has been kindled by the Spirit of God and you don't allow it to have its way in your life, it will not have the effect God intended. We cannot stay forever on the 'mount of transfiguration', basking in the light of our mountaintop experience (see Mk 9:1–9). But we must obey the light we received there; we must put it into action, no matter what the cost" (Chambers Mar 22).

When you are in a difficult situation, you may be faced with an army of emotions, most of which can be quite disruptive to whatever God has you pursuing. Very recently a "fear" serpent slithered into my life , from an area I hadn't previously seen as scary. I talked to God and – bottom line – he smacked down that slimy thing in no time! Here's how it went:

I called a friend, told her, and began to pray, because only God can help me in a situation like this. God has said over and over in his Word, Don't be afraid. I am with you. So I called on him, and he was as good as his Word. Quickly – within 30 minutes of talking to God – he helped me. First, he showed me that it was fear I was experiencing, not some vague nervousness. He reminded me that Satan – not God – is the author of fear. And then he moved me to get his thoughts and help on the situation. I read several days of Oswald Chamber, around today's date. And found something that God already knew would be spot on. So God equipped me to face the fear and gave me spiritual ammunition to defend myself! Now does that eliminate the fear serpent forever? No, but all I have to do is throw him at God's feet whenever he resurfaces!

Plus, there was a bonus: I tucked this little bit into the book, so you could benefit from what God had showed me!

"Your duty in service and ministry is to see that there is nothing between Jesus and yourself. Is there anything between you and Jesus even now? [and for me, the answer was yes – fear!] If there is, you must get *through* it, not by ignoring it as an irritation, or by going up and over it, but by facing it and getting it into the presence of Jesus Christ. Then that very problem itself, and all that you. have been through in connection with it, will glorify Jesus Christ in a way that you will never know until you see him face to face" (Chambers, October 3). Isn't God good?

Obstacle 5: A lack of restraint and self-discipline (twin sisters)

We'll work with one example — watching your mouth — but of course there are many others. If your life is beset by another self-discipline problem, like anger, procrastination, or excesses with food, alcohol, etc., then that's the one you will want to talk to God about. Believe me, he is the only one who can help us out of our particular ditch!

Jesus says: The mouth speaks the things that are in the heart. Mt 12:34b NCV
Jesus says: It is the thought-life that defiles you. For from within, out of a person's heart, come evil thoughts, sexual immorality, theft, murder, adultery, greed, wickedness, deceit, eagerness for lustful pleasure, envy, slander, pride, and foolishness. All these vile things come from within; they are what defile you and make you unacceptable to God. Mk 7:20–23 NLT Mt 15:19
Jesus says: There's nothing done or said that can't be forgiven. But if you deliberately persist in your slanders against God's Spirit, you are repudiating the very One who forgives. If you reject the Son of Man out of some misunderstanding, the Holy Spirit can forgive you, but when you reject the Holy Spirit, you're sawing off the branch on which you're sitting, severing by your own perversity all connection with the One who forgives. Mt 12:31–32 MSG Mk 3:28–29

James practically majored on the notion of watching your mouth! Here are just a few examples:
Jas 1:19–20 . . . be quick to hear, slow to speak, slow to anger.
Jas 1:26 ESV If anyone thinks he is religious and does not bridle his tongue but deceives his heart, this person's religion is worthless. Jas 3:5–12 and 4:11

Obstacle 6: A judgmental and critical spirit

We can become self-righteous and forget that judging is God's job. Can God use you to convey his concern about the wrong behavior of others? Yes he can, but if he does, it will look nothing like the usual criticism and judging that goes on in this world! So, if someone says to you, "God says you're a hopeless screw-up", that person is either lying or wrong or both!

Like most people, I can be a walking billboard for critical thoughts and words. But Jesus was crystal clear about this: Watch *your own* behavior. Don't major on judging others. Don't criticize. Don't condemn. If you have any doubts about this, take a look at any of Jesus' comments below, and the many comments by other figures in the Bible. Criticism rarely gives us a positive result, especially if it is not submitted first to God.

"If you have been shrewd is finding out the short-comings of others, remember that will be exactly how you will be measured . . . This eternal law works from God's throne down to us (see Ps 28:25–26). [Which begs the question] Who of us would dare to stand before God and say, 'My God, judge me as I have judged others'?" [Chambers, June 22] Maybe this is something we can work on, a bit at a time? I certainly hope so!

Jesus says: . . . First take the log out of your own eye, and then you will see clearly to take out the speck that is in your brother's eye. Lk 6:42 ESV, RSV Mt 7:4–5
Jesus says: [37] Judge not, and you will not be judged; condemn not, and you will not be condemned; forgive, and you will be forgiven; [38] give, and it will be given to you. Good measure, pressed down, shaken together, running over, will be put into your lap. For with the measure you use it will be measured back to you. Lk 6:37–38 Mt 7:1-2
Jesus says: You judge me with all your human limitations, but I am not judging anyone. And if I did, my judgment would be correct in every respect because I am not alone — I have with me the Father who sent me. Jn 8:15–16 NLT

Many times, God's word tells us that God will judge his people. Never avenge yourself. Leave it to God who says, "Vengeance is mine". Here are a few examples:

Rom 2:1 -11 [1] . . . In passing judgment on another you condemn yourself, because you, the judge, practice the very same things. [2] We know that the judgment of God rightly falls on those who practice such things . . .

Jas 2:4–9, 12–13 NIV . . . Judgment without mercy will be shown to anyone who has not been merciful. Mercy triumphs over judgment!

Obstacle 7: Judging, criticizing and condemning often join with their buddies, hypocrisy and self-righteousness.

This is a recurring theme of Jesus and appears throughout Scripture. If you preen and pretend, if you are a hypocrite, or self-righteous, if you talk about God but don't walk his way, you are not of God and you are not living in truth. When we judge others or posture before them, we are in serious danger of becoming self-righteous. And Jesus is *no fan* of that!

Jesus says, about hypocrisy and self-righteousness:

Jesus says: (in this parable about a tax collector who recognizes his own sin, while a Pharisee thanks God that he is not like other men) I tell you, this man [the humble tax collector] went down to his house justified, rather than the other. For everyone who exalts himself will be humbled, but the one who humbles himself will be exalted. Lk 18:9–14

Jesus says: When you pray, don't be like the hypocrites who love to pray publicly on street corners and in the synagogues where everyone can see them. I assure you, that is all the reward they will ever get. Mt 6:5 NLT

Jesus says: You are also called upon to exercise self-denial and self-discipline, but it must be genuine. There is some reward in merely talking about self-denial and giving the appearance of being this way, but you should seek to please God in this, and not merely for appearance's sake. Mt 6:16–18 WMF

Jesus says: First wash the inside of the cup, and then the outside will become clean, too . . . Hypocrites! . . . you are like white-washed tombs — beautiful on the outside but filled on the inside with dead people's bones and all sorts of impurity . . . inside your hearts are filled with hypocrisy and lawlessness. Mt 23:26–28 NLT Lk 11:39–44 (see Ps 5:9 and Ezek 37)

And there are many Biblical references to hypocrisy that share Jesus' impatience. And there are many warnings against sacrificing, praying, and fasting as external exercises, instead of turning your heart toward God.

Obstacle 8: Satan's "all or nothing" lie
Satan's strategy is to first come selling doubt. Here's a small example. You plan to spend a half-hour on Bible reading, but something comes up, and you have to leave your house. Now the enemy wants to con you into thinking that the ten minutes of praying you do in the car is worth nothing. "Why would God want only a few minutes with you?" he asks. "You've failed." But your job as a believer is to shake off this lie. Don't wallow in it! Just go back to your one-on-one with God. Our relationship with God can't be judged as "all or nothing." So don't fall for the enemy's lies.

> NO MATTER WHAT THE OBSTACLES — INCLUDING OUR OWN STRESS,
> SORROW, AND PAIN — JESUS CAN PROVIDE 'LIVING WATER' AND
> DRAW US INTO A LIFE OF FREEDOM AND FOLLOWING GOD.

You know that phrase "hitting bottom"? Well, some of us have had days or weeks where we felt *below* bottom! But the fact is, no matter how stressed we are or how bad we are feeling, God can help us the entire way. He sees it as a two-way street, if we will just turn and take his hand. But he does not ask us to follow him only in our own strength. As we've read in abundance in earlier chapters, God loves us, and he gives us all the tools we need to equip and support us. You can fully rely on God's equipping in your life! Trust me, it happens even when you have no idea what's coming!

Consider Jesus' conversation with the woman at the well (John 4), when she asks him where can she find the "living water" he talks about. His answer is for us, as well as her!
Jesus says: [10] . . . If you knew the gift of God, and who it is that is saying to you, 'Give me a drink', you would have asked him, and he would have given you

living water. [11] The woman said to him, 'Sir, you have nothing to draw water with, and the well is deep. Where do you get that living water?'

[13] **Jesus said to her,** "Everyone who drinks of this water will be thirsty again, [14] but whoever drinks of the water that I will give him will never be thirsty again. The water that I will give him will become in him a spring of water welling up to eternal life." Jn 4:10–14

Jesus' words about living water have two meanings. Literally, the phrase "living water" refers to fresh spring water (Gen 26:19; Lev 14:6), but Jn 7:38–39 identifies this "living water" as the Holy Spirit dwelling within a believer. (Jn 7:38–39 cf. Jer 2:13; Ezek 47:1–6; Zech 14:8; also Isa 12:3))

"Suppose that you have a deep 'well' of hurt and trouble inside your heart, and Jesus comes and says to you, 'Let not your heart be troubled'. . . (Jn 14:1). Would your response be to shrug your shoulders and say, 'But, Lord, the well is too deep, and even you can't draw up quietness and comfort out of it.' [But of course] Jesus doesn't bring anything up from the wells of human nature — He brings them down from above.

"The thing that approaches the very limits of Jesus' power is the very thing we as disciples of Jesus ought to believe he will do. When we get into difficult circumstances, we say 'Of course, he can't do anything about this.' We struggle to reach the bottom of our own well, trying to get water for ourselves. [But] the well of your incompleteness runs deep" (Chambers Feb 27).

Think of how thirsty you have been in your life. If you are like me, there have been times when you've been seriously desperate for help, for comfort, for compassion, for wisdom, for peace. But it goes against my human nature to easily turn things over to God. So I do a lot of pointless head banging (as I've confessed before), because I look to myself and not to God. And for most of us, that's a part of the Christian life that needs daily tending. Again, we need to look to God instead of to ourselves. If I say the simplest "Oh God, I am helpless and hopeless. Please save me", then there is "water" aplenty to help me in my worst times. We can have the water, and we can share it with others, all by asking.

WHEN GOD HELPS YOU *GAIN* NEW GROUND, HE WILL HELP
YOU TO HOLD AND DEFEND THAT NEW GROUND

By the first week of October 2014, I'd had a lively week or three (appendicitis and emergency surgery), so I really had nothing to do but think. Anyway, I'd been thinking about relationships, and God. And I focused on the fact that *gaining new ground*, with God and in relationships, must be followed by *holding and defending that new ground*. Otherwise (and let's all say this together out loud, because it's really that obvious) *we stand a good chance of losing the new ground!*

Now, while this seems obvious, we often let it sneak away without noticing it. And then, what? We are back where we started. Say you have a relationship with a long, troubled history. God miraculously intervenes and heals the thing between you, and you stand on brand-new, baby-fresh innocent ground. You are both surprised, astonished, and thrilled. But the very next day, God is good enough to warn you: you will need to defend this miracle against your own memories and all those, "Yeah, but remember when . . . ?" moments.

What God wants for you and for me is to move forward, without feasting one more time on all those bad times! But our human nature doesn't always cooperate. So in this particular case, my friend and I resolved to stand firm and defend our healing from all possible attacks. We are both holding the new ground with joy and determination, because it was — and is — so precious to us!

Want another example? Say I resolve, as the mother of grown sons, not to interfere and give unwanted and un-asked-for advice. All seems to be going well, and then I backslide. And I find myself wanting to give advice or be too touchy for my own good. Then, if I'm not careful, it would be oh-so-easy to roll back a few (or many) steps from the new ground.

No matter who we are and what our background is, we are tempted to look back, like Lot's wife (an unfortunate Biblical character) who turned into a pillar of salt! We all have a past with individuals and relationships, but with God's help — and only with his help — we can live firmly in the *now,* in that eternal life that God has for us today, tomorrow, and forever. It's complicated (we are people after all). But

God is most definitely in our corner on this whole thing — until we develop enough sense to get into *his* corner. We just need to keep our eye on the ball (the new ground) and how precious it is to us. It's worth recognizing and then defending, not in a stubborn, stupid, this-conflict-isn't-really-happening way, but in the light of faith. And faith says: All things are possible with our God! And it's a daily thing, because if you are anything like me, it's natural and tempting to go backwards instead of walk forward in victory. But God has promised us victory, if we will just cooperate!

Father, you are the Creator of everything in heaven and on earth, including me. You understand me, and you stand ready to help me BE and BECOME what you want for me. Too often, as you know, I can be too stubborn and willful to see the things that get between you and me – the barriers, the character flaws, etc. So I stumble on without your wisdom and your power. Do with me what you've done in the past few weeks. Make it impossible for me to miss what is strangling me, character-wise. You know how very much I love you. And I am happy to be in your potter's hands as you continue to mold me into a likeness of Christ. Amen, CGS

PRAYER AND MEDITATION FOR CHAPTER 8

CHAPTER 9 OUTLINE: WE CAN WALK ON WATER — AND LAND — TO ACCOMPLISH GOD'S ETERNAL PLANS AND PURPOSES FOR THIS WORLD AND FOR US. OR WE CAN SAY NO TO GOD.

Introduction

Walking on water — and on land — is a great picture of what we are asked to do today. In the process, God wants to mold us into Jesus' image — holy as he is holy — so that we can follow God's path and serve him and his purposes. And day by day, I am learning what Jesus wants me to do and how to follow him.

1. God knows and wants what is best for me.
2. Jesus is the light of the world . And he came to bring us abundant life and relationship with God. We walk in the light as he is in the light. 1 Jn 1:7
3. God offers us a clear choice: spiritual life or death, light or darkness.
4. I must cooperate with God's plan to transform me into the image of Christ. I can't stay where I am and go with God In his hands, I become a new creation, from the inside out. And he is never done with me. When I am cooperating, here's what the sequence looks like:
   * "His Spirit will direct my mind to my sin, so I can break free. And it won't be a vague sense of sin, but focusing on the concentration of sin in some specific, personal area of my life" (Chambers July 3).
   * I confess my sins to God. I admit my mistakes. I repent/turn away from my sin and towards God. Then I move on.

* I can't stay where I am and go with God. I must make adjustments. So I determinedly demolish some things within me and determinedly discipline others. Then I add what I need from God!

* If I stubbornly cling to some of my old ways, God will remind me again and again of how and why to do things his way, until I change. He is never done with me!

* I lean on God and accept his help as I walk away from my sin, and as I continue in his presence and in his ways, not my own. If I trip, he helps me up, dusts me off, and sets me again on the right path

5. I am blessed to be a blessing, and God wants me to consider *his* will and purpose for my life and for this earth in everything I do.

6. God is my foundation, my reason for courage. He says, Trust me and do not worry! (remember chapter 6?)
   Remember, it is not God's job to fix my every problem.

7. My motto on this journey: God, you are great. God, take my hand. And God, take my mouth! (or anything else that needs work)

CHAPTER 9

WE CAN WALK ON WATER — AND LAND — TO ACCOMPLISH GOD'S ETERNAL PLANS AND PURPOSES FOR THIS WORLD AND FOR US. OR WE CAN SAY NO TO GOD.

"You call me out upon the waters, the great unknown where
feet may fail. And there I find You in the mystery. In oceans
deep my faith will stand. And I will call upon Your name
And keep my eyes above the waves. When oceans rise, my soul will
rest in Your embrace, for I am Yours and You are mine"
(Lyrics from the moving song "Oceans, Where Feet May Fail," from
Hillsong United's album, *Zion*.)

INTRODUCTION

God did not send his Son into the world to condemn the world, but in order that the world might be saved through him (Jn 3:17). Good News, isn't it? *But Jesus did not come just to die. He also came to live and show us how to live God's way.* God wants to mold me into the image of Christ. I am to live a holy life according to his Word. And I am to follow God's heart and will for my life. This is a lifelong process, but it cannot begin or continue without faith in God. And a key is to be brave and continually stay open to the scrutiny of God himself. When we keep our eyes on God, we are on the right path!

Immediately after Jesus had fed the five thousand (Mt 14:13–21), we hear the famous story of Peter and the disciples in a storm. You may know the story. The disciples are in a boat during a storm, afraid. And then Jesus appears, walking on the water:

²⁴ Meanwhile, the disciples were in trouble far away from land, for a strong wind had risen, and they were fighting heavy waves. ²⁵ About three o'clock in the morning Jesus came toward them, walking on the water. ²⁶ When the disciples saw him walking on the water, they were terrified. In their fear, they cried out, 'It's a ghost!' ²⁷ But Jesus spoke to them at once. 'Don't be afraid' he said. 'Take courage. I am here!' ²⁸ Then Peter called to him, 'Lord, if it's really you, tell me to come to you, walking on the water.' ²⁹ 'Yes, come,' Jesus said. So Peter went over the side of the boat and walked on the water toward Jesus. ³⁰ But when he saw the strong wind and the waves, he was terrified and began to sink. 'Save me, Lord!' he shouted. ³¹ Jesus immediately reached out and grabbed him. 'You have so little faith,' Jesus said. 'Why did you doubt me?' ³² When they climbed back into the boat, the wind stopped. ³³ Then the disciples worshipped him. 'You really are the Son of God!' they exclaimed. Mt 14:22–32

Oh Peter, my brother! How I love you. And I love this story because I can see myself in you: bold, impetuous, passionate, charging around, often without carefully calculating the risks. Even messing up from time to time, while some of the other disciples are being more cautious and wise. In the craziest of situations, Peter, you head out toward Jesus, and keep your eyes on him. What an example for us all!

We can have these bold times ourselves, and they are wonderful, no matter what the circumstance. But there are *other* times when I don't see Jesus in the situation (because I'm not looking) and I stay huddled in the boat, afraid. Or I make a show of stepping out, only to be distracted after a few steps by circumstances, fear, or even other folks. Then, splish, splash, I am taking a bath! Down I go, soaking wet and gulping for air. Can you relate?

GOD KNOWS AND WANTS WHAT IS BEST FOR US.

Over and over, Jesus tells us what God wants us to be like. He can lay out a path for us, maybe even one we would never have even considered on our own. And you know it is good, because it's God's idea! But remember, we are always free to choose. God is not a policeman wanting to spoil our fun. And he is not a puppet master, forcing us to go where he wants us to. He wants us to love him with all our heart, soul, mind, and strength. He wants us to love other people as we love him. And he wants our lives to show it! From the very beginning, and for generations, God has loved and watched us. In fact, he had a plan long before any of us could spell the word "plan".

Jesus says: Seek first God's kingdom and His righteousness. Mt 6:25,31–33

Jesus says: Go and sin no more. Jn 8:11 Jn 5:14

Jesus says: Blessed are those who hunger and thirst for righteousness, for they shall be satisfied. Mt 5:6

Jesus says: Blessed are the pure in heart, for they shall see God. Mt 5:8

Jesus says: [20] "But I warn you — unless your righteousness is better than the righteousness of the teachers of religious law and the Pharisees, you will never enter the Kingdom of Heaven! Mt 5:20 NLT

Jesus says: You therefore must be perfect, as your heavenly father is perfect. Mt 5:48 (echoes Lev 19:2)

Ps 33:10–12 . . . [11] The counsel of the Lord stands forever, the plans of his heart to all generations . . .

Ps 139:16 "Your eyes saw me when I was formless. All my days were written in your book and planned before a single one of them began."

Eph 1:9–14 NLT tells us, "[9] God has now revealed to us his mysterious plan regarding Christ . . . At the right time he will bring everything together under the authority of Christ — everything in heaven and on earth. [11] Furthermore, because we are united with Christ, we have received an inheritance from God, for he chose us in advance, and he makes everything work out according to his plan . . .

Eph 2:10 NLT We are God's masterpiece. He has created us anew in Christ Jesus, so we can do the good things he planned for us long ago.

JESUS IS THE LIGHT OF THE WORLD. WE WALK
IN THE LIGHT AS HE IS IN THE LIGHT. 1 JN 1:7

God says, I will lead the blind in a way that they do not know,
in paths that they have not known I will guide them.
I will turn the darkness before them into light. Isa 42:16

Jesus came to bring us abundant life, and that life is the light that leads
us today. His light, shining into and through us into others, blazes into
the darkness. And the darkness has not – and cannot ever – overcome
that light. We just need to take off our blinders to see it! (See Jn 1:4–5
and others.) That does *not* mean walking in the light of our own conscience or in the light of a sense of duty. Jesus walks in resurrection life,
and that is the light we are to walk in (Chambers Feb 28).

From the start, God wanted nothing more than to bring light to his
people, first the Jews and then the rest. He is the fountain of life, the
light by which we see (Ps 36:9 NLT). See Mt 5:14, 16 (using the imagery
of Isa 60:1–3) Jn 8:12.

Jesus says: God did not send his Son into the world to condemn the
world, but in order that the world might be saved through him . . .
And this is the judgment: the light has come into the world, and people loved
the darkness rather than the light because their deeds were evil . . . But whoever does what is true comes to the light . . . Jn 3:17, 19–21 ESV
Ps 37:5–6 NIV Commit your way to the LORD; trust in him and he will do this:
He will make your righteousness shine like the dawn, the justice of your cause
like the noonday sun.
Peter put this beautifully in 1 Peter 2:9–10: " [9] . . . You are a chosen race, a royal
priesthood, a holy nation, a people for his own possession, that you may proclaim the excellencies of him who called you out of darkness into his marvelous
light. [10] Once you were not a people, but now you are God's people; once you
had not received mercy, but now you have received mercy."

Jn 1:4–5, 9 In him [Jesus] was life, and the life was the light of men. The light shines in the darkness, and the darkness has not overcome it . . . The true light . . . was coming into the world.
Rom 13:12–14 . . . Cast off the works of darkness and put on the armor of light . . . put on the Lord Jesus Christ.
1 Pet 2:9–10 (You can also find some of these same thoughts in Ex 19:5–6, Mal 3:17, and in Rev 1:6 and 5:10.)

FROM THE VERY BEGINNING, GOD OFFERS US A CLEAR CHOICE: SPIRITUAL LIFE OR DEATH, LIGHT OR DARKNESS

> [12] [Give] thanks to the Father, who has qualified you to share
> in the inheritance of the saints in light. [13] He has delivered us
> from the domain of darkness and transferred us to the
> kingdom of his beloved Son. Col 1:12–13

We have said this many times before. God, through Jesus, has done so much for us. But God gives us a choice: Follow him or don't. Pursue spiritual life and light, or death and darkness. Scripture is *full* of this!

Deut 30:11–20 ESV [11] This commandment . . . is not too hard for you, neither is it far off . . . [14] But the word is very near you. It is in your mouth and in your heart, so that you can do it . . . [16] If you obey the commandments of the Lord your God that I command you today, by loving the Lord your God, by walking in his ways, and by keeping his commandments and his statutes and his rules, then you shall live and multiply, and the Lord your God will bless you in the land that you are entering to take possession of it. [17] But if your heart turns away, and you will not hear, but are drawn away to worship other gods and serve them, [18] I declare to you today, that you shall surely perish . . . [19] I call heaven and earth to witness against you today, that I HAVE SET BEFORE YOU LIFE AND DEATH, blessing and curse. Therefore choose life, that you and your offspring may live, [20] loving the Lord your God, obeying his voice and holding fast to him, for he is your life and length of days . . .

Eph 5:1–2 AMP [1]Therefore be imitators of God [copy Him and follow His example], as well-beloved children [imitate their father]. [2] And walk in love, [esteeming and delighting in one another] as Christ loved us and gave Himself up for us, a slain offering and sacrifice to God [for you, so that it became] a sweet fragrance. [See Ezek 20:41.]

Jas 4:7–10 [7] Submit yourselves therefore to God. Resist the devil, and he will flee from you. [8] Draw near to God, and he will draw near to you. Cleanse your hands, you sinners, and purify your hearts, you double-minded. [9] Be wretched and mourn and weep. Let your laughter be turned to mourning and your joy to gloom. [10] Humble yourselves before the Lord, and he will exalt you.

"We must continually remind ourselves of God's purpose for our lives. We are not destined to happiness nor to health, but to holiness . . . The only thing that truly matters is whether a person will accept the God who will make him holy, and then have the right relationship with him. God has only one intended destiny for mankind — holiness . . . [But] God is *not* some eternal-blessing machine . . . and he did not come to save us out of pity. He came to save us because he created us to be holy. Atonement through the Cross of Christ means that God can put me back into perfect oneness with himself through the death of Jesus Christ, without a trace of anything coming between us any longer" (Chambers Sept 1).

I MUST COOPERATE WITH GOD'S PLAN TO TRANSFORM ME INTO THE IMAGE OF JESUS.

> **2 Chron 7:14** [One of my *very* favorite verses in the Bible.]
> **God says,** If my people who are called by my name
> humble themselves, and pray and seek my face and
> turn from their wicked ways, then I will hear from
> heaven and will forgive their sin and heal their land.

I can't stay the way I am and go with God at the same time (Blackaby, 19). God wants to mold me into the image of Christ. And I need to cooperate. As part of this, I need to determinedly demolish some things in my character and determinedly discipline others. (For more, see chapter

8.) I must also ask God to equip me for the job by adding qualities with a supernatural component only he can supply: his wisdom, his patience, his forgiveness, his courage, and more. In his hands, I become a new creation, from the inside out! And he is *never* done with me. Be encouraged! Peter and John, along with the other disciples, were thoroughly ordinary people, like you and me.

Acts 4 gives an example of their boldness in speaking so dynamically before the authorities. Because they had followed Jesus, God had equipped these two unschooled, ordinary men for greatness. And although Jesus' brother James came a bit late to the notion of big half-brother as Messiah, he definitely got there! So we should all take heart! Coming late is *so much* better than never getting there!

"It is only when God has transformed our nature and we have entered into the experience of sanctification that the fight begins. The warfare is not against sin; we can never fight against sin because Jesus has conquered that in his redemption of us. The conflict is waged over turning our natural life into a spiritual life.

"God does not make us holy in the sense that he makes our character holy. *He makes us holy in the sense that he has made us [legally] innocent before him. Then we have to turn that innocence into holy character through the moral choices we make.* We have a tendency to forget that a person is not only committed to Jesus Christ for salvation, but is also committed, responsible, and accountable to Jesus Christ's view of God, the world, and of sin, and the devil. This means, as Romans 12:2 tells us, that each of us must recognize the responsibility to be transformed by the renewing of our own minds" (Chambers Sept 8, 9).

When I am cooperating with God, it's easy to see.
As we have discussed elsewhere, I need to remember that God's desire is for me to live with and in him, submitting, following his way, his path. And God wants me to examine my life and my actions, daily. When I fall off the horse (or meet the ox face to face), I just get back on my feet and get back to what God wants me to do.

When I follow Jesus one day at a time, I am truly in the center of God's will for my life. Jesus was clear about this! We will all stand before the Lord, individually, and give an account of what we have done in these bodies. "So, obedience is the pathway to freedom" (DeMoss 55).

Remember, God wants us to repent, change our ways, and turn back to him. He is waiting for us to realize our sin, confess and repent, and then turn to him for help in living his way, not our own. This can be an immediate move or a process (sometimes long), but either way, God is active if we cooperate. Then, like Isaiah, we can be healed and freed from that particular sin. And once we have shed that sin, then God can use us, as he did Isaiah. It might be helpful to revisit the four basic steps a believer takes to follow Jesus (from chapter 2).

STEP 1: Repent and believe in the gospel.
* "His Spirit will direct my mind to my sin, so I can break free. And it won't be a vague sense of sin, but focusing on the concentration of sin in some specific, personal area of my life" (Chambers July 3).
* I confess my sins to God and turn away from them.

STEP 2: Deny yourself and follow Jesus.

STEP 3: Jesus says, "If you love me, keep my commandments."
Jn 4: 15. This includes honoring the law and teachings of the Old Testament.

STEP 4: Keep focused on Jesus, as he and the Father guide us.
* I lean on God and accept his help as I walk away from my sin, and as I continue in his presence and in his ways, not my own.
* If I trip, he helps me up, dusts me off, and sets me again on the right path
* If I stubbornly cling to some of my old ways, God will remind me again and again of how and why to do things his way, until I change. He is never done with me!

"To be born of God means that I have his supernatural power to stop sinning. (see 1 John 3:9) The Bible never asks, 'Should a Christian sin?'

Instead, it emphatically states that a Christian must not sin. The work of the new birth is being effective in us when we do not commit sin. It is not merely that we have the power not to sin, but that we have actually stopped sinning. Yet 1 John 3:9 doesn't mean that we cannot sin. It means that if we will obey the life of God in us, then we do not have to sin" (Chambers Aug 15).

Isaiah 6:5 "Woe is me, for I am undone! I am a man of unclean lips." Now who of us hasn't felt like that? Once Isaiah acknowledged his sin, God reaches out and touches his lips, removing his sin. That cleansing, healing touch transformed Isaiah, and it can transform us, if we do what Isaiah did.

Col 3:1–17 If then you have been raised with Christ, seek the things that are above, where Christ is, seated at the right hand of God. [2] Set your minds on things that are above, not on things that are on earth. [3] For you have died, and your life is hidden with Christ in God. [4] When Christ who is your life appears, then you also will appear with him in glory. [5] Put to death therefore what is earthly in you . . . anger, wrath, malice, slander, and obscene talk from your mouth. [9] Do not lie to one another, seeing that you have put off the old self with its practices [10] and have put on the new self, which is being renewed in knowledge after the image of its creator . . .

Sometimes "experts" talk about all this as if it's easy to jettison our old ways. But often, it is not.

There are areas of our lives where we are happy with our behavior. Then there are others where we are more or less content (or maybe apathetic would be a better word). We may not realize there are problems that could use some tweaking. Or we may be deliberately clinging to some old familiar ways that are downright unhealthy and ungodly. And finally, there are certain areas where we know we need lots of help. James 1:4 encourages us that if we are patient and steadfast, persistent and enduring, then we can be perfect and complete, lacking in nothing. Perfection is a process, and my own experience is that I am either *in* that flow or *out*, *in* that groove or *not*, hitting the sweet spot *or missing it*. But even if I am slacking off, God is committed and willing to help me make the changes I must make to get back in the groove and move forward!

"Ultimately, God will allow nothing to escape. Every detail of our lives is under his scrutiny. God will bring us back in countless ways to the same point over and over again . . . until we learn the lesson, because his purpose is to produce the finished product. It may be a problem arising from our impulsive nature, but again and again, with the most persistent patience, God has brought us back to that one particular point. Or the problem may be our idle and

wandering thinking, or our independent nature and self-interest. Through this process, God is trying to impress upon us the one thing that is not entirely right in our lives" (Chambers July 31).

I AM BLESSED TO BE A BLESSING. GOD WANTS ME TO CONSIDER HIS WILL AND PURPOSE FOR MY LIFE AND FOR THIS EARTH IN EVERYTHING I DO.

Now the Lord said to Abram, "Go from your country and your kindred and your father's house to the land that I will show you. ²And I will make of you a great nation, and I will bless you and make your name great, so that you will be a blessing . . ." Gen 12:1–3 (another favorite verse!)

Yes, God has a plan. But you may be thinking, surely he's looking at the big picture and isn't interested in every single little thing we do. Ah, but he is. And somehow he manages "big picture" and "micro pics" just fine. Just read some of the Bible verses in this book. God's plans and purposes are for the benefit of the world and for our personal salvation and our purification. Remember, God offers us a choice — *choose life or choose death* — and he never gives up on us while we still have breath!

So if God has a plan and we believe he is a good and powerful Father, wouldn't we want to consult that plan in every part of our lives? Micah 6:8 says we should not ignore the will of God when we plan. But how often do we think of that? I'll admit it, not enough! But I know that God created us so that we might seek him and reach out and find him. He is not far from each one of us. In him, we live and move and exist. We are his offspring (Acts 17:26–28).

Rivers of Living Water

Jesus says: Whoever drinks of the water that I will give him will never be thirsty again. The water that I shall give him will become in him a fountain of water springing up into everlasting life. Jn 4:14

"The picture our Lord described here is not that of a simple stream of water, but an overflowing fountain. Continue to 'be filled' (Eph 5:18) . . . and the sweetness of your vital relationship to Jesus will flow as generously out of you as it has been given to you. Focus on the Source so that out of you 'will flow rivers of living water' — irrepressible life. (Jn 7:38) . . . Stay at the Source, closely guarding your faith in Jesus Christ and your relationship to him, and there will be a steady flow into the lives of others with no dryness or deadness whatsoever" (Chambers Sept 7).

GOD IS OUR FOUNDATION AND OUR REASON FOR COURAGE. TRUST HIM AND DO NOT WORRY.

The good news is that God is not some disinterested old man twiddling his thumbs in the sky (as I probably thought when I was younger). He cares about us, and he is actively involved with us. He cares and he helps. This is one of the grand themes throughout scripture.

Once I accept Jesus as Lord and Savior, I follow him and our loving Father. They both say to me: I will never leave you. You are never alone. Do not be afraid. Do not worry. God is loving and steadfast, with us always, and we can count on that, even more than we count on the rising sun each morning. This reassuring truth is simple, but not necessarily easy. So let's revisit what Jesus repeated over and over: Don't be afraid or worry. Trust me. Lean on me. I am with you. And practice, practice, practice. Matthew 10 is great for this, as is the book of Psalms. But the encouragement is elsewhere, as well.

Here's what Jesus had to say about worrying versus trusting him:

Jesus says: Peace I leave with you; my peace I give you. I do not give to you as the world gives. Do not let your hearts be troubled and do not be afraid. Jn 14:27 NIV

Jesus says: Fear not, little flock, for it is your Father's good pleasure to give you the Kingdom. Lk 12:32 KJV

Jesus says: Come to Me, all you who are weary and are heavy laden, and I will give you rest. Take My yoke upon you and learn from Me, for I am gentle and humble in heart, and you will find rest for your souls. For my yoke is easy and my burden is light. Mt 11:28–30 NASB

FINALLY: GOD, YOU ARE GREAT!
GOD, TAKE MY HAND. AND GOD, TAKE MY MOUTH.

There is a real "rubber meets the road" quality to the Christian faith. And some of us linger too long before we plunge into a full life *as God wants us to.* Here is a story for our journey. And it shows that we must always be tuned in when God is talking!

A year or two before Stayton moved to heaven in 2013, I was trying to develop a short phrase I could memorize about God, to pull out when I was stressed beyond reason. Anyway, after a week or so of this, I told Stayton what I was doing and asked him, "How would you finish this phrase: God is . . . ?" Stayton beamed and said, "Oh, GOD IS GREAT!" And I just laughed at how right he was!

Later, I told this story to my friend Linda who always says, "GOD, TAKE MY HAND". No fancy phrases – just simply offering herself to God and going his way. So, as we talked and laughed about it, I told her that if I took Stayton's short phrase and combined it with hers, I would have the complete essence of this book!

But then this week, as this book is winding down, God (who always keeps on pitching) helped me see that there was one more phrase that I needed to add. I may have mentioned earlier that for all of my life, since I was a teenager, I have had a passion for helping the underdog. From a girl who was ground on by a teacher unfairly – to a clerk at work who was attacked by those in power – or a friend who has been cheated out of her home, I've taken their part and defended them. And I don't regret it. But in the last instance, I found it impossible to keep my mouth shut in the face of the enemy. So I wasn't as effective as I wanted, and I was furious a lot of the time. Friends Shelley and Tanya gave me some good coaching on being quiet when it was called for, and I knew they were right. But it was *so* hard and not my natural inclination! So God gave me this phrase, GOD, TAKE MY MOUTH! Ouch and thank you, Father! Can you relate? Or is there something else you should substitute for "mouth" – that needs work in your life? It's not an easy question, but it is well worth asking.

Dearest Father, I know if I make something other than you my first priority, I have made a choice, even if it's unconscious. If I'm a slave to anything — anger, food, pride, drugs, perfectionism, an unbridled mouth, you name it — I have responsibility because somewhere in the past I have surrendered to that thing. And by the same token (and here's the good news): If I follow and obey you and live the Jesus way, I can make repeated choices to yield myself to you. Please help me daily to evaluate my choices and my life, and ask for your power and wisdom to sync my life with my faith. If I keep my eyes on you, then my life will show that you really are my Number 1!

God, thank you for being so direct and clear with me, without yelling or abusing or turning your back on me. You gave us free will and you gave us a choice (although a few times I've wondered why). You don't hide the path to you or play tricks with us. You just tell us the truth: "Come to me, follow me, and live in — and with — me. Then life will be rich for you." (And I'm *not* talking luxury cars here!)

Jesus, I came to you fairly late (OK, very late!). But you knew all along that a woman like me, with a bit of a hard head, would need to fall in love with you instead of just signing some ritualistic agreements. And you were so right. I will never be able to say enough about how much I love you *and* our Dad! Hugs all around! *CGS*

PRAYER AND MEDITATION FOR CHAPTER 9

CHAPTER 10 OUTLINE: LIVE AND LOVE THE JESUS WAY. LOVE OTHERS, DO GOOD, GIVE, AND TEND HIS SHEEP. BE AT PEACE, SHOW MERCY, FORGIVE, AND DON'T TAKE OFFENSE.

The more you consider the " simple" list above, the more you'll discover that we desperately need God's help if we are to do anything at all in this arena. So what's the good news? When God calls us to do something and we follow him, he will also equip us.

We all have "natural affections – people we like and others we don't. Yet that must never rule our Christian life.

1. God calls and equips me to love others as much as I love myself, and as much as Jesus loves me. God's love and our love for him, is central to the many "fruits of the spirit" (Gal 5:22–23). These are the result of a life spent following God. They enrich and enable us at every step.
2. I agree with Jesus that it is my job to:
    Do good. Give. Tend his sheep.
3. How does Jesus deal with people who struggle? And how should we? Grace, mercy, compassion
4. Seek peace and pursue it.
5. Love your enemies.
6. Treat others the way you want to be treated.
7. Live with reasonable expectations of your fellow man.
8. How should we? With grace, mercy, compassion
9. Forgive and do not take offense. Or prepare to meet "Taking Offense", the ugly little sister of unforgiveness.

CHAPTER 10

LIVE AND LOVE THE JESUS WAY. LOVE OTHERS, DO GOOD, GIVE, AND TEND HIS SHEEP. BE AT PEACE, SHOW MERCY, FORGIVE, AND DON'T TAKE OFFENSE.

Jesus says: The person who trusts me will not only do what I'm
doing but even greater things, because I, on my way to
the Father, am giving you the same work to do that I've
been doing. You can count on it. Jn 14:12 MSG

Jesus says: . . . Live out this God-created identity the way our Father
lives toward us, generously and graciously, even when we're at our
worst. Our Father is kind [merciful]; you be kind.   Lk 6:35–36 MSG

GOD CALLS AND EQUIPS US TO LOVE OTHERS
AS MUCH AS WE LOVE OURSELVES,
AND AS MUCH AS JESUS LOVES US

God's simple (?) "to do" list above – which starts with loving others –
would be quite daunting if we tried to accomplish it in our own strength.
Clearly, we need God's help if we are to do anything at all in this arena. So
what's the good news? When God calls us to do something and we follow
him, he will also equip us. So let's keep our eyes on that very big truth!
And experience the many "fruits of the spirit" (Gal 5:22–23) that come
from a life spent following God. They enrich and enable us at every step.

Godly love is unselfish, unconditional, and flows from his Holy
Spirit within you. Throughout the New Testament, God makes it perfectly clear: We who love God, should also love others. But what about

all those "unlovable" types, you may wonder? Don't worry. Our own love, feeble at times, will be intertwined with God's love, which is ever present and as durable as eternity. And between God and us, there will be plenty to go around!

Of course, we all have "natural affections – people we like and others we don't. Yet that must never rule our Christian life . . . We are to 'walk in the light and have fellowship with one another' (1 Jn 1;7), even with those toward whom we have no affection" (Chambers Sept 20).

On the flip side, love does not mean that you make the other person your "god." And you shouldn't expect him or her to complete your life. Only Jesus can do that! But with God's help, we can love the lovable and the unlovable. After all, hasn't God managed that in our case?

What Jesus says about loving others:
[46] If you love only those who love you, what reward is there for that? Even corrupt tax collectors do that much. [47] If you are kind only to your friends, how are you different from anyone else? Even pagans do that. [48] But you are to be perfect, even as your Father in heaven is perfect. Mt 5:38-48
Jesus says: You must love the Lord your God with all your heart and with all your soul and with all your strength and with all your mind; and your neighbor as yourself. Lk 10:27 [reflecting Lev 19:18; Deut 6:5.]
Jesus says: Love your neighbor as yourself. Mt 19:19b and Mt 22:39; Mk 12:31; Lk 10:27 (All cited from Lev 19:18) (And then he went even further.)
Jesus says: This is My commandment, that you love one another as I have loved you. Greater love has no one than this, than to lay down one's life for his friends. Jn 15:12–13 NKJV Mt 22:39 and in Lk 10:27

Other Scripture speaks often of love for others.
Here are some:
Gal 5:14 AMP 14 For the whole Law [concerning human relationships] is complied with in the one precept, You shall love your neighbor as [you do] yourself. [Lev 19:18.]
Eph 5:2 AMP And walk in love, [esteeming and delighting in one another] as Christ loved us and gave Himself up for us, a slain offering and sacrifice to God [for you, so that it became] a sweet fragrance. [Ezek. 20:41]

1 Jn 4:11–12 NIV . . . If we love one another, God lives in us and his love is made complete in us.

2 Jn 6 MSG Love means following his commandments, and his unifying commandment is that you conduct your lives in love. This is the first thing you heard, and nothing has changed.

DO GOOD, GIVE, AND TEND GOD'S SHEEP

This is part of what the Bible calls "good works" (Mt 5:14–16). Thanks to Jesus, our Christian faith is a loving, living, working faith. Some folks spend a lot of time debating which is most important —faith or good works — although Jesus clearly linked the two in his teaching. And nowhere does he say that "good works" will save us. These arguments often take up more time and energy than good works would! That isn't what God has in mind. He wants both!

When Jesus appeared a third time to the disciples after his resurrection, he had this famous conversation with Peter:

[15] When they had finished breakfast, Jesus said to Simon Peter, "Simon, son of John, do you love me more than these?" He said to him, "Yes, Lord; you know that I love you." He said to him, "Feed my lambs." [reflecting the imagery of God as all powerful, and yet still a shepherd in Isaiah 40:10–11] [16] He said to him a second time, "Simon, son of John, do you love me?" He said to him, "Yes, Lord; you know that I love you." He said to him, "Tend my sheep." [17] He said to him the third time, "Simon, son of John, do you love me?" Peter was grieved because he said to him the third time, "Do you love me?" and he said to him, "Lord, you know everything; you know that I love you." Jesus said to him, "Feed my sheep . . . [19] . . . [and] "Follow me." Jn 21:15–19

Oswald Chambers observes, correctly, that we (God's sheep) can be "extraordinarily peculiar, some unkempt and dirty, some awkward or pushy, and some that have gone astray. But it is impossible to exhaust God's love, and impossible to exhaust my love if it flows from the Spirit of God within me" (Chambers Mar 3). So God has no plans to deliver or release us from this important commission!

At the beginning of his public ministry, Jesus gave us a pattern to follow.

Jesus says: The Spirit of the Lord is on me, because he has anointed me to preach good news to the poor. He has sent me to proclaim freedom for the prisoners and recovery of sight for the blind, to release the oppressed, to proclaim the year of the Lord's favor. Lk 4:18–19 NIV (quoting Isa 61:1–2)

Jesus says: Do good . . . expecting nothing in return . . . Lk 6:35

Jesus says: If you give, you will receive. Your gift will return to you in full measure, pressed down, shaken together to make room for more, and running over. Whatever measure you use in giving — large or small — it will be used to measure what is given back to you. Lk 6:38 NLT Mk 4:24 Mt 7:1–2 (reflecting the ideas of Prov 11:24–25 and others)

Sadly, Luke 6:38 (above) is often quoted as some sort of prosperity formula, a tit-for-tat gimmick to get God to give us all the things on our material wish list. But that is inconsistent with the overall word of God. And it reeks of what Oswald Chambers calls "miserable commercial self-interest" (Chambers Mar 12). If we give to God and others and are enriched in return, it is so that we will have the resources to help spread the love and good news of Jesus Christ throughout the world. Blessed to be a blessing!

Jesus says: Great gifts mean great responsibilities; greater gifts, greater responsibilities! Lk 12:48 MSG   In his story of the sheep and goats, Jesus says that the "sheep" (those who take care of the needy) are blessed and will inherit the kingdom. Those who do not (the "goats") will be cast into eternal fire. Here he explains this to the blessed ones:

Jesus says: I was hungry and you gave me food, I was thirsty and you gave me drink, I was a stranger and you welcomed me, I was naked and you clothed me, I was sick and you visited me, I was in prison and you came to me . . . As you did it to one of the least of these my brothers, you did it to me. Mt 25:35–40 ESV (expands Isa 58:6–7; Isa 61:1)

Titus 2:14 [14] [God through Jesus] gave himself for us to redeem us from all lawlessness and to purify for himself a people for his own possession (see Ezek 37:23; Ex 19:5) who are zealous for good works. (Titus 3:8; Eph 2:10).

Titus 3:3–8 MSG When God, our kind and loving Savior God, stepped in, he saved us from all that. It was all his doing; we had nothing to do with it [not even our "'good works'"]. He gave us a good bath, and we came out of it new people, washed inside and out by the Holy Spirit. Our Savior Jesus poured out new life so generously. God's gift has restored our relationship with him and given us back our lives. And there's more life to come — an eternity of life! You can count on this.

WHAT SHOULD WE DO WHEN WE ENCOUNTER PEOPLE WHO STRUGGLE? HOW DID JESUS DEAL WITH THOSE FOLKS? CAN WE FOLLOW HIM AND SHOW HIS GRACE, LOVE, MERCY, AND COMPASSION?

Mercy can be defined as compassion and kindness toward the miserable and afflicted, a readiness to help, to spare, and to forgive [Lk 1:50 AMP and Mt 12:7 AMP]. But in some cases, receiving mercy can also mean *not* getting what you deserve! If I observe my Father's mercy toward me, I can learn to be merciful, as he is merciful.

I am at the stage in this book when I should *not* be adding another word! But I attended a funeral on Saturday (Sept 12, 2015), where I felt God was talking straight to me! Toby Shockey (my friend Joy's son) was speaking at his aunt's funeral and his topic was "How does Jesus deal with people who struggle?" (John 8: 1+)

Toby opened by saying that the family agreed that he should speak about his aunt as she was. A woman who made some good decisions, which she was glad for later. And a woman who – like us all – had made some bad decisions which she regretted. In short, she struggled, as we all do at some time or another. And then Toby began to tell the story of Jesus' dealing with a woman who had obviously made at least one bad decision. And I'm thinking this is a VERY strange story for a funeral. But I am hooked by his topic, so my ears perk up for sure!

The woman in this familiar Bible story is caught in the act of adultery by a group of men and thrown at the feet of Jesus. (Toby asks, *How* do they know? And, *Where* is the man?) The men want to stone (kill) her. After some back and forth, Jesus says to the men, "All right, but let the man who has never sinned throw the first stone!" Their response? Toby says the only sound we hear is stones dropping to the ground. And the men all slip away. Jesus asks the woman, "Where are your accusers? Didn't even one of them condemn you?" "No, Lord," she said.

And Jesus said, "Neither do I condemn you. Go and sin no more." And Toby asks us to notice the order of these two statements. The first statement – I do not condemn you – comes first and has no conditions. Even more amazing yet is that this Jesus – the Son of God – is the one who will later go to the cross and take on this woman's punishment.

So what is our response to people who – like us – can be a mess sometimes? We don't have to pretend something isn't what it is, but we are called to respond with grace. And what about me? Wouldn't I want others to treat me with the same mercy? Are there people in our lives who also need this grace? This compassion? Instead of judgment and endless advice on "how to fix it"?

Toby concluded by reminding us that Jesus came to the broken, those just like us. So we must look every day for an opportunity to show this grace ourselves. Could this message be any better for me? Or you? Jesus could have responded another way. After all he was divine, and this woman was just damaged goods. How glad I am that he responded – and continues to respond – with such love, grace, mercy and compassion!

Jesus says: Be merciful, even as your Father is merciful. Lk 6:36
Blessed are the merciful, for they shall receive mercy. Mt 5:7 ESV
Jesus says: Go and learn what this means, "I desire mercy and not sacrifice." For I came not to call the righteous, but sinners Mt 9:13 and later in Mt 12:7. (building on Hos 6:6 where God says, "I desire steadfast love and not sacrifice.")
Ex 34:6 -7 . . . a God merciful and gracious, slow to anger, and abounding in steadfast love and faithfulness.
Lam 3:21–23 AMP [21] But this I recall and therefore have I hope *and* expectation: [22]It is because of the Lord's mercy *and* loving-kindness that we are not consumed, because His [tender] compassions fail not. [Mal 3:6.] [23]They are new every morning; great *and* abundant is Your stability *and* faithfulness. [Isa. 33:2.]

Jas 2:13 NASB Judgment will be merciless to one who has shown no mercy; mercy triumphs over judgment.

For more on mercy, see chapters 1, 7, 8 and 12.

SEEK PEACE AND PURSUE IT
1 PETER 3:11B, CITING PSALM 34:14

Peace with others is something we all yearn for, but it can be difficult to find. In fact some of us have a very low concentration of natural peace and serenity in our DNA. And yes, I am one of those. That is why God's peace is so very critical! Like forgiveness, peace has a supernatural component. In fact, *God's peace* is the ingredient that makes the whole "peace stew" work!

I'm not proud to admit that I often don't realize I need God's peace until I am halfway up the crazy and ticked-off tree! There's only one good thing about that. When his peace does come to me, I recognize it instantly. If you're anything like me, let's agree that we can do better and start asking for peace, early and often!

Jesus calls us to peace with one another

Jesus says: Blessed are the peacemakers, for they shall be called sons of God. Mt 5:9 [or as the Amplified Bible puts it] Blessed (enjoying enviable happiness, spiritually prosperous — with life, joy, and satisfaction in God's favor and salvation, regardless of their outward conditions) are the makers and maintainers of peace, for they shall be called the sons of God. Mt 5:9 AMP

Jesus says: Be reconciled to your brother. Mt 5:22–24

Jesus says: Peace I leave with you; my peace I give to you. Not as the world gives do I give to you. Let not your hearts be troubled, neither let them be afraid. Jn 14:27

Jesus says: These things I have spoken to you, that in me you may have peace. In the world you will have tribulation; but be of good cheer; I have overcome the world. Jn 16:33 NKJV

For other Scripture references on peace, see:

Re pursuing peace, see Mk 9:50b, Rom 14:19; Heb 12:14; Rom 12:18)

Eph 2:14 He is our peace, who has made us both [Jews and Gentiles] one, and has broken down the dividing wall of hostility.

Col 3:12–17 ESV, RSV . . . Put on love, which binds everything together in perfect harmony . . . Let the peace of Christ rule in your hearts . . . Let the word of Christ dwell in you richly . . . See also 2 Cor 13:11; 1 Thess 5:13;

For more on peace, see Introduction and chapters 1-7 and 12.

LOVE YOUR ENEMIES

Jesus says: You have heard that the law of Moses says, 'Love your neighbor and hate your enemy.' But I say, love your enemies! Pray for those who persecute you! In that way, you will be acting as true children of your Father in heaven. For he gives his sunlight to both the evil and the good, and he sends rain on the just and on the unjust, too. If you love only those who love you, what good is that? Even corrupt tax collectors do that much. If you are kind only to your friends, how are you different from anyone else? Even pagans do that. But you are to be perfect, even as your Father in heaven is perfect. Mt 5:43–48 NLT Lk 6:27–28, 32

Jesus says: I tell you, love your enemies. Help and give without expecting a return. You'll never, I promise, regret it. Live out this God-created identity the way our Father lives toward us, generously and graciously, even when we're at our worst. Our Father is kind; you be kind. Lk 6:35–36 MSG

Rom 12:21 Do not be overcome by evil, but overcome evil with good.

1 Pet 3:9 NIV Do not repay evil with evil or insult with insult, but with blessing . . . so that you may inherit a blessing.

LIVE WITH REASONABLE EXPECTATIONS

"The days that I keep my gratitude higher than my expectations —
Well, I have really good days." Ray Wylie Hubbard

My expectations, like Kudzu, need some pruning. How about yours?
Expectations are a natural part of relationships. But there are times when expectations creep out of their boundaries and take over, like

Kudzu. Kudzu is a climbing, coiling, and trailing perennial vines native to much of eastern Asia, southeast Asia, and some Pacific Islands. When it is introduced into a new land, it can be invasive and is considered a noxious weed. It out-competes other species for light, climbs over trees or shrubs, and grows so rapidly that it suffocates and kills its 'host' by heavy shading.

So, yes, sorry to say, expectations are often like Kudzu! Carefully controlled, expectations are healthy and useful. Otherwise, they can be quite harmful to our relationships. Want an example? My husband and I loved and adored each other – and much, much more. But because I am human, it was easy to expect more. So even though he was a wonderful man, I could still get irritated because he often needed to be right. Uncommon? I think not. All of us – including me – like to be right, and some of us absolutely *must* be right. Irritating? Oh yeah!

This one thing was truly small in the grand scheme, and yet I would hammer at it from time to time because I expected him to change. (It probably didn't help that I was raised by a very overbearing father – how's that for an excuse from a grown woman?) Of course all of this was as much about how I saw myself as how he saw himself. But I was never smart enough to see that and adapt. So it wasn't until he began to fail, say, seven years before his death, that I dropped my unrealistic expectation as a natural outcome of our new reality. Frankly, it was a relief and a reality check to focus instead — and only — on what was truly important: him and me together, forever.

God, help us examine our expectations, to see if they've become like Kudzu, choking the life out of us and the things (and people) around us that deserve to thrive! Are our expectations in line with your desire for these relationships: For a spouse? Our children? Our *grown* children? Our best friend? Our colleagues at work? Our pastor? An estranged relative? Are our expectations reasonable? And if not, please help us get us in line with you.

TREAT OTHERS THE WAY YOU WANT TO BE TREATED. DO
GOOD. DO NOT JUDGE OR CONDEMN. GIVE.

God says: [9] "This is what the LORD Almighty said: 'Administer true
justice; show mercy and compassion to one another. [10] Do not oppress
the widow or the fatherless, the foreigner or the poor. Do not
plot evil against each other . . . Zech 7:9–14 NIV

Jesus is very concerned with how we treat others:

Jesus says: Treat others as you want them to treat you. This is what the Law and
the Prophets are all about. Mt 7:12 CEV Lk 6:31

Jesus says: Do good . . . expecting nothing in return . . . Lk 6:35

Jesus says: Do not judge, and you will not be judged. Lk 6:37

Jesus says: Do not condemn, and you will not be condemned. Lk 6:37

Jesus says: Forgive, and you will be forgiven; Lk 6:37 NRSV Mt 7:1–5

Jesus says: Give away your life; you'll find life given back, but not merely
given back — given back with bonus and blessing. Giving, not getting, is
the way. Generosity begets generosity. Lk 6:38 MSG Mk 4:24–25 [And if
you have any doubts about how strongly Jesus felt about this, check out Mt
25:31–46]

Jesus says: But [dedicate your inner self and] give as donations to the poor
of those things which are within [of inward righteousness] and behold, everything is purified and clean for you. Lk 11:41 AMP

Jesus says: You have heard . . . "An eye for an eye and a tooth for a tooth." But
I say to you, Do not resist an evil-doer. But if any one strikes you on the right
cheek, turn the other also; and if any one wants to sue you and take your coat,
give your cloak as well; and if any one forces you to go one mile, go also the
second mile. Mt 5:38–41 NRSV Lk 6:29 (Here, Jesus transforms Ex 21:24; Lev
24:20; and Deut 19:21.)

FORGIVE AND DON'T TAKE OFFENSE – OR ELSE GET READY TO MEET "TAKING OFFENSE", THE UGLY LITTLE SISTER OF UNFORGIVENESS

Forgiveness doesn't mean we are unhurt or undamaged by a slight or a terrible wrong. And it doesn't mean we invite the same hurt again. It means, instead, that we lay down the anger and the hurt, and move on. Truth be told, this may be a process rather than a 'once and done' deal. I am definitely a work in progress in this area, but it's worth persisting, trust me. Some people will fail you, and you will fail them at times, as well. So you will have endless opportunities in your life to practice forgiving and being forgiven.

Forgiveness has a supernatural component that we cannot ignore or do without. And here's an understatement alert: Without God's help, it is difficult to forgive, to let go, and to move on. But happily, we do have God's help. And when we ask for his power and his grace to do the right thing, he is ready and more than willing to supply them. Sometimes, he helps even when we don't ask, even though we are perfectly aware that our unforgiveness is wrong. I have personally experienced God's intervention to clear the logjam of a long-standing hardness of heart on both sides (described in chapter 8). There was no mistaking this. *It was totally God.* But we both understood that God expected us to do our part and stand and defend this new holy ground.

Jesus says: Acquit and forgive and release (give up resentment, let it drop), and you will be acquitted and forgiven and released. Lk 6:37b AMP
Jesus says: Pray . . . forgive us our sins, just as we have forgiven those who have sinned against us. Mt 6:9, 12 NLT Lk 11:4
Jesus says: Whenever you stand praying, forgive, if you have anything against anyone, so that your Father who is in heaven will also forgive you your transgressions. Mk 11:25 NASB (and the same thought is found in Mt 6:14.)
Jesus says: If you forgive men when they sin against you, your heavenly Father will also forgive you . . . Mt 6:14–15 NIV
Jesus says: If you continue in my word, you are truly my disciples, and you will know the truth, and the truth will make you free . . . So if the Son makes you free, you will be free indeed. Jn 8:31–36

Jesus says: [speaking after his resurrection] . . .
If you forgive someone's sins, they're gone for good. If you don't forgive sins, what are you going to do with them? Jn 20:22–23 MSG

Taking offense: the Ugly Little Sister of Unforgiveness

Pastor Brian Leifeste's sermon on taking offense, or refusing to, is one I will never forget. The message was a real eye opener for me, and I quote it all the time. It points out that unforgiveness is too hot a potato to hang on to, bringing far more pain to the carrier than to anyone else. And the same is true of taking offense. The opportunity to take offense can come through true injustice or through the perception of injustice. It's what we do with that "opportunity" that counts. In fact, Brian describes two doors that open to us whenever we see the opportunity to take offense.

The first choice is the door of offense — choosing to take offense, which leads to traps and bondage. I can still hear Brian describing a hunter spreading corn before a wild hog, luring him further and further into the trap, into enemy territory. That's quite a visual of how enticing it can be to take offense!

Brian says that when we take offense (versus refuse to take it), we are separated from one another and cannot walk in the light, in true fellowship. We erect walls which keep things out, yes, but walls also keep things in. Our hurt is so big, that all we can see is us! And when we take offense, we become more and more self-seeking, self-oriented. And the love of God inside us grows cold. (Mt 24) We are alone, imprisoned in the heart. And this is *not* God's will.

The second door or choice before us is to refuse to pick up the offense and, instead, forgive. Even when the offense is real, we gain nothing by picking it up and carrying it all the way to the trap! So release the ones who have been unjust, unfair, and/or cruel. Let God set you free. Jesus was our model in all this. Although he was tempted to feel angry and take offense, he didn't go there! True forgiveness requires the power and grace of God, and it is *not* based on how you feel. Instead it is based on the grace of God within us that gives us the strength to do what we cannot do alone. Grace and love can draw us out of our imprisoned heart (Leifeste 2011).

As I've said, Brian's sermon really peaked my interest. And I found a book which is a great companion, entitled *The Bait of Satan: Living Free From the Deadly Trap of Offense 20th Anniversary edition 2014.* Author John Bevere explains that the Greek word for "offend" in Luke 17:1 comes from the Greek word *skandala*, which originally referred to the part of the trap which the bait was attached. Hence, the word signifies laying a trap in someone's way. In the New Testament it often describes an entrapment used by the enemy.

And [Jesus] said to His disciples,
Temptations (snares, traps set to entice to sin) are sure to come, but woe to him by *or* through whom they come! Luke 17:1 AMP.

Father, I can have the hardest of hearts, and I need you to help me identify and break the logjams that "guard" them. Like anyone else, I can justify a hard heart. In many of these situations, the facts as I remember them are absolutely correct, and the people involved did hurt me terribly. But you know that, Father, and you still want my heart soft.

Jesus, you have held me close and told me that you can love me when others should have, but did not. I know what you want me to do about unforgiveness. Help me to come to you — as often as I need — to make my heart soft and forgiving. And give me amnesia of those wounds of the past. Teach me that I can be hurt and still forgive. Whisper in my ear. Remind me that forgiving is not the same as embracing an old offender. Forgiving is divine, and taking offense is not! I can only do this with your help. I love you so much!   *CGS*

PRAYER AND MEDITATION FOR CHAPTER 10

CHAPTER 11 OUTLINE: JESUS CALLS US TO SHARE THE TRUTH OF GOD WITH OTHERS — IN LOVE — AND HELP OTHERS BECOME TRUE DISCIPLES

Jesus says: . . . God is not a secret to be kept.
We're going public with this . . . Mt 5:14, 16 MSG

INTRODUCTION — Four key truths (out of many) for the believer's own life and his/her mission to share God's love with the world:

- First, Jesus wants to break down relational barriers, so that he can have a dialogue between the "lost" and the "found".
- Second, Jesus addresses our brokenness, asking us to expose our deepest hurts and failures before him. Then . . .
- Third, Jesus desires to fill the emptiness of our lives, where we live on the edges of deceit [and defeat] and fill us with himself.
- Fourth, Jesus is relentless in his pursuit of humanity — and that's you. If you came here with a longing, Jesus is what you're after. Jesus wants you and HE is your answer (this series of four from Rice 2015)

1. What is it like to have a call on your life? Includes a reference to John 17. And we hear of the amazing example of William Tyndale. Don't we yearn to hear God say of us "Love drives such a man/or woman. God drives such a man/or woman"?
2. God plans to reach the world, and I am part of that. Telling people about God is step one.

- It's a blessing to be able to do that. And I should always remember that the gospel is our source of joy!
- I am a disciple of Jesus. I am equipped for this, even if it seems like a pretty tall mountain to climb!
- Share the good news of God: Father, Son, and Holy Spirit. Lk 12:8–9 Mt 10:32–33 . . .
- Go and proclaim the kingdom of God. Lk 9:60b (which Jesus describes as his own work, as well, in Lk 4:42–43; Lk 8:1; 16:16; Mt 4:23; 24:14; Acts 8:12

3. Step 2 is to make disciples: baptize, disciple, and teach new believers. And encourage and other Christians Mt 28:18–20; Mt 5:19b God is all about discipleship!

4. Finally, some real life examples of people sharing God's word with the world

JESUS CALLS US TO SHARE THE TRUTH OF GOD WITH OTHERS — IN LOVE — AND HELP OTHERS BECOME TRUE DISCIPLES

Jesus says: . . . God is not a secret to be kept.
We're going public with this . . . Mt 5:14, 16 MSG

Jesus says (speaking after his resurrection and immediately
before he ascends into Heaven): You will receive power when the
Holy Spirit has come upon you; and you shall be My witnesses both
in Jerusalem, and in all Judea and Samaria, and even to the remotest
part of the earth. Acts 1:8 NASB

Rom 1:16 WMF I am not ashamed of the good news . . .
for in [it] is the very power of God revealed, a power capable
of providing salvation to everyone that will believe . . .

Rom 10:13–15 NIV Everyone who calls on the name of the
Lord will be saved. How, then, can they call on the one they have not
believed in? And how can they believe in the one of whom they have not
heard? And how can they hear without someone preaching to them?
And how can they preach unless they are sent? As it is written, 'How
beautiful are the feet of those who bring good news!'

INTRODUCTION

In late July 2015, I'd been through the editing process and *thought* I was about ready to put this book to bed (or as my younger son says, put shoes on that puppy and let it walk out the door!). But then, the last Sunday in July (today as I write this), I heard a sermon by Pastor Rusty Rice with four on-target points that speak to the believer's own life and his/ her mission to share God's love with the world. I thought, oh, this is good! Let's tuck it into chapter 11. So here it is.

God, through Jesus, has many truths he wants us to remember –for the believer's own life and for his/her mission to share God's love with the world. First, Jesus wants to break down relational barriers, so that he can have a dialogue between the "lost" and the "found". Second, Jesus addresses our brokenness, asking us to expose our deepest hurts and fail-ures before him . . . Because . . . Third, Jesus wants to heal the emptiness of our lives – where we live on the edges of deceit [and defeat] – and fill us with his life and his character. And Fourth, Jesus is relentless in his pur-suit of humanity, and that's you and me. If you came here with a longing, Jesus is what you're after. Jesus wants you. HE is your answer (Rice 2015).

WHAT IS IT LIKE TO HAVE
GOD'S CALL ON YOUR LIFE?

First, let's look again at John 17, where Jesus pours out his heart to his Father in heaven on the night before he died. In these excerpts, Jesus explains God's "call" on his life:

> Jn 17: 2–4 MSG You put [me, your Son] in charge of every-thing human, so he might give real and eternal life to all in his charge. And this is the real and eternal life: That they know you, the one and only true God, and Jesus Christ, whom you sent. I glorified you on earth by complet-ing down to the last detail what you assigned me to do . . . Jn 17:18–19 MSG In the same way that you gave me a mission in the world, I give them a mission in the world. I'm consecrating myself for their sakes, so they'll be truth-consecrated in their mission.

Obviously this is important to Jesus, so it is important to me. Like you, I have a specific history, spiritually and otherwise. Remember, my husband and I came very late to the realization that God wanted a personal relationship with us, through his Son Jesus. So almost from the first day that we met Jesus on a personal basis, we wanted to share that Good News with everyone we met. It's *the most* important topic for us.

Beth Moore puts it well: "Press on for a fresh reminder that your life has great significance and perfect timing. And press on for encouragement to train and mobilize others . . . If you have placed your faith in Jesus Christ as your personal Savior, then, child of God, you have a ministry — a way we've each been called to serve Christ. It is the ever-accruing collection of your life works for the glory of God. It's not about where you receive a paycheck; it's the means by which you live out your divine purpose. It can take place in secular or sacred environments. In fact, God fulfilling in you what you were born to do can render a secular environment beautifully sacred.

"Each believer has 'a God-ordained ministry'. It is the reason God left you on this planet after you received Christ and became a citizen of heaven. You won't be satisfied until you are living it out, because God wired you with a compulsion to do it" (Moore 2014, 141, 142).

Then Beth describes the passion and courage of William Tyndale for his God (quoting from an excellent biography by David Teems). Tyndale translated Scripture into English at great peril — and ultimately death — to himself.

"To William Tyndale, the Word of God is a living thing. It has both warmth and intellect. It has discretion, generosity, subtlety, movement, authority. It has a heart and a pulse. It keeps a beat and has a musical voice that allows it to sing. It enchants and it soothes. It argues and it forgives. It defends and it reasons. It intoxicates and it restores. It weeps and it exults. It thunders but never roars. It calls but never begs. And it always loves. Indeed, for Tyndale, love is the code that unlocks and empowers the Scripture. His inquiry into Scripture is always relational, never analytic" (Teems, page xvii).

In early August 1536, before a gathering of bishops, Tyndale had been ceremonially and publically stripped of his priesthood and condemned to die. He was executed on Friday, October 6, 1536, "for the most heinous of crimes. He'd dared to translate the Scriptures into English. And he'd done so at great loss and constant risk. Proficient in multiple languages, including Hebrew and Greek, he labored tirelessly, moved constantly, and evaded authorities until, finally, the New Testament was birthed in 1526 with the distinct cries of an English infant" (Teems quoted by Moore, 2014, 152, 255).

I love these final lines, speaking of Tyndale: "Discipline alone lacks the heat to keep a long, arduous work aflame amid the ruination of reputation and the loss of home, country, and companionship. Love drives such a man. God drives such a man" (Moore 2014, 152).

GOD PLANS TO REACH THE WORLD
THROUGH JESUS, AND I AM PART OF THAT

> At my age and stage, I agree whole-heartedly with Paul, when he says
> in Acts 20:24 NLT: My life is worth nothing to me unless I use it for
> finishing the work assigned me by the Lord Jesus . . . telling others
> the Good News about the wonderful grace of God. CGS

As a follower of Jesus, I am to share the good news of God — Father, Son, and Holy Spirit. And I am to go and proclaim the Kingdom of God. It's a blessing to be able to do that. And I want to always remember that the gospel is my source of joy. My prayer is that you will see it the same way!

In the Old Testament, God insisted that all the Hebrew people know his words, his laws, and his ways. Now God, through Jesus, expands this, so that the whole world can know God. And remember that new believers receive *all* of God: Father, Son, and Holy Spirit. That's Jesus' model, and it is ours as well.

Charles Spurgeon describes the joy of sharing and hearing the Gospel. "The invitations of the Gospel are invitations to happiness. In delivering God's message, we do not ask men to come to a funeral, but to a wedding feast! If our errand were one of sorrow, we might not marvel if men refused to listen to us. But it is one of gladness, not sadness . . .

"When the coming of Christ to the earth was first announced, it was with . . . the choral symphonies of holy angels (Lk 2:14). And as long as the Gospel shall be preached in this world, its main message will be one of joy.

"It is a source of joy to those who proclaim it, for unto us is this Grace given — that we should preach among the Gentiles the unsearchable riches of Christ (Eph 3:8). And it is a source of joy to all who hear it aright and accept it. The simplest telling out of the Gospel is of itself a most delightful thing! And if our hearts were in a right condition, we would not merely be glad to hear of Jesus over and over again, but the story of the love of our Incarnate God and of the redemption worked by Immanuel would be the sweetest music that our ears ever heard" (Spurgeon 1874).

Jesus said to them, [43]"I must preach the good news of the kingdom of God to the other towns as well; for I was sent for this purpose." [44] And he was preaching in the synagogues of Judea. Lk 4:23–44   Mk 1:39
And Jesus said to him, "Leave the dead to bury their own dead. But as for you, go and proclaim the kingdom of God." Lk 9:60
Jesus says (Mt 10:32–33) [32] So everyone who acknowledges me before men, I also will acknowledge before my Father who is in heaven, [Rom. 10:9, 10; Heb. 10:35; Rev. 3:5], [33] but whoever denies me before men (Mk 8:38; 2 Tim 2:12; 2 Pet 2:1; 1 Jn 2:23;), I also will deny before my Father who is in heaven. (Mt 7:23; 25:12; Lk 13:25)

By God's grace, this sharing of the gospel, near and far, is an honor for any Christian. If you've never tried it, please do! Personally, I do it because I love God, because Jesus gave his all to save me, and because now I am God's daughter, wanting everyone to know my "Dad".

The apostle Paul called believers "letters" sent out to the world from God (2 Cor 3:2–3). And that's a great picture, meaning that those around us are watching and "reading," not just our words proclaiming Jesus, but also our lives! And watch out if our lives don't fit what we say! "Then, like a witness who contradicts himself on cross-examination, [our] testimony goes for nothing" (Finney 1839).

Jesus says: . . . Go in to all the world and preach the gospel to the whole creation . . . Mk 16:15–16 [Some ancient texts omit Mk 16:9–20]

Jesus says: I tell you, all those who stand before others and say they believe in me, I, the Son of Man, will say before the angels of God that they belong to me. But all who stand before others and say they do not believe in me, I will say before the angels of God that they do not belong to me. Lk 12:8–9 NCV Mt 10:32–33

Jesus says: If anyone is ashamed of me and my words, the Son of Man will be ashamed of him when he comes in his glory and in the glory of the Father and of the holy angels. Lk 9:26 NIV Mk 8:38

Jesus says: He who is not with me is against me. Mt 12:30 Mk 9:40 Lk 11:23

Jesus says: Go and proclaim the kingdom of God. Lk 9:60b [which Jesus said in Lk 4:43 was his own mission, as well]

Jesus says: . . . God is not a secret to be kept. We're going public with this . . . Mt 5:14 MSG

Jesus says: As you go, preach this message: 'The kingdom of heaven is near'. Heal the sick, raise the dead, cleanse those who have leprosy, drive out demons. Freely you have received, freely give. Mt 10:1, 7–8 NIV
Mk 6:7, 12–13 Lk 9:1–2 and later, in Lk 10:1–2, 8–9

Jesus says: The harvest is plentiful, but the workers are few. Ask the Lord of the harvest, therefore, to send out workers into his harvest field. Mt 9:37–38 NIV and in Lk 10:2 and in Jn 4:35

Jesus says: The gospel must first be preached to all nations. Mk 13:10

[Speaking after the resurrection]
Jesus says: Go into all the world and preach the gospel to every creature . . . Mk 16:15–18 NKJV

Jesus says: Repentance and forgiveness of sins should be preached in his [the Christ's] name, to all nations . . . Lk 24:47

Telling your own faith story.
As part of sharing the Gospel – telling God's story – you can also tell your own story, clearly and simply. And remember, everybody's story is different: yours, mine, and those who listen to us. Life is messy. There

is absolutely no need to disclose every detail when telling your story, but it will be helpful for pre-Christians and others to understand that while life is hard at times, God is with us all the time! He may rescue us from a bad spot, or he may guide us through it. But either way, he is our all-loving and all-powerful God, not some magician to supply your every whim. So seriously consider including times when you felt desperate or lost, a "desert" experience, dry and painful.

But don't be fearful when you do acknowledge Jesus.

Jesus says: . . . Do not worry about what to say or how to say it. At that time you will be given what to say, for it will not be you speaking, but the Spirit of your Father speaking through you. Mt 10:19–20 NIV Mk 13:11 Lk 12:11–12 (reflects Ex 4:10–17 and Jer 1:6–10)

Jesus says: They will lay their hands on you and persecute you . . . This will be a time for you to bear testimony . . . I will give you a mouth and wisdom, which none of your adversaries will be able to withstand or contradict . . . By your endurance, you will gain your lives. Lk 21:12–19 (reflecting Ex 4:10–17)

Isa 49:6 God says: I will make you as a light for the nations, that my salvation may reach to the end of the earth.

Isa 55:9–12 NLT [God says] [9] For just as the heavens are higher than the earth, so my ways are higher than your ways and my thoughts higher than your thoughts. [10] The rain and snow come down from the heavens and stay on the ground to water the earth. They cause the grain to grow, producing seed for the farmer and bread for the hungry. [11] It is the same with my word. I send it out, and it always produces fruit. It will accomplish all I want it to, and it will prosper everywhere I send it. [12] You will live in joy and peace. The mountains and hills will burst into song, and the trees of the field will clap their hands!

Dan 12:3 ESV And those who are wise shall shine like the brightness of the sky above; and those who turn many to righteousness, like the stars forever and ever.

Ezek 33:11 God takes no pleasure in the death of the wicked, but wants them to turn back from their wicked ways and live!

1 Pet 3:15 . . . Always be prepared to make a defense to any one who calls you to account for the hope that is in you, yet do it with gentleness and reverence.

THE OTHER PART OF SPREADING THE GOSPEL
IS TO MAKE DISCIPLES, BAPTIZE, AND TEACH

Jesus says [after his resurrection]: [18] . . . "All authority in heaven
and on earth has been given to me. [19] Go therefore and make disciples
of all nations [Gr *ethnos*: races, people groups], baptizing them in the
name of the Father and of the Son and of the Holy Spirit, [20] teaching
them to observe all that I have commanded you. And behold, I am
with you always, to the end of the age." Mt 28:18–20 NIV

I am a disciple of Jesus. And I trust that I am equipped for this, because
I trust that God does the equipping. (Talk about taking plain dough and
turning it into a wonderful cookie!)

"Discipleship represents nothing less than God's ultimate restoration of his universal people to the original creation-design and purpose
— to walk with God (Gen 5:22–24) and to be restored as true image-
bearers of God (Rom 8:29; 1 Cor 15:49; 2 Cor 3:18; Col 3:10).

"Discipleship is not merely a certain code of conduct for the disciples. It means joining the people of God in God's creation, coming
under his eternal covenant and kingly rule, and living in dependence
on God rather than independence from him. We ultimately see that
discipleship in Mark and elsewhere flows from dependence upon the
Master's captivating and exemplary person, formative teaching, and
atoning work" (ESV GTB Notes on Mk).

Jesus says: . . . Whoever obeys the commands and teaches other people to obey
them will be great in the kingdom of heaven. Mt 5:19 NCV

But Jesus also cautions us to be wise as well as evangelistic. There is no point
in your wasting good teaching and true inspiration on insensitive and antagonist
people. It would be like insisting on putting a pearl necklace on a pig. Mt 7:6 WMF

[11] And He Himself gave some *to be* apostles, some prophets, some evange-
lists, and some pastors and teachers, [12] for the equipping of the saints for the
work of ministry, for the edifying of body of Christ, [13] till we all come to the
unity of the faith and of the knowledge of the Son of God, to a perfect man, to
the measure of the stature of the fullness of Christ;

¹⁴that we should no longer be children, tossed to and fro and carried about with every wind of doctrine, by the trickery of men, in the cunning craftiness of deceitful plotting, ¹⁵but, speaking the truth in love, may grow up in all things into Him who is the head, Christ, ¹⁶from whom the whole body, joined and knit together by what every joint supplies, according to the effective working by which every part does its share, causes growth of the body for the edifying of itself in love. Eph 4:11–16 NKJV

God is all about discipleship.

- Teach God's words to your children: Deut 6:6–7, 20–25; 11:18–19; 32:46–47
- Display his words for all to see: Deut 6:8–9 and 11:20 -21
- Read God's words aloud [to everyone]: Deut 31:9–13
- I am a servant of Christ and a steward of the mysteries of God. 1 Cor 4: 1
- Let the word of Christ dwell in you richly, teach and admonish one another in all wisdom, and sing psalms and hymns and spiritual songs with thankfulness in your hearts to God. And whatever you do, in word or deed, do everything in the name of the Lord Jesus, giving thanks to God the Father through him. Col 3:16–17
- Preach the Word; be prepared in season and out of season; correct, rebuke and encourage — with great patience and careful instruction . . . 2 Tim 4:1–5 NIV

FINALLY, HERE ARE SOME REAL LIFE EXAMPLES OF SHARING GOD'S WORD WITH THE WORLD.

Let me salute just a few of the magnificent people I know personally, who have heard and answered God's call.
Scott and Vicki McCracken headed out for the mission field shortly after graduating college. In the many years they have served God, they have led countless people to an understanding and love for Jesus. And they have built disciples to do the same, in their loving ministry to non-Christians and Christians alike. These two have the finest characters

you could ever find, and Stayton and I were blessed to work with them as we traveled for short-term missions (two or so months at a time).

Brenda Lange was loving God and minding her own business (horses in Texas) when God called her to go to Africa and take care of orphans. He was quite specific about her ministry, even given her instructions on how the little huts or houses should be constructed. She has done this amazing work for many years now, *with* a giant heart for her kids and the Lord and *without* a single prissy moment (I'm guessing).

Sam and Fran Holdsambeck were middle-aged when God called them to overseas missions. When I first met them, they were ministering to Muslim refugees in a southern European country. Since that time, they have served in several countries in the Middle East, and have only recently (Spring 2015) come home for the next stage of their lives.

Peter and Pat Robinson were in the same Youth With A Mission discipleship class with us. As different from each other as chalk and cheese, these two were both delightful, and we've called them friends ever since. As Brits, they had an exciting life as teachers overseas, in Africa, and then in Hong Kong. But their true love was God, and it showed through both of them in ways that delighted us (and God too, of course)!

Jim and Michelle Hasbrouck were living a happy and financially successful life in Texas as a young family with two darling kids. In 2004, in a dramatic and gutsy move, they sold their house and went to an African country, at God's calling. And they have lived and served there ever since.

Evy and Costa Soulitzis have consistently served God through their very little church and its very big missions calling. To do this, they have turned their back on some lucrative opportunities, and instead followed their God as he pointed them to children and adults who needed them.

Al and Lynne Stahl knew they were headed to overseas missions by the time they had graduated from college. Now they have two grown sons and are still going strong in God's chosen field, reaching out to people in largely Muslim countries with the truth about Jesus and his love for them.

John and Joy Raney have loved God with their whole hearts since before we met them in 1993, at Youth With a Mission (YWAM). In fact, I nominated John as the person I'd like to be trapped on a desert island with, because he knew more about God than anyone I'd ever met. And his way of explaining faith was so down to earth (my kind of guy). He and Joy have made stellar partners, and I can only imagine how very much God loves them. We certainly do!

John Gentles was, like us, new to missions when we met in 1993. And we fell in love with this delightful and crazy man who loves God with such a passion. John didn't have to go overseas to serve God. He worked, and works, with the poor and hopeless, wherever he finds them. And I remember a time when that "hopeless" person was me. When I was close to madness myself, he served my husband with his heart, hands, and feet, when no one else would.

So, what do these people have in common?

- Every one of them loves God and listens to him.
- Not one of them is perfect, fancy, or famous.
- They hear God when he calls, and they are open to obeying him.
- They opted to share God with people full time, versus pursuing a possibly lucrative career.
- They didn't bargain with God or tell him they would only serve in safe, easy ministries. Not one of them is doing something you or I couldn't do, if God asked us, and then equipped us, *and we cooperated with his call on our lives.*

Jesus, I am so grateful for the wonderful hearts of the people who serve in the mission field, at home and overseas. They are indeed letters from you, the Christ, to the world — written not with ink but with the Spirit of the Living God— not on tablets of stone (as in Ex 24:12), but on tablets of human hearts. When I join them, even for short-term missions, I too become a "letter" to those who

have not yet met you. (Drawn from 1 Cor 3:2–3) How blessed can a person be!

I am grateful for the two or three months per year Stayton and I were able to go on overseas mission trips. We always felt that we gained more than we gave, because we learned so much, met people of stellar passion, and grew closer and closer to you everyday.

I will never forget the examples of courage and faith that we have witnessed. John and Joy, for example, were, and are, irresistible to us, because they have always combined such class with a hair-on-fire love for Jesus. Thank you for their lives, Jesus, and for the opportunity Stayton and I had to meet them at Youth With A Mission. They spoke truth in love all the time, and they are always in our hearts, no matter where we are respectively in the globe, or beyond!

Beth Moore described William Tyndale this way: "Discipline alone lacks the heat to keep a long, arduous work aflame amid the ruination of reputation and the loss of home, country, and companionship. Love drives such a man. God drives such a man" (Moore 2014, 152).

Father, please help me give what's left of my life, so that one day those who knew me can say,

"Love drove such a woman.
God drove such a woman." CGS

PRAYER AND MEDITATION FOR CHAPTER 11

CHAPTER 12 OUTLINE: RELISH THE ABUNDANT LIFE THAT COMES FROM FOLLOWING AND TRUSTING GOD. REMEMBER, THE CHOICE IS YOURS.

INTRODUCTION. There is nothing like enjoying God's presence and finding satisfaction in him. Discover the truth about your spiritual life – which is between you and God alone — from today until the end of your life on earth — and beyond.

1. God created every one of us capable of accepting Jesus, who can bring us to the Father. Jesus promises us eternal life with God as soon as we believe and follow him. (Our choice remember?) And that life begins the day we accept him, not when we die and go to heaven. So I live in the kingdom of God now, not just later in heaven.

2. Because of Jesus, God has prepared a banquet, and an amazing array of gifts for us, in this world, and in the next. But I do not love Jesus to get those things; I get those things because I love and follow him.

3. It is an amazing privilege to know, believe, and trust God. So get up your courage. Take a step on that giant trampoline and fly, baby, fly.

4. There is abundant fruit that is produced in our lives when we walk with God's Spirit. Galatians 5:22–26

5. There is a joy in God's presence that comes from my obedience and my covenant relationship with God through Christ.

6. When we walk with God, we can experience his peace. Peace and God are absolutely linked. Peace and righteousness (not perfection) are linked. And Jesus brings peace to my heart, if I let him.

7. God shares his wisdom and power with us, if we are asking in Jesus' will, not our own.

8. And when we do fall, he is there to help us up and back onto his path.

9. Sadly, some may never experience the glories we have discussed in this chapter. But that can change !

    *   Some just want that ticket to heaven, but not a head-over-heels love relationship with their Savior

    *   Some who initially say "yes" turn their backs on God.

    *   Others feel that once they say yes to Jesus and have that ticket in hand, they can just sit down and rest on their pew.

10. Scripture tells us that our choices – to follow God or not – have consequences.

11. Life with God is not all sunshine and merry-go-rounds. But God is with me, on the mountaintops and in the valleys. I am not alone.

12. When my physical body dies, I believe that my spirit will go immediately to heaven to be with God.

RELISH THE ABUNDANT LIFE THAT COMES FROM FOLLOWING AND TRUSTING GOD. REMEMBER, THE CHOICE IS YOURS.

God raised Jesus and he will raise me up by his power. 1 Cor 6:14

"The Father loves the Son extravagantly. He turned
everything over to him so he could give it away [to us]–
a lavish distribution of gifts. That is why whoever accepts and
trusts the Son gets in on everything, life complete and forever!"
(John the Baptist speaking in Jn 3:35–36 MSG)

INTRODUCTION

For it is time for judgment to begin at the household of God;
and if it begins with us, what will be the outcome for those
who do not obey the gospel of God? 1 Peter 4:17 NIV

"[In the verse above] Peter is not teaching that salvation is earned
through personal trials or works, but simply that those who
are saved are not exempt from temporal disciplinary judgments
which are the natural consequences of sin" (Raymer 1985).

God Created Every One Of Us Capable Of Accepting Jesus, Who Came To Bring Us To The Father.

Our Creator/Father gave every one of us an open shot at a love relationship with him.
He sent Jesus to bring us "home" to our Dad. And Jesus promises us eternal life with God and his Son as soon as we believe and follow him. (Our choice, remember?) That eternal life begins the day we accept him, not when we die and go to heaven. So I live in the kingdom of God now, not just later in heaven.

There is nothing like enjoying God's presence and finding satisfaction in him.
Sadly, some people never discover this truth. That's why I've taken the time to talk about some of the amazing things that can come into your life when you walk with God.

The truth about your spiritual life is between you and God alone – from today until the end of your life on earth – and beyond. He knows it all, of course, and it's important for you to search your heart so that you know the truth as well. The beauty is that no matter where we are spiritually, we can change, grow closer to Jesus, and learn to obey and follow him. Now! To begin, let's ask ourselves some hard questions:

* Am I a true follower of Jesus or am I, instead, some form of a "religious imposter"?
* Do I follow God from my heart, or just from the teeth out?
* Am I someone who "simply shrugs his shoulders" at things that matter to God, or do I obey him out of love and gratitude for his saving me and drawing me into a loving, personal relationship with him (phrases in quotes are from Chambers July 27).

This chapter discusses the rewards and consequences of following or not following God. Naturally, this topic brings up different viewpoints. Debates are a waste of time, so we won't be doing that. Either way, there is only one truth, which is God's alone. So let's agree to disagree, if we must, and move on to learning what Jesus and others in the Bible had to say.

Whoever accepts, trusts and follows Jesus . . .

If we follow Jesus' commands and walk with God, we can expect abundant and eternal life with God, beginning now!

Throughout this book, we have said that following Jesus is a lifelong process. We love him and learn to trust and obey him. He guides, directs, and lovingly disciplines us. Then we follow him and try to do things his way, not ours. When we stumble, he picks us up and sets us back on the right road. If we live for God this way, Jesus says we will see the rewards God gives the faithful, loving, and obedient. He's equally clear that those who disobey will experience inevitable consequences for disobedience. But God is not a scary Father, eagerly waiting for us to fail. He wants us to succeed, and that's why he sent Jesus!

JESUS PROMISES US ETERNAL LIFE WITH GOD, AS SOON AS WE BELIEVE AND FOLLOW HIM

We don't have to wait to die and go to heaven. I live in the kingdom of God now, not just later in heaven. And those who believe can face the last judgment with confidence.

Jesus says: (in Jn 5:24) . . . Whoever hears my word and believes him who sent me has eternal life. He does not come into judgment, but has passed from death to life. [see also Jn 3:18, 29; Jn 8:51; 20; 31; 1 Jn 3:14; 5:9–13]

Bottom line? [10] All who believe in the Son of God know in their hearts that this testimony is true. Those who don't believe this are actually calling God a liar because they don't believe what God has testified about his Son. [11] And this is what God has testified: He has given us eternal life, and this life is in his Son. [12] Whoever has the Son has life; whoever does not have God's Son does not have life. 1 Jn 5:10-12 NLT

BECAUSE OF JESUS, GOD HAS PREPARED A BANQUET, AND AN AMAZING ARRAY OF GIFTS FOR US, IN THIS WORLD AND IN THE NEXT

I heard a great story some years ago, told to make a point. There was a man who saved and saved money for a sailing ticket from England to America. Every day he stayed in his little cabin, eating the meager portions he'd brought with him for the trip. Finally, someone asked him why he didn't go into the dining room for meals. He replied that he didn't have the extra funds for food. Astonished, the person informed him that the meals were included in the transatlantic ticket.

Aren't we like this in many ways? God has a magnificent banquet for us — love, wisdom, peace, guidance, and a ticket to heaven — and still we don't dive in. Instead, we live pinched and sad little lives, while the Creator of the universe waits with open arms.

And finally, I've said this before, of course, but it bears repeating. Although God has many gifts and blessings for us, that is *not* why I love him. I love him because he is the ultimate loving, concerned Father, a life giver whom I need *with every part of me.* The goodies are just a bonus!

IT IS AN AMAZING PRIVILEGE TO KNOW, BELIEVE, AND TRUST IN GOD. SO GET UP YOUR COURAGE. TAKE A STEP ON THAT GIANT TRAMPOLINE AND FLY, BABY, FLY!

On October 20, 2012, I was reading *My Utmost for His Highest,* the wonderful devotional based on the teaching of Oswald Chambers. If you've never tried it, I urge you to because it is a thing of delight and challenge. Oswald doesn't write flowery greeting cards, with profuse and puffy platitudes. But that's why I love him, because he is a fearless truth teller! And I need that sock-it-to-me style of biblical truth.

Anyway, the question for that day was, "Is God's will my will?" (Tough, eh? I warned you about Oswald.) But it's a great question to ponder. And here is the essence of the answer, for Oswald and for us. It is clearly God's will that he and I be brought together, joined through Jesus, in loving relationship. Jesus came to accomplish just that, when he lived and died for us. So that is *God's will.*

But there is another part of that equation, and it is *me:* my own will, my mind and emotions, and resulting behavior. God could have easily set us up as puppets, with no choice in anything. But he did not. So while God has made his will perfectly clear in the Bible, he has also made our part in the deal also perfectly clear. We must exercise our own will and self-discipline, with God's ever-present help, to join in relationship with him.

Now we come to the trampoline.
(Were you wondering when we'd get here?) As I was reading in 2012, I got this picture of a huge powerful trampoline, bigger than you can imagine, and able to propel people to amazing heights. Imagine that is God's will. Now add your will. Picture yourself stepping onto that marvelous field and taking a few tentative jumps. Then see yourself jumping higher and higher, all because you have partnered with this great trampoline. You get it, don't you? I can tell, even from here. It's so simple, really. But I never saw it before today. And it was all because I was reading dear old Oswald Chambers. Is the jumping always safe? No! Are outcomes guaranteed? Again, no. Will I ever be hurt while spinning high above the earth? Probably! Will there be days when I refuse to get up on the great bouncy thing, or when I am too afraid or hurt to attempt even the smallest jump? Oh yes, for sure.

I've been a jumper now for some twenty years, and there have been wonderful times of soaring to the sky on the trampoline. But there have been many times when I've stayed off the trampoline. But I promise you, even if you stay away for a while, or fall off, even when you huddle on your bed and refuse to play, God is still there. He is pulling for you, pursuing you, and loving you. Every day he is helping me develop my faith in him, teaching me to *yield and trust.* And even when I'm a very slow student (and there are many times like that), he is still the loving teacher. He wants me to fly higher than I can possibly imagine, and combining my will with his is the only way that happens. So get up your courage, step out on that amazing field, and *jump.* I promise it is worth everything! You don't have to understand exactly how the trampoline works, or why. Just get up and jump. And if it's been a long time — or never — don't worry about that. God's will is there, for you, for me, always! How can we not love and embrace a God like that? So fly, baby, fly and enjoy every minute! I promise you, God will!

THERE IS ABUNDANT FRUIT THAT IS PRODUCED IN OUR LIVES WHEN WE WALK WITH GOD'S SPIRIT

No one ever produced an orange grove by sitting in a chair and wishing it so. Growing fruit requires a lot of effort and all sorts of elements: rich soil, decent weather, sufficient water and nutrients, and so on. It's the same when we talk about "spiritual fruit" in our lives. Not much happens unless we put some effort into it! But we aren't alone, because God's Holy Spirit is in there with us every step.

[16]So I say, let the Holy Spirit guide your lives ... [22]But the Holy Spirit produces this kind of fruit in our lives: love, joy, peace, patience, kindness, goodness, faithfulness, [23]gentleness, and self-control. There is no law against these things! [24]Those who belong to Christ Jesus have nailed the passions and desires of their sinful nature to his cross and crucified them there. [25]Since we are living by the Spirit, let us follow the Spirit's leading in every part of our lives. Gal 5:16–17 and 22:25 NLT.

What God is saying here is that we need to be led by the Holy Spirit – God's Spirit – rather than by our own cravings and desires. Then the Holy Spirit within us will produce, with our full cooperation, the kind of "fruit" that we all yearn for: love, joy, peace, etc. Now I don't know about you, but that sounds like a very good deal. But most of us find it hard to do our part — to give up on "doing things our way" and "pursuing our own desires," regardless of whether they sync with God's or not. So we may not experience the fruitfulness that is possible in our hearts, minds, and characters. Can this be remedied? Yes, we can focus, trust in God, and yield to his leading. And then we, too, can have the abundant fruit in our lives. I'm for trying more seriously than I have. How about you?

THERE IS JOY IN GOD'S PRESENCE

"The full flood of my life is not in bodily health, not in external
happenings, not in seeing God's work succeed, but in the
perfect understanding of God, and in the communion
with Him that Jesus Himself had." (Chambers Aug 31).

There is a joy of the Lord that comes from my love and my obedience
and my covenant relationship with God through Christ. You know I've
written about this elsewhere, but I think it's worth revisiting. The enjoyment, pleasure, satisfaction, and growth that come from being with
God are beyond description. Don't let anyone tell you it's all about head
knowledge and try to impress you with his or her vast scholarly investi-
gations. Yes, Jesus wants us to study, but with that, he wants us joined
together, heart to heart!

I often just close my eyes and imagine throwing my arms around
Jesus' neck. Talk about joy and satisfaction – for both of us!

**Jesus talks about his joy and our joy: He prays that his joy might remain
in us, and that our joy might be full.** Jn 15:11 "What was the joy that
Jesus had? It is an insult to use the word happiness in connection with
Jesus Christ. The joy of Jesus was the absolute self-surrender and self-
sacrifice of himself to his Father, the joy of doing that which the Father
sent him to do . . . Jesus prayed that our joy might go on fulfilling itself
until it was the same joy as his. Have I allowed Jesus Christ to introduce
his joy to me?

"Be rightly related to God, find your joy there, and out of you will
flow rivers of living water. Be a center for Jesus Christ to pour living water through. Stop being self-conscious, stop being a sanctified prig, and
live the life hid with Christ. The life that is rightly related to God is as
natural as breathing wherever it goes" (Chambers Aug 31; March 5 also
touches on joy).

AS WE WALK WITH GOD, WE CAN EXPERIENCE
GOD'S PEACE, A TRUE GIFT.

Peace and God — and peace and righteousness (*not* perfection) — are absolutely linked. Jesus brings peace to my heart, if I let him.

A personal story of God's amazing love, grace, and peace
On December 25, 2013, I wrote to my friends and family, sharing my heart four months after my husband's death on August 13. Looking back, it is good to remember how clearly I could see God's hand in my life. For all of our time together, I could not imagine a life without Stayton. I'm not being overly dramatic, just honest. From the first day I met him, I was captured and in love. So I could only see horrible grief and loneliness if I tried to live without him — the love of my life, the center of my universe, my best friend, my husband, and my fellow God-follower. But it turns out that God had other ideas, and I can't possibly express how surprised I am at this turn in my life.

Some people equate God's love and faithfulness with their own earthly success.
They question God's love if things go south in their life, their health, family, job, whatever. If things go well, they are quick to say it's because they are favored by God, but that leaves the question: What about the faithful Christians whose lives are in the toilet through no fault of their own?

Although I can't really explain it, I never once considered blaming God for Stayton's illness and his death. And I never questioned God when I was crazed with grief as my husband slipped inexorably away. That isn't me, and it never will be. So when I tell you (as I write this in December 2013) how well I am doing, despite my shock at this truth, don't for one minute think that I am saying that this is proof that God loves me. If I were in terrible trouble now, maybe lying collapsed in a darkened room, with worried friends keeping watch, I would still know that God loved me. And if my grief took a 180 degree turn in the future and I was prostrate for months, it would not mean that God had abandoned or rejected me. This isn't an opinion but a fact, based on my own solid experience with my Father.

I've been through seven years of happiness and sorrow with my darling man through his illness, and every step of the way, I understood that God loved us and would *never* leave us or forsake us. But having said that, I also want to shout this truth from the rooftops: God has blessed me with such a peace and understanding that I could never have expected. I never even asked for it! But this time for me has been so supernatural that even the word "miracle" seems too puny to explain it.

And looking back today, I understand that God's hand was busy all along — daily — since August 13, just as it was before August 13. For instance, since Stayton's death, God has led me into many projects for his grown kids and grandkids that have allowed me the pleasure of marinating hour after hour in the wonderfulness that was Stayton. I thought these projects were just for them, but in truth they enriched me in ways too numerous to count. And the examples just go on and on.

When Stayton first died, I felt like I was wrapped in cotton, briefly safe from whatever ravages awaited me. But as this time has gone on, I see that it's much more astonishing than that. I miss Stayton, and will until the day I die, but it's as if God is literally carrying me through this experience. And I truly mean it when I say I am shocked and grateful for every single minute of it. You know how it is when you have a bad cold? You think, if I can ever breathe easily again I will be so grateful and I'll never forget how bad this was. But that's not how it works, is it? We go back to breathing, and don't give it a second thought.

Well that is *not* what I am experiencing now. Many times each day, I marvel at how I am. There is only One who is responsible, and it ain't me, babe, I can promise you that. I walked (and sat) beside Stayton as he declined over seven years, and I began grieving on day one and it never fully left me. And how could it? It was a horrible loss! But at the same time, it was a tremendous honor to care for such a wonderful man. Oh yes, I experienced heavy sorrow, not to mention lots of flat-on-the-floor craziness. But God's goodness allowed me to gradually come to terms with my loss, gradually and gently.

Sometimes God whisks you from danger, but sometimes (as in our case) he does not. But in those difficult cases, he walks every step with you and loves you far more than any human can. And he provides you with loving friends who come alongside you and love you too. And when that part of the journey is over and the loss is "complete", God is innovative and clever beyond imagining as he heals you and holds you tight as you walk (and sometimes stumble) along.

I have loved God since 1993. But let me say this again: I never anticipated anything like this. I promise you, I did not. But I am beyond grateful to God, and more in love with Jesus than ever, because of his wisdom, compassion, and love for me. Baby, it's like ponies and ice cream compared to what I thought it would be. Tears come, yes; and tears go. I will love and miss Stayton until the day I die. But God is with me faithfully, every moment of every day! If things take a serious turn south, I may suffer more than I am suffering now. But I will never blame God for that suffering, and I will always know that he has my back!

GOD SHARES HIS WISDOM AND POWER WITH US,
IF WE ARE ASKING IN JESUS' WILL
DOING IT *HIS* WAY AND NOT OUR OWN

This is a wonder we can hardly comprehend! And if you haven't experienced this, if you aren't really into God, I highly recommend him. He's a dandy friend, a wise, loving counselor, and powerful as all get out! Try to find that in your regular circle of friends!

Halls of Wonder

My husband and I have a great story from 2006, which we've told often because it makes us laugh. We were walking through a long amazing "hall" at the Vatican Museum in Rome, making our way slowly to the famous Sistine Chapel, which we (and the crowds) were eager to see. Along this large gallery, we were blown away by the beauty: walls with huge ancient maps, magnificent ceilings with paintings and sculpture, the whole bit! Every inch of the gallery's barrel vault ceiling is covered with dazzling frescos. The colors are simply brilliant. And so we walked and walked along this space, in complete awe.

And then we realized we weren't yet in the Sistine Chapel! The Sistine Chapel, by comparison, was small and jammed with people, all staring at the ceiling, to the accompaniment of hushing guards trying to restrain the tightly packed crowd. Of course it was beautiful. But the great hall, which I learned later they called the Map Gallery, (among other things) was the most amazing to us, because it was so vast and beautiful.

Later, after we'd passed through the Sistine Chapel, we asked about the hall. But most of the staff were almost dismissive of it, because it wasn't the Sistine Chapel, with ceilings painted by the famous Michelangelo. When we asked who had done the work in the magnificent hall, they told us it was done, not by anyone famous, but by a school of painters during the same period, all greatly talented, but none with a famous name. Well, we're from Texas, baby, and they couldn't fool us! We thought it was fabulous, anyway. [Here's a link with images of the gallery. Check them out and you'll have small hint of what we saw. [touritaly.org/tours/ vaticanmuseum/Vatican03. htm]

In a way, it's a perfect comparison for life, isn't it? We have our eyes focused on a distant prize, and all the while we are wandering in halls of wonder!

AND WHEN WE DO FALL, HE IS THERE
TO HELP US UP AND BACK ONTO HIS PATH

Trapeze Artists and God.
Bible teacher Priscilla Shirer has a great way of explaining lofty and spiritual things by giving down-to-earth examples we all can understand. In her study, *One in a Million*, she gives us a picture of trapeze artists soaring in midair as they swing from one bar to another. When they release their grip on one bar, they do so with the knowledge that another awaits their grasp. They grow comfortable with letting go because someone trustworthy makes certain that another sturdy bar

arrives at just the right time. Then Priscilla links it to something precious by saying that, like the trapeze artists, we too can be confident because the God whom we love, also loves us. He never leaves us alone (Shirer 2010).

Pondering this in October 2012, I realized that God goes even further and gives us what the acrobat may not have: someone with us on the bar and with us in the air! It doesn't get much better than that. Do we ever fall or lose our grip? Sure! But if we do land on the net below (which he has placed there), he helps us crawl back up and start flying again! The only way we will never fly is if we cling to the ladder and refuse to take the leap with and toward God!

IN YOUR CURRENT LIFE AND DIRECTION, YOU MAY NEVER EXPERIENCE THE GLORIES WE HAVE DISCUSSED IN THIS CHAPTER. BUT THAT'S ENTIRELY UP TO YOU – AND IT'S NEVER TOO LATE TO CHANGE IT

You may have missed the entire Jesus train altogether, up to now.
Maybe you are like me and just didn't get it. Or maybe you didn't really care about God, figuring the whole thing was just a delusion.

But if you are reading this, it is not too late. God has put this book in your path for a good reason. You have nothing to lose and everything to gain by closing your eyes, putting your mental "arms" around God's neck, and begging for a love relationship for the two of you.

There are others who just want a ticket to heaven, but not a head-over-heels love relationship with their Savior.
But that's like settling for a meager meal when you can have an entire banquet! Some say that Christians will not face God's judgment. But I believe that God will hold everyone, including believers sure of their place in heaven, accountable for how they've lived their lives. God's Truth and Light came into the world through Jesus. And if we truly love Jesus, we will *want* to follow him, please him, and help him reach the world. It isn't fear that motivates us; it's love and gratitude!

Some who initially say "yes" turn their backs on God. Imagine what it would be like if we approached marriage that way. Say that two people agree to marry. They get the license and say their "I do's" in front of family and friends. Then they drive back to their house, and the wife begins a debate on just how little she can contribute and still have a marriage. She declares that she will not live with her husband, and she will not share her life with him. Or perhaps shortly after the wedding, the husband declares that he has no further interest in his wife, despite his promises earlier that day. He will not spend time with her. He will not support her. He cares nothing for her hopes, her plans, her wishes, or her feelings. Is he still married? Well, technically, yes. And he gets to count himself as married when people ask. But is he really part of a marriage? Our prayer is that you will not let that happen between you and God. Give him all you have, and you will never be sorry!

And others feel that once they say yes to Jesus and have that ticket in hand, they can just sit down and rest on their pew.
They aren't completely turning their back on God, but when you look up the word "lukewarm" in the dictionary, you may see their faces. And maybe God does too. These folks may likely say that there is no judgment for Christians, and even quote a few verses they think fit with that. But my view is that God will, and does, indeed hold us accountable, without necessarily canceling our "ticket". I believe that God will ask, at the end of our days on earth: "Did you love My Truth and follow My Light?" I want to look forward to answering that question. Don't you?

SCRIPTURE TELLS US THAT OUR CHOICES – TO FOLLOW GOD OR NOT –HAVE CONSEQUENCES.

Jesus says: Whoever refuses to obey any command and teaches other people not to obey that command will be the least important in the kingdom of heaven. But whoever obeys the commands and teaches other people to obey them will be great in the kingdom of heaven . . . Mt 5:19–20 NCV (expanding ideas in Deut 5:32 and others)

Jesus says: The way that I teach is a narrow way in that it is well defined. It is not easy to follow the straight path, but it is the way to a full and eternal life, while the undisciplined way is a way to destruction and death.
Mt 7:13–14 WMF (Also see Jer 21:8)

Jesus says: [17] For God did not send his Son into the world to condemn the world, but in order that the world might be saved through him. [18]Whoever believes in him is not condemned, but whoever does not believe is condemned already, because he has not believed in the name of the only Son of God. [19]And this is the judgment: the light has come into the world, and people loved the darkness rather than the light because their works were evil. [20] For everyone who does wicked things hates the light and does not come to the light, lest his works should be exposed. [21] But whoever does what is true comes to the light, so that it may be clearly seen that his works have been carried out in God." Jn 3:17–21

Jesus says: I am the resurrection and the life; he who believes in me, though he die, yet shall he live, and whoever lives and believes in me shall never die. Jn 11:25–26 (This builds on Deut 30:19 NIV: This day I call heaven and earth as witnesses against you that I have set before you life and death, blessings and curses. Now choose life, so that you and your children may live.)

Jesus says: Knowing the correct password — saying 'Master, Master' for instance — isn't going to get you anywhere with me. What is required is serious obedience — doing what my Father wills. I can see it now — at the Final Judgment thousands strutting up to me and saying, 'Master, we preached the Message, we bashed the demons, our God-sponsored projects had everyone talking.' And do you know what I am going say? 'You missed the boat. All you did was use me to make yourselves important. You don't impress me one bit. You're out of here.' Mt 7:21–23 MSG

Jesus says: So why do you call me 'Lord', when you won't obey me? I will show you what it's like when someone comes to me, listens to my teaching, and then obeys me. It is like a person who builds a house on a strong foundation laid upon the underlying rock. When the floodwaters rise and break against the house, it stands firm because it is well built. But anyone who listens and doesn't obey is like a person who builds a house without a foundation. When the floods sweep down against that house, it will crumble into a heap of ruins. Lk 6:46–49 NLT Mt 7:24–27

Take care of those in need or don't. Either way has consequences.

Jesus says: When the Son of Man comes in his glory, and all the angels with him, he will sit on his throne in heavenly glory. All the nations will be gathered before him, and he will separate the people one from another as a shepherd separates the sheep from the goats. He will put the sheep on his right and the goats on his left. Then the King will say to those on his right, "Come, you who are blessed by my Father; take your inheritance, the kingdom prepared for you since the creation of the world. For I was hungry and you gave me something to eat, I was thirsty and you gave me something to drink, I was a stranger and you invited me in, I needed clothes and you clothed me, I was sick and you looked after me, I was in prison and you came to visit me." . . . "I tell you the truth, whatever you did for one of the least of these brothers of mine, you did for me."

Then he will say to those on his left, "Depart from me, you who are cursed, into the eternal fire prepared for the devil and his angels. For I was hungry and you gave me nothing to eat, I was thirsty and you gave me nothing to drink, I was a stranger and you did not invite me in, I needed clothes and you did not clothe me, I was sick and in prison and you did not look after me." . . . "I tell you the truth, whatever you did not do for one of the least of these, you did not do for me." Then they will go away to eternal punishment, but the righteous to eternal life. Mt 25:31–46 NIV (expands Isa 58:6–7 and 61:1)

God's heart is consistent throughout scripture. Yes, there are consequences that result from our behavior, good and bad. But we also see God's mercy, a promise of hope for those who turn their hearts back to him.

Leviticus 26, Deuteronomy 28, and Deuteronomy 30 are entire chapters devoted to the importance of going God's way, not our own. God isn't shy about telling us the consequences of obedience and disobedience. And although there is a lot of discussion of "law" in the Old Testament, God's heart is consistent throughout Scripture: Do what I ask of you, or I will be displeased.

2 Chron 7:14 – again! If my people who are called by my name humble themselves, and pray and seek my face, and turn from their wicked ways, then I will hear from heaven, and will forgive their sin and heal their land.

Isa 58:6–12 [6] Is not this the fast that I choose: to loose the bonds of wickedness, to undo the straps of the yoke, to let the oppressed go free, and to break every yoke? [7] Is it not to share your bread with the hungry and bring the homeless poor into your house; when you see the naked, to cover him, and not to hide yourself from your own flesh?

⁸ Then shall your light break forth like the dawn, and your healing shall spring up speedily; your righteousness shall go before you; the glory of the Lord shall be your rear guard. ⁹Then you shall call, and the Lord will answer; you shall cry, and he will say, 'Here I am' . . . ¹⁰ If you pour yourself out for the hungry and satisfy the desire of the afflicted, then shall your light rise in the darkness and your gloom be as the noonday. ¹¹And the Lord will guide you continually and satisfy your desire in scorched places and make your bones strong; and you shall be like a watered garden, like a spring of water, whose waters do not fail . . .

Eph 5:6–21 ⁶ Let no one deceive you with empty words, for because of these things the wrath of God comes upon the sons of disobedience.
⁷ Therefore do not become partners with them; ⁸ for at one time you were darkness, but now you are light in the Lord. Walk as children of light
⁹ (for the fruit of light is found in all that is good and right and true),
¹⁰ and try to discern what is pleasing to the Lord. ¹¹ Take no part in the unfruitful works of darkness, but instead expose them . . . ¹⁵ Look carefully then how you walk, not as unwise but as wise, . . . but be filled with the Spirit . . . ²⁰ giving thanks always and for everything to God the Father in the name of our Lord Jesus Christ . . .

Col 1:21–23 ²¹ And you, who once were alienated and hostile in mind, doing evil deeds, ²² he has now reconciled in his body of flesh by his death, in order to present you holy and blameless and above reproach before him, ²³ if indeed you continue in the faith, stable and steadfast, not shifting from the hope of the gospel that you heard, which has been proclaimed in all creation under heaven . . .

Heb 10:19–31, 39 . . . ²² Let us draw near with a true heart in full assurance of faith, with our hearts sprinkled clean from an evil conscience and our bodies washed with pure water . . . ³⁰ For we know him who said, "Vengeance is mine; I will repay." And again, "The Lord will judge his people." ³¹ It is a fearful thing to fall into the hands of the living God. . . .
³⁹ But we are not of those who shrink back and are destroyed, but of those who have faith and preserve their souls.

1 Pet 4:17–19 [17] For it is time for judgment to begin at the household of God; and if it begins with us, what will be the out-come for those who do not obey the gospel of God? [18] And "If the righteous is scarcely saved, what will become of the ungodly and the sinner?" [19] Therefore let those who suffer according to God's will entrust their souls to a faithful Creator while doing good.

2 Pet 3:7–15 . . . [8] But do not overlook this one fact, beloved, that with the Lord one day is as a thousand years, and a thousand years as one day.

[9] The Lord is not slow to fulfill his promise as some count slowness, but is patient toward you, not wishing that any should perish, but that all should reach repentance. [10] But the day of the Lord will come like a thief, and then the heavens will pass away with a roar, and the heavenly bodies will be burned up and dissolved, and the earth and the works that are done on it will be exposed.

LIFE WITH GOD IS *NOT* ALL SUNSHINE AND MERRY-GO-ROUNDS, ALTHOUGH SOME MAY SAY SO

God is with us, on the mountaintops and in the valleys. There will be difficulties, even with life abundant and everlasting. CGS

You may notice that I come back to this point often, but there's a good reason for it. My dear friends in Colorado, John and Joy, are some of the finest followers of Jesus I have ever known (and the people who introduced me to my darling Oswald!). Some years back, Joy was told by well-meaning friends, "If you only had more faith, your daughter Dawn would be healed." I was outraged, and, even as a very new Christian, I knew that was bull! Since then, I've heard people say, "Pray in just the right way and all success will come your way." But the truth is that suffering and sorrow come to everyone. God permits it, for various reasons, but he never leaves us alone or forsakes us in those times. And if someone tells you otherwise, just put it in the "round file" and never think about it again! Because we are *not* alone!

Jas 1:12–15 [12] Blessed is the man who remains steadfast under trial, for when he has stood the test he will receive the crown of life, which God has promised to those who love him. [13] Let no one say when he is tempted, "I am being tempted by God," for God cannot be tempted with evil, and he himself tempts no one. [14] But each person is tempted when he is lured and enticed by his own desire. [15] Then desire when it has conceived gives birth to sin, and sin when it is fully grown brings forth death.

Brother Lawrence, our French monk from the late 1600s, said "'We ought to give ourselves up to God . . . and seek our satisfaction only in the fulfilling of his will, whether he leads us by suffering or by consolation.' He fully expected that his life would bring his turn of pain and suffering. But he was not uneasy about it, for he knew very well that as he could do nothing by himself, God would not fail to give him the strength to bear it . . . The goodness of God assures us that he will not forsake us utterly, and that he will give me strength to bear whatever evil he has permitted to happen to me. Therefore I resolve to fear nothing" (Brother Lawrence, 16,18, 24).

WHEN MY PHYSICAL BODY DIES, I BELIEVE MY SPIRIT WILL GO IMMEDIATELY TO HEAVEN TO BE WITH GOD.

To die to this earth is to live with the Lord in Heaven. But, and please hear this, only God has all the details on this subject. And since I am so *not* God, I'll just leave all those details to him! Our earthly bodies, which will die and decay or be burned, will be different when they are resurrected. They will be spiritual bodies. And that's very good news for me! How about you?

Jesus says: (to the man dying beside him on a cross) Truly, I say to you, today you will be with me in Paradise. Lk 23:43
1 Cor 15:35–53 . . . These perishable bodies of ours are not able to live forever.
2 Cor 5:1–9 We know that if the tent that is our earthly home is destroyed, we have a building from God, a house not made with hands, eternal in the heavens. . . . We know that while we are at home in the [physical] body, we are away from the Lord, for we walk by faith and not by sight . . . We would rather be away from the body and at home with the Lord [but] whether we are at home or away, we make it our aim to please him.

It's Sunday, September 27, 2015, and I am writing one more time to say how grateful I am that God is so active in my life. I love and need his every hug and nudge and firm tap on the head!

This morning I woke up and asked him to please help me become more peaceful, more gentle, more accepting. I would like that, really. God didn't reply, so he probably filed it away for future attention. But then he gave me three small but specific changes to make to this book – two in the introduction and one in chapter 10. So I got up and did just that. And once more I was grateful for his direction, even when I sometimes think it's mine!

Today at sundown is the first day of the Jewish Feast of Tabernacles [or Feast of Booths/ Sukkot]. God told Moses to begin this celebration in Leviticus 23:33-44. [See also Num 29:12; Deut 16:13-15; Ezra 3:4; Neh 8:14; Ezek 45:25; Hos 12:9; Zech 14:16; John 7:2]. It was to celebrate God's protective care during the 40-year period in the wilderness between Egypt and Canaan when Israelites lived in tents (thus the name Feast of Tabernacles, or "booths," Lev 23:43). And it also celebrates "God's present goodness and provision with the completion of the harvest. Sukkot is the last of seven biblically mandated feasts or celebrations. It was also the most joyful and was the only feast in which the Israelites were commanded by God to rejoice" (Rosenberg 2015). It is still celebrated by Jews around the world.

For the first time in memory, I am contemplating this important feast on its first day of celebration. And I believe that is God's intent, for several reasons. First, I am finishing this book today and coming to a time of celebration of sorts. I don't feel joy exactly, but I think God wants that for me. Also tonight was the rare occurrence of a lunar eclipse, happening on the same day as the beginning of the Feast of Tabernacles. And third, I believe this Feast links to an important event in the Christian faith. Just last week I was in a Bible study looking at Mark 9:1-8 and Jesus' transfiguration on the mountain-top. The three disciples with Jesus – Peter (my fav), John, and James – were understandably unsettled, even terrified. Peter pops up to suggest that they erect tents for Jesus and Moses and Elijah. Some may see different motives for Peter and that's fair enough. He was outspoken and bold, but he was also the first disciple to acknowledge Jesus as Messiah. And he was a huge part of the church, after Jesus went home. But I love Peter – a good man, passionate for Jesus, but flawed like us all! Wishing he could stay on the mountaintop forever – and who wouldn't? Beyond that, I think Peter was tapping into his Jewish faith and heading for something familiar in a most strange but wonderful situation. And that familiar thing was the Feast of Tabernacles, which Peter had no doubt celebrated all of his life and which Jews have celebrated since the days of Moses.

Jesus, I address these last words to you, and to our Father who graciously sent you to me. Thank you *so much* for entrusting this book project to me. It has been a delight and a great privilege over several years to share your love with the people who will read this book when it is published. You have loved me and made me a part of your family. Please continue to help me live up to this great blessing! Clothe me with your mercy, kindness, humility, gentleness, and patience. Even more than all this, please help me clothe myself in love.

Let your peace, Jesus, control my thinking. (a big job but totally do-able!) Let me always be thankful for everything you gave – and give – me so that I can follow you all the days of my life. Christ, let your teaching live in me richly. I want my life to focus on our Father and on you, to whom I owe so much. Everything I do or say should be done to honor and obey you, Jesus, and our Dad. In all I do, I give thanks to God our Father and to you, dear brother, Jesus (drawn from Col 3: 12–17 NCV).

We are almost done now, Father. Help me let go of this book and put it into your marvelous hands. The writing process, spanning several years, has been a beautiful and perpetual gift from you to me. Now, after several months with the publisher, it is almost ready to be printed. You know that some aspects of this publishing process have delighted me, while others have not. For my part, Father, I confess that I did not consult you as often as I should have. The result was predictable, now that I look back on it, with times when I felt frustrated and just plain crazy.

I thank you so much, Father, that you finally stepped in – close to the end of the publishing process – and showed me an important and divine truth which I too often forget. Let me cling to that truth today and every day: It is only YOU who have the right to be in control of this – and every – process. This is your book and I am your daughter. I have engaged good folks to help me turn the manuscript into a book. But help me to remind myself daily that YOU – not me and not the people I've engaged – are in charge.

Father and Son, bless those who will pray for and help with the entire process of getting this book into the hands of those who need it. And bless those who will read this book or even just parts of it. Finally, comfort me as I let it go into the world! I will miss it for sure! But I know we will work together very soon, and however that looks, I am ready when you are.

Blessings and hugs all around heaven and earth,
Your adoring daughter, Claudia – September 27, 2015

PRAYER AND MEDITATION FOR CHAPTER 12

STUDY HELPS . . . QUESTIONS TO PONDER, FOR INDIVIDUALS AND GROUPS (ADAPTED FROM *DAY BY DAY THE JESUS WAY*, THIRD PRINTING)

Heart to Heart with God is a great tool for individual meditation and for discussion in a group setting. There is an introduction section and twelve chapters in the book, so I suggest you address one section per week (including the introduction). I'd do four weeks, then take a break, then resume for another four, and so on. That way everyone stays fresh. But it's all up to you, of course!

I urge you to open your group to believers *and* to inquirers, people who are curious about Jesus and the Christian faith. I like a group size of four to twelve. Group sessions should be about one and a half to two hours. If you like, you can serve coffee and/or snacks before the meeting. This allows people to relax. Then start and end the discussion session on time. Some will stay beyond that for visiting, etc. But those who must leave can do so without missing the heart of the session.

Pray to begin each session. Make the prayer simple and brief, so that all members of the group can be comfortable. And encourage confidentiality within the group. Follow the wise saying, "What's said here, stays here."

The group "leader" is in truth not a leader or a teacher or a guru, but a facilitator, a host/hostess. He or she is simply a member of the group who is charged with keeping things on track, lovingly. There are no "experts" and no "dummies" in this process, just folks traveling a path together.

Everyone in the group should practice love, forgiveness, mercy, and mutual respect with one another. The more open and honest the group members are, the more God can work in their hearts and minds. No one — especially the leader — should dominate the conversation. All questions, viewpoints, and opinions are valid and should be encouraged. There are no "bad" questions! Affirm with comments like: Yes; Thank You; OK; I hadn't thought of it that way; and It's a difficult issue isn't it? Encourage people to build on their comments with remarks like: Can you tell us more about that? Can you explain what you mean by that? Can you give an example?

It's always fine to ask if anyone else has a different viewpoint.
Allow a free discussion of thoughts, impressions, questions — all of it! People should be free to express themselves *and* free to hold off until they're more comfortable in the group.

SOME POSSIBLE DISCUSSION STARTERS OR QUESTIONS
TO PONDER IN THE WEEKLY SESSION

- Let's look at the main topics within this week's chapter. Which of them caught the most attention for you? Can you tell us why?
- What's another main topic that grabbed you? Or challenged you? Or both?
- Which quote of Jesus' stood out the most for you this week? Why?
- Let's talk about one new idea that came to you this week. Or perhaps something you've heard before that hit you this week in a different way? What other ideas do people have?
- Before you read this week's section of the book, what was your concept of Jesus? How has this been strengthened or changed?
- How does this apply to your life? Who do you know who would benefit from this week's section? (Names aren't necessary, unless you choose.) A friend? Family member? Non-churchgoer? What would you want them to know?
- Are there things from this week's reading that are easier said than done? Let's hear some examples.
- Did you have an opportunity to practice something from this week's reading? How did it go?
- Sometimes, when we read the words of Jesus, questions or doubts come up. Questions are perfectly natural, even desirable. Did you have questions or doubts this week? What were they?
- Why is this week's topic important to believers? To the body of Christ?
- In what ways did you experience God's presence this week? Was it related to the reading for the week?
- What are some things in your life that are keeping you from living these words from Jesus? How can you get back into the "groove"?
- Did God seem close or far off this week? Can you say why? How can we (the group) pray for you?
- What could a struggling believer hang on to from this week's reading? Something to encourage, guide, uplift?
- Did you get any clear-cut "marching order" from God this week?
- How can this group help you? What stands in your way?

REFERENCE LIST

The reference system I use is explained in the Copyright section at the front of the book. Here is a list of the resources that were used in this book (in addition to the various Bible versions and the Hebrew-Greek resources listed in the copyright section).

ANDRUS, CONNER. 2014 When he was 9-years old, Conner shared with his grandmother Carolyn a visual of satisfying thirst in a desert, which I used in chapter 1.

BARRETT, TYE. "Wayward Ones," song from album of same name, by The Gladsome Light.

BARRY, J. D., HEISER, M. S., CUSTIS, M., MANGUM, D., & WHITEHEAD, M. M. (2012). Notes on John 17 from *Faithlife Study Bible.* Bellingham, WA: Logos Bible Software.

BARRY, JOHN D. AND VAN NOORD, REBECCA . 2012. Logos edition with KRUYSWIJK, R. *Connect the Testaments: A One-Year Daily Devotional with Bible Reading Plan.* Feb 18 entry — Dwelling in the Wilderness. Bellingham, WA: Lexham Press.

BELL, MARTIN. 1968. *The Way of the Wolf* (New York: Seabury Press, 1968), 43. Tim Hansel quoted from this book in his book, *Holy Sweat,* p 42. So of course I was intrigued and had to find a copy of *Way of the Wolf* for myself. I was not disappointed!

BILLHEIMER, PAUL E. 1975. *Destined for the Throne* (Fort Washington, PA: Christian Literature Crusade) p 107.

BLACKABY, HENRY AND RICHARD with Claude King.   Aug 1996. *Experiencing God . . . Knowing and Doing the Will of God.* Revised and expanded. [Softcover workbook] Lifeway Press, Nashville, TN..

BOUNDS, E. M. (1999). *Power through Prayer.* Chapter 5. Logos Edition. Oak Harbor, WA: Logos Research Systems, Inc. *Power Through Prayer* is called by many "the greatest book on prayer ever written." Edward McKendree Bounds (1835–1913) was a Methodist minister and devotional writer.

BROTHER LAWRENCE 2007. *The Practice of the Presence of God, with Spiritual Maxims.* The edition I used was published by Spire Books, a division of Baker Publishing, Grand Rapids, Mi. 22nd printing, June 2007. Brother Lawrence was a humble cook living in a French monastery in the late 1600s. He did not actually pen this great spiritual classic himself. Rather, it was compiled from his letters and from a short work he wrote entitled "Maxims," which was found among his possessions after his death. It also includes summaries of spiritual discussions that Abbe Joseph de Beaufort had with Brother Lawrence.

BROWN, R. (1982; Logos 1988). *The message of Hebrews: Christ above all* (p. 63). Notes on Heb 2:10–13. Leicester, England; Downers Grove, IL: InterVarsity Press.

CARPENTER, E. E. and COMFORT, P. W. (2000). In *Holman Treasury of Key Bible Words: 200 Greek and 200 Hebrew words defined and explained* (p. 347). Nashville, TN: Broadman & Holman Publishers.

CHAMBERS, OSWALD. 1927, 1986, 1992. *My Utmost for His Highest.* First Copyright 1927, Oswald Chambers Publication Assn. Copyright renewed 1963 by Oswald Chambers Publications Assn., Ltd. All rights reserved. I love Oswald and I appreciate the "'classic'" language version — *My Utmost for His Highest: Selections for the Year.* Grand Rapids, MI: Oswald Chambers Publications; Marshall Pickering, 1986. Most of my references, however, are from the 1992 language-gently-updated edition (my description) in today's language edited by James G. Reimann and distributed by Barbour Publishing Inc. This is my most frequently quoted source. If I do quote from the "classic" version (not edited by Reimann), I will say so.

CHAMBERS, OSWALD. 1947. *Biblical ethics.* Hants UK: Marshall, Morgan & Scott. Copyright 1947 Oswald Chambers Publications Association. [Source: these lectures were given by Oswald Chambers at The Bible Training College, 1911–1915; League of Prayer meetings in Britain, 1909–1915; and Zeitoun YMCA Huts, classes for soldiers in Egypt, 1917. Quote in chap 4 is fromSpiritual Construction part 2).

COWMAN, LETTIE BURD (1925). *Streams in the Desert.* Los Angeles, CA: The Oriental Missionary Society.

DEMOSS, NANCY LEIGH 2001 *Lies Women Believe and the Truth That Sets Them Free.* Moody Publishers, Chicago, Il.

EDERSHEIM, ALFRED (1883 1ˢᵗ ed; 1886 2ⁿᵈ ed). *The Life and Times of Jesus the Messiah* (Vol. 2, pp. 519–528). Bellingham, WA: Logos Bible Software. From his Chapter 11: The Last Discourses of Christ – The Prayer of Consecration (John 14, 15, 16, 17).

Chap 4 quote re. "innermost sanctuary"/John 17 from Book 5, chapter 11 p 528); Chap 5 quote re. "unlimitedness of prayer" from Book 5, chapter 11, page 52. Edersheim (March 7, 1825 –March 16, 1889) was a Jewish convert to Christianity and a Biblical scholar known especially for this book *The Life and Times of Jesus the Messiah* (1883). Edersheim divides his work into five sections, or books.

ELLEL MINISTRIES 2015 website content ellel.org/uk/about/
Ellel Ministries is a non-denominational Christian ministry that began in England in 1986 and is now established in over 20 countries around the world. For more, also see http://www.peterhorrobin.com/ellel-ministries

ELLIOT, ELISABETH 1982. *Discipline: The Glad Surrender.* Published by Revell, division of Baker Publishing Group, Grand Rapids, MI. Elliot says more in fewer pages than almost anyone I've read. Her insight and faith are treasures!

FINNEY, PROF CHARLES G. 1839. Speaking in lecture March 27, 1839, printed in *The Oberlin Evangelist.* Lecture VII. Glorifying God. Text.--I Cor. 10:31 http://www.gospeltruth.net/1839OE/390327_glorifying_god.htm

FRANGIPANE, FRANCIS 1997 *The Three Battlegrounds* by Francis Frangipane, © 1989. 21ˢᵗ printing Dec 1997. 145 pp. Arrow Publications, Cedar Rapids, Iowa.

GEISLER, N. L. 1985. Section on Colossians. In J. F. Walvoord and R. B. Zuck (Eds.), *The Bible Knowledge Commentary: An Exposition of the Scriptures* (Vol. 2, pp. 672–673). Wheaton, IL: Victor Books.

GRAHAM, BILLY 1997. Article in *San Antonio Express News,* August 1997

HANSEL, TIM 1987. *Holy Sweat.* Word Books Publishing, Waco Texas. 1987 Hansel lived 1941–2009, . I heartily recommend this book, – with its tremendous out-of-the-box ideas and approach.

HAYFORD, JACK 1977. *Prayer is Invading the Impossible* (South Plainfield, NJ: Logos International 1977; revised ed. Bridge Publishing 1995), p 92 of 1977 edition. Hayford serves as Chancellor of The Kings University (formerly The King's College and Seminary) in Los Angeles and Dallas, which he founded in 1997. From 2004 to 2009, he also served as President of The International Church of the Foursquare Gospel. He is probably best known, however, as "Pastor Jack," founding pastor of The Church On The Way in Van Nuys, California, where he served as senior pastor for more than three decades.

HENRY, MATTHEW 1706 (and editor SCOTT, T for Logos edition 1997). *Matthew Henry's Concise Commentary.* Logos Edition 1997. Notes on Eph 1: 9–14 and Rev 21 and 22. Originally written in 1706. Oak Harbor, WA: Logos Research Systems. This is a smaller devotional commentary on the Bible, and provides a condensed look at nearly every verse in the Bible. Matthew Henry lived

1662–1714. His reputation rests upon his renowned commentary, *An Exposition of the Old and New Testaments* (1708–10, known also as *Matthew Henry's Commentary on the Whole Bible*). He lived to complete it only as far as to the end of the Acts, but after his death, other like-minded authors prepared the remainder from Henry's manuscripts. This work was long celebrated as the best English commentary for devotional purposes and the expanded edition was initially published in 1896. Charles Spurgeon used Henry's commentary and commended it heartily, saying: "Every minister ought to read it entirely and carefully through once at least."

HILLSONG UNITED. Song "Oceans (Where Feet May Fail)" is track #4 on the album Zion, 2013. It was written by Joel Houston, Matt Crocker, Salomon Lighthelm. Lyrics published by © EMI MUSIC PUBLISHING.

HOLMAN QUICKSOURCE GUIDE FOR UNDERSTANDING THE BIBLE 2002 Easley, Kendell H. Nashville, TN: Bible Publishers, 2002.

HORROBIN, PETER J. 1994. *Healing Through Deliverance . . . Book 1 - The Biblical Basis,* 2nd edition. Sovereign World Ltd., Kent, England. Printed in England by Clays Ltd, 1994 (There was a second book in the series, *Healing Through Deliverance – Book 2. The Practical Ministry.* But my quotes are from book 1.) At time of writing, Horrobin was Director of Ellel Ministries, Centres for Training and Ministry in Christian Healing and Counseling. Presently (July 2015) he is Director of the work of Ellel Ministries International and Chairman of the 11-strong Executive Leadership of the international ministry, now with operating centres in twenty different countries, and with students who have trained with the ministry working in well over forty different countries.] His website is http://www.peterhorrobin.com.

HUBBARD, RAY WYLIE. 2012. A great line about expectations from "Mother Blues," a song from Hubbard's album *Grifter's Hymnal.* "The days that I keep my gratitude higher than my expectations — Well, I have really good days."

LEIFESTE, PASTOR BRIAN 2011. From sermon on Forgiveness, part of a series titled "No Ordinary Family" by Brian and Sallie Leifeste, Northpoint Church, New Braunfels, TX, March 2011. www.thenpc.com

L'ENGLE, MADELEINE. 1988 (Pronounced LENG el) [1918–2007] Two-Part Invention: The Story of a Marriage, The Crosswicks Journal, Book 4. Farrar, Straus and Giroux, NY, NY. October 1988. p 124.

L'ENGLE, MADELEINE 1980 *Walking on Water: Reflections on Faith and Art.* From the chapter "Healed, Whole and Holy" 1980. Wheaton: Harold Shaw Publishers. (Attribution given by author Kaye Dacus in her blog http://kayedacus.com /2010/08/24/what-are-your-qualifications/).

LEWIS, C. S. 1952 *Mere Christianity,* London: Collins, 1952, pp. 54 – 56. (In all editions, this is Bk. II, Ch. 3, "The Shocking Alternative.")

LUCADO, MAX. 2007. *3:16: . . . The Numbers of Hope.* Thomas Nelson, Nashville, TN. 2007. pp 185–186

MANSER, MARTIN H. 1999. "Hope" in *Dictionary of Bible Themes: The Accessible and Comprehensive Tool for Topical Studies.* London: Martin Manser.

MCDOWELL, JOHN 1992. *His Image . . . My Image.* First published in the USA 1984 by Here's Life Publishers Inc., San Bernadino, CA 92402. First British edition 1985. Reprinted 1988, 1989, 1992. These notes taken from last British edition, produced and printed in England for Scripture Press Foundation (UK) LTD, Raans Road, Amersham-on-the-Hill, Bucks HP6 6JQ by Nuprint Ltd, 30b Station Road, Harpenden, Herts AL5 4SE ISBN 0 946515 04 2

MILTON, JOHN 1667. *Paradise Lost* – an epic poem in blank verse by the 17th-century English poet John Milton. The first version, published in 1667, consisted of ten books with over ten thousand lines of verse. *Paradise Lost* was followed by *Paradise Regained*

MOORE, BETH 2009. *Breaking Free* – updated edition . . . The Journey, The Stories. Lifeway Press, 2009 rev. [softcover workbook]

MOORE, BETH 2011. *James . . . Mercy Triumphs.* Lifeway Press, Nashville, TN. 2011. [softcover workbook]

MOORE, BETH 2014. *Children of the Day, 1 and 2 Thessalonians.* LifeWay Press, Nashville, TN, 2014.

MURRAY, ANDREW 1897, 1981; 1981 edition, titled *The Ministry of Intercessory Prayer* (Minneapolis: Bethany House Publishers) pp 22–23. [(original date under the title The Ministry of Intercession]

PRIOR, D. 1985. *The message of 1 Corinthians: life in the local church.* Logos Edition. Leicester, England; Downers Grove, IL: InterVarsity Press.

RAYMER, ROGER M, 1985 Section on 1 Peter in *The Bible Knowledge Commentary: An Exposition of the Scriptures* .1985.

RICE, RUSTY. 2015 sermon July 26, based on John 4. Rusty is executive pastor at Oakwood Baptist Church in New Braunfels, Texas.

RICHARDSON, JACOB 2012 conversation with Jacob, my grandson.

ROBERTS, DR. MARK D 2011. A sermon titled "What was the message of Jesus?" April 11, 2011. Dr. Roberts is a pastor, author, retreat leader, speaker, and blogger. Since October 2007 he has been the Senior Director and Scholar-in-Residence for Laity Lodge, a multifaceted ministry in the Hill Country of Texas. http://www.patheos.com/ community/markdroberts/series/what-was-the-message-of-jesus/. © 2011 by Mark D. Roberts and Patheos.com. acknowledge the source of this material: http://www.patheos.com/blogs/markdroberts/.

ROGERS, GINGER 2015 Bible study notes on *Take Me to the Rock that is Higher Than I* (Ps 61:2) September 2015. Ginger is one of my very closest friends and this book's dearest heart-partner!

ROSENBERG, JOEL 2015 *The Feast of Tabernacles – Sukkot* www.joshuafund.com/learn/newsarticle/the_feast_of_tabernacles_sukkot2

ROTHSCHILD, JENNIFER 2011. *Walking by Faith . . . Lessons Learned in the Dark.* Lifeway Press. Nashville, TN. 2003. 11th printing 2011.

SHEETS, DUTCH 1996 *Intercessory Prayer* (Published by Regal Books from Gospel Light, Ventura, CA. 264 pp.

SHIRER, PRISCILLA 2010. *One in a Million* (LifeWay Press. Nashville, TN

SHOCKEY, TOBY 2015 September 12 – Speaking at his aunt's funeral

SKOGLUND, ELIZABETH, writes this in *The Whole Christian*, 1976: "The problem is not . . . the Scriptures but rather that the words pride and humility are not correctly understood in the total light of Scripture. Pride in the biblical sense involves a not-honest estimate of oneself. Real humility is simply an absence of concentration upon oneself. It means that while I accept myself, I don't need to prove my worth excessively either to myself or to others. "(Quoted by McDowell 39–40.)

SMITH, RON 1994. *Hooked on the Word.* ©1994 by Ron Smith. West Shore Books, a part of Youth With A Mission, Lakeside, Montana.

SPURGEON, CHARLES (C.H.) 2008 *Morning by Morning: The Devotions of Charles Spurgeon.* Expanded, indexed, and updated in today's language by Jim Reimann, Editor. (Spurgeon original was 1865) Zondervan (Grand Rapids, MI: 2008).

SPURGEON, CHARLES 2010. *Evening by Evening: The Devotions of Charles Spurgeon.* Expanded, indexed, and updated in today's language by Jim Reimann, Editor. (Spurgeon original was 1868.) Zondervan (Grand Rapids, MI. 2010).

SPURGEON, CHARLES (C. H.) (1858). *The Saint and His Savior: The Progress of the Soul in the Knowledge of Jesus* (pp. 217–221). Section 6. New York: Sheldon, Blakeman & Co.

SPURGEON, CHARLES (C.H.) 1860. *Special Thanksgiving to the Father* Sermon No. 319, Delivered on Sabbath evening, Jan 15, 1860, At New Park Street Chapel, Southwark. Vol 6. www.spurgeongems.org.

SPURGEON, CHARLES 1862. *A Psalm for the New Year*. NO. 427. Jan 5, 1862, at the Metropolitan Tabernacle, Newington [London]. http://www.spurgeon-gems.org/vols7-9/chs427.pdf.

SPURGEON, CHARLES 1874. *Marvelous Things*. No. 3086. Delivered 7 May 1874. Published Apr 2, 1908, by Rev. C. H. Spurgeon at the Metropolitan Tabernacle, Newington [London]. Available online at spurgeongems.org/vols52-54/chs3086.pdf.

SPURGEON, CHARLES 1891. *A Harp of Ten Strings*. Sermon (No. 2219) intended for reading 20 Aug 1891. At Metropolitan Tabernacle, Newington. www.spurgeon.org/sermons/2219.htm.

STANLEY, DR. CHARLES (CF) 1996. *Listening to God*. Nashville: T. Nelson Publishers. LOGOS edition.

STANLEY, DR. CHARLES (CF) 2000. *Into His Presence* (pp. 20–21). January 19 entry. Nashville, TN: Thomas Nelson Publishers. Here he is quoting J.I. Packer in his book Knowing God.

STANLEY, DR. CHARLES CF 2005. From Notes on Job 25:4 in Life Principle 12 from Stanley, C. F. (2005). *The Charles F. Stanley Life Principles Bible: New King James Version* (Job 25:4). Nashville, TN: Nelson Bibles.

STIER, JIM, in his article entitled "No Matter What You Think . . . God is Crazy About You." Published in the FOCUS Newsletter, YWAM Tyler, date unknown. Jim Stier is a former president of Youth With A Mission (YWAM), and served as YWAM's International Director of Evangelism and Frontier Missions and national director for YWAM Brazil and all Portuguese speaking nations. FOCUS address is YWAM, P.O. Box 4600, Tyler,TX 75712 Ph 903-882-5591 editorial@ywamtyler.org.

STILL, PASTOR RAY. Pastor of Oakwood Baptist Church, New Braunfels, Texas.

STONE, SAM E. 1995. *Characteristics of a Live Church . . .* [adapted by CGS for Characteristics of a Live Follower of Christ]. Sermon Outlines on Galatians,

Ephesians, Philippians, Colossians. (S. E. Stone, Ed.) pp. 51–55). Cincinnati, OH: Standard].

STOTT, JOHN 1984. From *Understanding the Bible by John Stott* (revised edition London: Scripture Union, 1984); Page 134. First published 1972. Excerpted in "Authentic Christianity . . . From the Writings of John Stott" (compiled by Timothy Dudley-Smith), p. 400, by permission of InterVarsity Press, 1996.

STOTT, JOHN 2003 *What Christ Thinks of the Church: An Exposition of Revelation 1–3* (Grand Rapids, Baker: 2003) p 58.

STRONG'S EXHAUSTIVE CONCORDANCE, ©1980 and 1986, and assigned to the World Bible Publishers Inc. All rights reserved. My primary reference for definitions of Biblical Hebrew and Greek words.

TEEMS, DAVID 2012. *Tyndale: The Man Who Gave God an English Voice* (Nashville, TN: Thomas Nelson).

TOZER, A. W. 1960 first edition *How to be Filled with the Holy Spirit.* pp 56–57, Christian Publications, Incorporated; Publication date: 1/1/2002. Pages: 124. Tozer (4-21-1897 to 5-12-1963)

WIERSBE, W. W. 1992. *Wiersbe's Expository Outlines on the New Testament* (pp. 855–856 notes on Revelation 21:6). Wheaton, IL: Victor Books.

WILLARD, DALLAS 1998. *The Divine Conspiracy . . . Rediscovering Our Hidden Life in God.* HarperSanFrancisco, a division of HarperCollins Publishers. San Francisco, CA. First Edition

ADDITIONAL SCRIPTURE FOR CHAPTER 1

GOD'S LOVE

2 Chron 20:21b; Ps 36; 5, 7, 10; Song of Solomon 8:6–7

Ps 42:8 By day the Lord commands his steadfast love, [Ps. 44:4; 68:28; 71:3; 133:3] and at night his song is with me, [Job 35:10; Ps. 4:4; 16:7; 63:6; 77:6; 119:55, 62, 148;149:5] a prayer to the God of my life.

GOD WANTS ALL TO BE SAVED.

Ezek 18:23, 31– 32 and 33:11; Ps 89:24–36 ; Isa 43:1–7; 44:2–5; 54:10; and 63:7–9, 10–14;

Isa 66:13–14 As one whom his mother comforts, so will I comfort you . . .

Jer 7:25–26; 9:24 ; 13:11 and 29:11–13; Jer 31:3, 9, 20, 25, 33–34

Ezek 34:1–10; Hos 6:6 ; 11:3–4; and 14:4, 8; Micah 7:18–20

Rom 10:21 (quoting Isa 65:2); 2 Cor 5:17–19; 2 Cor 6:18 (reflecting Isa 43:6–7 and Hos 1:10); Eph 2:4–10; 1 John 3:1 and 4:14–21 NIV

God says . . . How I would set you among my sons, and give you a pleasant land, a heritage most beautiful of all nations. And I thought you would call me, My Father, and would not turn from following me. Surely, as a treacherous wife leaves her husband, so have you been treacherous to me . . . Return, O faithless sons; I will heal your faithfulness. Jer 3:19–20, 22

1 Cor 1:23–25 [23] . . . We preach Christ crucified, a stumbling block to Jews and folly to Gentiles, [24] but to those who are called, both Jews and Greeks, Christ the power of God and the wisdom of God. [25] For the foolishness of God is wiser than men, and the weakness of God is stronger than men.

GOD IS PRAISE-WORTHY

Deut 10:17–21 [17] For the Lord your God is God of gods and Lord of lords [Josh 22:22; Ps 136:2; Dan 2:47; 11:36], the great, the mighty, and the awesome God, who is not partial and takes no bribe. [18] He executes justice for the fatherless and the widow, and loves the sojourner, giving him food and clothing. [Ps 68:5; 146:9; [c 24:17; E 22:22] [20] . . . You shall serve him and hold fast to him, and by his name you shall swear. [21] He is your praise. He is your God [Ps 22:3; 109:1; Jer 17:14], who has done for you these great and terrifying things that your eyes have seen. [2 Sam 7:23; Ps 106:21, 22]

Isa 45:1–12 AMP; Jer 10:6–7 [6] There is none like you, O Lord [ch 49:19; Ex. 15:11; Ps. 86:8, 10] ; you are great, and your name is great in might. [7] Who would not fear you, O King of the nations? For this is your due [ch 5:22; Rev 15:4] . . . there is none like you.

Rom 11:33 [Col. 2:3; Ps. 139:6]; Rom 16:27; 1 Cor 1:18

1 Cor 1:28–29 [28] God chose what is low and despised in the world, even things that are not, to bring to nothing things that are, [29] so that no human being might boast in the presence of God. [30] And because of him you are in Christ Jesus, who became to us wisdom from God, righteousness and sanctification and redemption . . . [See also Isa 9:6; 11:2; 1 Cor 1:24; Col 2:2–3]

1 Cor 8:6 NIV   There is but one, unchanging God, the Father, from whom all things came and for whom we live; and there is but one Lord, Jesus Christ, through whom all things came and through whom we live.

Eph 1:17–23 gives us a great depiction of God's wisdom and power. Here are many cross-references that fit throughout this passage, so that if you are curious and want to read more, you'll know where to start.

Verse 18 see Acts 26:18; Heb 6:4 and 10:32; Rev 3:17, 18

Verse 19 see Dan 4:30; Eph 3:7 and 6:10; Phil 3:21; Col 1:29; 2:12]

Verse 20 See Mk 16:19; Acts 2:33; 1 Pet. 3:22]

Verse 21 [Eph 4:10; Col 2:10; See Jn 3:31. 1 Cor 15:24], and above every name that is named [Eph 3:15; Phil 2:9; Heb. 1:4], not only in this age [Mt 12:32]

Verse 22 And he put all things under his feet [cited from Ps 8:6; See 1 Cor 15:27] and gave him as head over all things to the church [1 Cor 11:3; Eph 4:15; 5:23; Col 1:18; 2:10, 19;], [23] which is his body, the fullness of him who fills all in all. [Jer 23:24; Jn 1:16; Eph 3:19; Col 3:11]

Rev 11:15 Then the seventh angel blew his trumpet, and there were loud voices in heaven, saying, "The kingdom of the world has become the kingdom of our Lord and of his Christ, and he shall reign forever and ever."

Rev 19:6–8 [6] Then I heard what seemed to be the voice of a great multitude, like the roar of many waters and like the sound of mighty peals of thunder, crying out, "Hallelujah! For the Lord our God the Almighty reigns. [7] Let us rejoice and exult and give him the glory, for the marriage of the Lamb has come, and his Bride has made herself ready; [8] it was granted her to clothe herself with fine linen, bright and pure" —for the fine linen is the righteous deeds of the saints.

GOD IS WISE AND POWERFUL.

1 Sam 2:3; Isa 28:29

Wonderful in counsel [Jer. 32:19; [ch 9:6], Excellent in wisdom

Isa 40:28 See also Job 9:4; 28:12–24; Ps 92:5; Eccl 8:17

Power belongs to God. Ps 62:11; Power and glory Ps 63:2

Great is our Lord, abundant in power; his understanding beyond measure. Ps 147:5

God's wisdom is superior to human wisdom Isa 55:9 (See also Job 21:22)

And is exhibited in creation Jer 10:12 See also Job 28:25–27; 37:14–16; Ps 104:24; 136:5;

Prov 3:19–20; Isa 40:12–14;

Exhibited in historical events Isa 31:2; Job 12:13–25; Dan 2:20–22

Exhibited in knowing the human mind 1Ch 28:9 See also Ps 139:2,4,6

And God's wisdom is given to human beings   2 Ch 1:11–12; Ezra 7:25;

Prov 2:6; Eccl 12:11; Dan 2:23; 1Co 2:6–16; Eph 1:17 ; Eph 3:10; Jas 1:5

Rom 11:33 Oh, the depth of the riches and wisdom and knowledge of God! [Col. 2:3;

[Ps. 139:6] Rom 16:25+; 1Sa 16:7; 1Ki 3:28; Isa 28:24–29; Luke 11:49

1 Cor 1:18 For the word of the cross is folly to those who are perishing, but to us who

are being saved it is the power of God . . .

GOD IS GOOD AND FAITHFUL AND GREATLY TO BE PRAISED. AND I HAVE

CONFIDENCE IN HIS CHARACTER.

He has many amazing qualities to share. (See 1 Chron 16:25; Ps 31: 19; Ps 58:1; Ps 96:4;

Ps 119:68; Ps 145:3)

God is good. Ps 136:1 Give thanks to the lord for he is good.

Ps 145:9 The LORD is good to all and his mercy is over all that he has made.

God is merciful. Deut 4:31; Rom 9:14–16, 18 (reflects Ex 33:19)

God is patient, steadfast, and encouraging. Rom 15:5 Ps 57:10

He is our God of peace. Rom 15:33; Phil. 4:9 ; 1 Thess 5:23;

2 Thess 3:16; Heb 13:20–21

He is my refuge, my shield, my strength, and my rock. Ps 71:3, 7;

Ps 73:28; Ps 61:1–4; Ps 91:1–2;

God is righteous. Ps 36:6

God is our salvation. Ps 68:19–20; Ps 79:9

God is our shepherd. Ps 78:52; Ps 80:1; Isa 40:11; Jer 31:10; Ezek 34:11,12, 23, 30–31; Jn

10:11; Heb 13:20; 1 Pet 2:25; 5:4

God is enough. He is with me always, and I can trust him completely. Eph 3:16–19; Heb 13:20-21; 1 Pet 3:13-17 ; 5:7–10

And the Psalms are full of this imagery that God is enough: Ps 18:30, 31–32, 35, 46; Ps 27:1, 13, 14 and 31:24; Ps 44:6–8; Ps 57:1 ; Ps 63:7–8; Ps 55:22 Cast your burden on the LORD, and he will sustain you.

Ps 34:15,19 AMP: The eyes of the Lord are toward the [uncompromisingly] righteous and His ears are open to their cry. Many evils confront the [consistently] righteous, but the Lord delivers them out of them all.

Ps 73:23–26, 28 [David speaking to God] I am continually with you. You hold my right hand. You guide me with your counsel, and afterward you will receive me to glory . . . And there is nothing on earth that I desire besides you . . . God is the strength of my heart and my portion forever .

Ps 103:1–18 [1-2 NASB] . . . Bless the Lord, O my soul, and all that is within me, bless his holy name! . . . and forget none of his benefits . . . [11-13 AMP] For as the heavens are high above the earth, so great are His mercy and loving-kindness toward those who reverently and worshipfully fear Him. As far as the east is from the west, so far has He removed our transgressions from us. As a father loves and pities his children, so the Lord loves and pities those who fear Him [devotion with reverence, worship, and awe]

Rom 8:14–17 CEV Only those people who are led by God's Spirit are his children . . . call him our Father . . . share in the glory of Christ.

1 Cor 1:9 AMP God is faithful (reliable, trustworthy, and there-fore ever true to his promise, and He can be depended on) . . .

ADDITIONAL SCRIPTURE FOR CHAPTER 2

JESUS, THE SON OF GOD, IS THE WAY, THE TRUTH, AND THE LIFE

God sent Jesus to live and die for us. Jesus was – and is - God's rescue plan for us! Ps 34:20; 49:15; Ps 79:9; 118:22; Isa 53:5; Isa 61:1; Lk 4:18-19; 1 Cor 1:10; 1 Cor 3:3

Jesus is the Christ, the Messiah, the Son of God born to a virgin

Deut 13:1-5 and 18:20-22 for two tests of prophet's authenticity

Isa 5:20-21; Jer 2:8 ; 5:30-31; and 6:13 (repeated in 8:10-12); Jer 6:31 (repeated in Jer 8:10-12); Ezek 22:23-28; Hos 4:4-6; Mal 2:7-9

Acts 20:29-30 where Paul uses images from Mt 7:15 and Ezek 22:27; 2 Cor 11:3-4: Galatians 1:6-9; Col 2:18-19; 1 Tim 6:20-21; 2 Tim 3:12-17 and 4:2-4; Heb 13:9; 1 Jn 2:18-25 and 4:1-6 ; 2 Jn 7-11; Jude 3-4 and 17-23; Rev 13:11-18

I BELIEVE GOD AND I BELIEVE IN GOD.

And I accept and believe that Jesus is who he says he is – the Son of God, the Messiah, my Lord, and my Savior.

Jesus says: Strive to enter by the narrow door; for many, I tell you, will seek to enter and will not be able. Lk 13:24+

Jesus says: . . . If you do not believe that I am the one I claim to be, you will indeed die in your sins. Jn 8: 24 NIV

Jesus says: If God were your Father, you would love me, because I came from God and only from him. He sent me. I did not come on my own. Jn 8:42 CEV

Jesus says: He who believes in me, believes not in me, but in him who sent me. And he who sees me sees him who sent me.   Jn 12:44-45 and again in Jn 14:9

Jesus says: . . . If you are thirsty, come to me and drink! Have faith in me, and you will have LIFE-GIVING WATER flowing from deep inside you, just as the Scriptures say. Jn 7:37-38 CEV   (building on Isa 55:1) [Jesus' words (above) reflect the many times in the Old Testament that God is referred to as a fountain or source of living water. More examples: Ps 36:9 ; Is 44:3; Isa 58:11 ; Jer 2:13; 17:13; Ezek 47; Zech 14:8.

Jesus says: Heaven and earth will pass away, but my words will never pass away. Lk 21:33 NIV   Mt 24:35   Mk 13:31

Jesus says: If God were your Father, you would love me, because I came from God and only from him. He sent me. I did not come on my own. Jn 8:42 CEV

Jesus says: He who believes in me, believes not in me, but in him who sent me. And he who sees me sees him who sent me.   Jn 12:44-45 and in Jn 14:9

Jesus says: He who receives you receives me, and he who receives me receives him who sent me. Mt 10:40; Also in Mk 9:37; Lk 10:16; and in Jn 13:20

Jesus says: I tell you the truth, if you have faith as small as a mustard seed, you can say to this mountain, 'Move from here to there' and it will move.

Jesus says: This is the work (service) that God asks of you: that you believe in the One Whom He has sent [that you cleave to, trust, rely on, and have faith in His Messenger]. Jn 6:29 AMP

Jesus says: The way that I teach is a narrow way in that it is well defined. It is not easy to follow the straight path, but it is the way to a full and eternal life, while the undisciplined way is a way to destruction and death. Mt 7:13-14 WMF (See Jer 21:8)

Remember, God patiently beckons us to live and walk with him.
He sent Jesus to show us how. Acts 16:31; Rom 10:9;
1 Cor 1:30 NLT God alone made it possible for you to be in Christ Jesus. For our benefit God made Christ to be wisdom itself. He is the one who made us acceptable to God. He made us pure and holy, and he gave himself to purchase our freedom

TO SERVE GOD, I MUST FOLLOW HIM, AND THAT MEANS FOLLOWING JESUS.
Jesus is my model
STEP 1: Repent and believe in the gospel.
Jesus says: Sit down and count the cost [of following me] . . . Lk 14:28
Jesus says: If you try to keep your life for yourself, you will lose it. But if you give up your life for me, you will find true life. Lk 9:24 NLT Mt 16:25 Mk 8:35 (Same idea is found in Mt 10:39 and in Lk 17:33 and in Jn 12:25.)
Jesus says: On Judgment Day, the Ninevites will stand up and give evidence that will condemn this generation, because when Jonah preached to them they changed their lives. A far greater preacher than Jonah is here, and you squabble about 'proofs'. Mt 12:41 MSG Lk 11:32
Jesus told a number of parables about repentance and God's forgiveness.
The underlying truth: "There is joy before the angels of God over one sinner who repents." Lk 15:10
Many of these parables are in Luke 15, the "lost and found" chapter:
The story of recovering a lost sheep Lk 15:3-7 Mt 18:12-14
The story about the joy of finding a lost coin. Lk 15:8-10 :
The story of the prodigal son Lk 15:11-32

STEP 2: Deny yourself and follow me.
Jesus says: Any person who sacrifices by leaving friends, families or glorious plans and follows me for my sake or as a witness for the good news, such a person shall be rewarded, even on this earth, in spite of tough persecutions, but such a person shall also acquire eternal life. Mk 10:29-30 WMF Lk 18:29-30 Mt 19:29-30

STEP 3: Jesus says: if you love me, keep my commandments. Jn 4: 15 This includes honoring the law and teachings of the Old Testament.

Jesus says: If anyone keeps my word, he will never see death. Jn 8:51

Jesus says: All of us must quickly carry out the tasks assigned us by the one who sent me, because there is little time left before the night falls and all work comes to an end. Jn 9:4 NLT

Jesus says: I did not come to judge the world, but to save it. There is a judge for the one who rejects me and does not accept my words; that very word which I spoke will condemn him at the last day. Jn 12:47-48

Jesus says: Man shall not live by bread alone, but by every word that proceeds from the mouth of God. Mt 4:4 Lk 4:4 (quoting Deut 8:3)

Jesus says: Whoever does the will of my Father in heaven is my brother, and sister, and mother. Mt 12:50   Mk 3:35   Lk 8:21

Jesus says: . . . If you would enter life, keep the commandments . . . and follow me. Mt 19:16-21   Mk 10:17-21   Lk 18:18-22

STEP 4: Keep focused on Jesus, as he guides us.

Jesus says: If a man loves me, he will keep my word, and my Father will love him, and we will come to him and make our home with him. Jn 14:23

Jesus says: You, therefore, must be perfect, as your heavenly Father is perfect. Mt 5:48 (building on Lev 11:44-45; 19:2; 20:26). (Mt 5:48 AMP describes "perfect" as growing into complete maturity of godliness in mind and character, having reached the proper height of virtue and integrity.)

Jesus says: The way that I teach is a narrow way in that it is well defined. It is not easy to follow the straight path, but it is the way to a full and eternal life, while the undisciplined way is a way to destruction and death. Mt 7:13-14 WMF   (expanding Jer 21:8 and others) [and for more on pursuing righteousness, please check out Chap 6]

Jesus says: [After describing himself as the bread of life and the eternal quenching of thirst in Jn 6:35, 50-51] . . . Unless you eat of my flesh and drink of my blood, you don't have a part in my program. Those that do eat of my flesh and drink of my blood have eternal life. It is all a matter of involvement. You must receive me, share my work, suffer, be a working part of my program, then you are receiving my flesh and my blood as spiritual bread and wine. I am not talking about ordinary bread and wine, but as symbols. Jn 6:53-58 WMF

More on this: Isa 57:15; Rom 8:9-11; 1 Cor 3:16; 2 Cor 1:21-22;

2 Cor 6:16 . . . I will live in them

Eph 2:19-22; Eph 3:14-19 . .Christ may dwell in your hearts through faith

Col 1:27 NASB . . . Christ in you, the hope of glory

Col 2:6-7; Col 3:11 NASB . . . Christ is all, and in all [believers].

Jas 4:8a; 1 Jn 2:4-6, 24, 27-29; 1 Jn 3:24 and 4:4, 13-16

More references to confession, repentance, and turning back to the Lord

Lev 26:40-42 ; Deut 30:1-10; Deut 4:25-31; Hos 5:15 - 6:2; Joel 2:12-13 ; Mal 3:6-7

Ps 32:1-5 ; Ps 51:6-14 . . . create in me a clean heart, O God, and put a new and right
spirit within me . . . ; Prov 28:13 ; Isa 1:15-20 and 43:25; Jer 7:5-7 ;18:7-11;
Lam 3:40-42 ; Ezek 14:6; 18:21-29; Ezek 33:11-20; Ezek 18:31-32 . . .
Cast away from you all the transgressions which you have committed against me, and
get yourselves a new heart and a new spirit! Why will you die, O house of Israel? For I
have no pleasure in the death of anyone, says the Lord God; so turn and live . . .

Acts 2:38-39; 3:19-21; Acts 8:22-23; 17:30

Rom 2:4-5 NRSV Do you not realize that God's kindness is meant to lead you to repentance? But by your hard and impenitent heart you are storing up wrath for yourself on
the day of wrath, when God's righteous judgment will be revealed.

2 Cor 7:10; 1 Pet 2:21; James 2:19

1 Jn 1:8-10 . . . If we confess our sins, he is faithful and just, and will forgive our sins and
cleanse us from all unrighteousness.

Jesus also spoke about honoring the law and teachings of the Old Testament.

Jesus says: Until John the Baptist began to preach, the laws of Moses and the messages
of the prophets were your guides. But now the Good News of the Kingdom of God is
preached, and eager multitudes are forcing their way in. But that doesn't mean that
the law has lost its force in even the smallest point. It is stronger and more permanent
than heaven and earth. Lk 16:16-17 NLT

Jesus says: . . . If you wish to enter into life, keep the commandments . . .
and come, follow Me. Mt 19:16-21 NASB   Mk 10:17-21   Lk 18:18-22

Here are the Ten Commandments (1-4):

Command 1 --You shall have no other gods before me. Ex 20: 3; Deut 4:39 and 5:7 [These are
specific references, but of course, this idea runs throughout the OT. Jer 7 is just one example.]

Jesus says: Call no man your father on earth, for you have one Father, who is in heaven. Neither be called masters, for you have one master, the Christ. Mt 23:9-10

Command 2 -- no graven image . . . Ex 20:4-6, 22-26; Lev 19:4; Deut 4:23-24; 5:8-10

Jesus says: . . . You cannot serve God and mammon (deceitful riches, money, possessions, or whatever is trusted in). Mt 6:24 AMP   Lk 16:13

Command 3 -- You shall not use or repeat the name of the Lord your God in vain. [that is, lightly or frivolously, in false affirmations or profanely] . . . Ex 20:7 AMP; Lev 19:12; Numbers 30:2; Deut 5:11 and 23:21-23   See also James 5:12

Jesus says: You have heard . . . 'You shall not swear falsely' . . . But I say to you, Do not swear at all, either by heaven . . . or by earth . . . Let what you say be simply 'Yes' or 'No'. Mt 5:33-37

Command 4 -- Remember the Sabbath day, to keep it holy. Ex 20:8-11; Lev 19:3; Deut 5:12 -15. But Jesus did not support a ritualistic, legalistic observance of the Sabbath.

Jesus says: that the Sabbath was made for man, not vice versa. Mk 2:27

Jesus says: he was Lord of the Sabbath. (Mk 2:28, Mt 12:8), and when rebuked for healing on the Sabbath, he answered them, My Father is working still, and I am working . . . Jn 5:17

Commandments 5 - 9 were repeated by Jesus in one series which appears in three of the gospels: Mt 19:18-19; Mk 10:19; Lk 18:20. And he went on to elaborate on several of these.

Command 5 – Honor your father and mother.   Then you will live a long, full life in the land the Lord your God will give you. Ex 20:12 NLT; Lev 19:3; Deut 5:16; Expanded in Mt 15:3-6; Mk 7:9-13

Command 6 – You shall not kill. Ex 20:13 ; Deut 5:17; Expanded in Mt 5:21-24

Command 7 – You shall not commit adultery. Ex 20:14; Deut 5:18   Expanded in Mt 5:27-32 and in Jn 8:3-11

Jesus says Let him who is without sin among you be the first to throw a stone. Jn 8:7 [And when some Pharisees tried to test him by asking whether there was any cause for lawful divorce] Jesus says: ... It was because you were so hard-hearted that Moses allowed you to divorce your wives, but from the beginning it was not so. And I say to you, whoever divorces his wife, except for unchastity, and marries another commits adultery. Mt 19:3-9 NRSV Mk 10:6-9 See also Deut 24:1-4; Prov 6:32; Mal 2:13-16

Command 8 – You shall not steal. Ex 20:15; Lev 19:11; Deut 5:19; Isa 61:8

Command 9 – You shall not witness falsely against your neighbor.

Ex 20:16 AMP; Lev 19:11-12;   Deut 5:20

Command 10 -- You shall not covet . . . anything that is your neighbor's.

Ex 20:17 NKJV   Deut 5:21   Expanded in Lk 12:15-21

The New Testament writers agreed with Jesus that the law given by God to Moses was still important. One good example is Gal 3: 21-29

THROUGHOUT, JESUS AND THE FATHER PROMISE TO GUIDE US AS WE FOLLOW AND OBEY

Jesus confirms the many OT scriptures that repeatedly tell us to focus our whole minds and hearts on what God has told us to do, to walk in all his ways, and to teach our children these commands. And the rewards are clear.

Deut 6:6-9, 20-25 NRSV Keep these words that I am commanding you today in your heart. Recite them to your children and talk about them when you are at home and when you are away, when you lie down and when you rise. . . . .

Deut 30:11-20 ESV . . . The word is very near you. It is in your mouth and in your heart, so that you can do it. . . (reflected later in Rom 10:6+)

Ps 103:17-18 MSG God's love, though, is ever and always, eternally present to all who fear him . . . as they follow his Covenant ways and remember to do whatever he said

Jesus says: You are my friends if you do what I command. Jn 15:14

More on this: Deut 4:1-2, 6, 9, 13-14, 39-40; Deut 29:18-19 ; Deut 10:12-13;   11:18-25; 15:4-6; and   26:16-19; Deut 28 and   32:46-47; Deut 30:19-20; Jer 21:8; Joshua 1:6-9; 1 Samuel 15; Ps 37:23 and 119 (among many others)

Prov 4:11-13, 20-22, 25-27; 7:2; Eccl 12:13-14; Jer 7:22-28

Rom 2:13: Rom 6:17-18 ; Jas 1:22-25; Jas 2:14, 26 and   4:17

1 Jn 1:6-9 and 2:3-6 ; 1 Jn 3:10, 22-24   and 5:3 ; 2 Jn 6, 7-9 NCV

God and Jesus: The Alpha and the Omega (speaking in John's vision)

Rev 1:8; 21:6; 22:13; [Isa. 41:4; 43:10; 44:6] "Eternal life and lordship characterize God (1:8) and his Christ, who is coming soon" (ESV Study Bible).

Rev 1:8 'I am the Alpha and the Omega', says the Lord God, 'who is and who was and who is to come, the Almighty'. Here God gives his titles, Alpha and Omega, the Beginning and the End, as a pledge for the full performance (Henry 1706, Notes on Revelation).

Rev 21:6 ⁶ It is done. I am the Alpha and the Omega, the beginning and the end. I will give to the one who thirsts from the spring of the water of life without cost.

God's "It is done!" parallels Christ's "It is finished!" (Jn 19:30) The same Lord who started creation will also finish it; He is Alpha and Omega (the first and last letters of the Greek alphabet) (Wiersbe 1992 pp. 855–856).

And the 'spring of the water of life' is the throne of God and the Lamb (Rev 22:1), a throne of grace (Heb. 4:16) because here the thirsty drink without payment, by God's free gift (Isa. 55:1) (ESV Study Bible).

Rev 21:7 ⁷ He who overcomes will inherit these things, and I will be his God and he will be My Son.

JESUS AND THE KINGDOM OF HEAVEN/ THE KINGDOM OF GOD

¹⁴ Now after John was arrested [Mt 4:12; 14:3; Lk 3:20; Jn 3:24], Jesus came into Galilee, [Mt 4:17, 23] proclaiming the gospel of God, ¹⁵ and saying, "The time is fulfilled, [Dan. 9:25; Gal 4:4; Eph 1:10; Lk 21:8; Jn 7:8] and the kingdom of God is at hand; [See Mt 3:2] Repent and believe in the gospel." [Acts 19:4; 20:21; Heb 6:1]

Jesus says: Seek first God's kingdom and his righteousness.

Jesus says: Make sure that the light you think you have is not really darkness. If you are filled with light, with no dark corners, then your whole life will be radiant, as though a floodlight is shining on you. Lk 11:35-36 NLT   Mt 6:22-23

Jesus says: While you have the Light, believe in the Light [have faith in it, hold to it, rely on it], that you may become sons of the Light and be filled with Light. Jn 12:36 AMP

Jesus says: . . . Go, and sin no more. Jn 8:11 KJV and earlier in Jn 5:1

Jesus says: Fear not, little flock, for it is your Father's good pleasure to give you the kingdom. Lk 12:32

Jesus speaking in John's vision: Those whom I [dearly and tenderly] love, I tell their faults and convict and convince and reprove and chasten [I discipline and instruct them] . . . Rev 3:19 AMP (affirming Prov 3:12 and Prov 12:1, and also appearing in Heb 12:5-6). For more on this, see Chapter 6.

Col 1:13-14 (with expanded references) ¹³ [God the Father] has delivered us [1 Thess. 1:10] from the domain of darkness [Lk 22:53; Eph 6:12], and transferred us to the kingdom of his beloved Son [2 Peter 1:11], ¹⁴ in whom we have redemption, the forgiveness of sins.

ADDITIONAL SCRIPTURE FOR CHAPTER 3

FROM THE MOMENT WE ACCEPT JESUS AS LORD AND SAVIOR, WE BECOME A NEW CREATION AND RECEIVE THE MIND OF CHRIST AND ABUNDANT LIFE.

Jesus says: My prayer is . . . that they will be one, just as you and I are one, Father – that just as you are in me and I am in you, so they will be in us, and the world will believe you sent me. Jn 17: 21 NLT

Rom 8:9 – 11 But you are not in the flesh, you are in the Spirit, if the Spirit of God really dwells in you. Any one who does not have the Spirit of Christ does not belong to him . . . If the Spirit of him who raised Jesus from the dead dwells in you, he who raised Christ Jesus from the dead will give life to your mortal bodies also through his Spirit which dwells in you.

He gives me everything I need to handle what's ahead.

Deut 11:8+ NLT Be careful to obey every command I am giving you today, so you may have strength to go in and take over the land you are about to enter.

Rom 16:25-27 NLT [25] Now all glory to God, who is able to make you strong . . .

1 Cor 3:16 I am God's temple. God's Spirit dwells in me.

1 Cor 2:16; 3:9; 6:19; 2 Cor 1:21-22; Eph 1:3,13-14; 2:19-22; and 3:14-19

2 Tim 1:13-14 . . .[14] By the Holy Spirit who dwells within us, guard the good deposit entrusted to you.

1 Jn 5: 3-5, 20 . . . [20]The Son of God has come and has given us understanding so that we may know him who is true . . . the true God.

The Holy Spirit ministers to me. He comforts us. He teaches, directs, and opens our minds to the mind of Christ.

Jesus says: When you are arrested, don't worry about what to say in your defense, because you will be given the right words at the right time. For it won't be you doing the talking – it will be the Spirit of your Father speaking through you. Mt 10:19-20 NLT [also in Lk12:11-12 and in Mk 13:11-12 Lk 21:14-15 ; and reflects Ex 4:10-12, 15-16 and Jer 1:6-9]

Jesus says: He will come to you from the Father and will tell you all about me. And you must also tell others about me because you have been with me from the beginning. Jn 15:26-27 NLT (See Acts 5:32)

Jesus says: When he comes, he'll expose the error of the godless world's view of sin, righteousness, and judgment: He'll show them that their refusal to believe in me is their basic sin; that righteousness comes from above, where I am with the Father, out of their sight and control; that judgment takes place as the ruler of this godless world is brought to trial and convicted . . . Jn 16:8-11 MSG

If we walk with God, his Holy Spirit will equip and empower us. 1 Cor 12; 1 Cor 14; Eph 4:7-16; 1 Pet 4:10-11

1 Cor 1:4-9 NIV ⁴ I always thank God for you because of his grace given you in Christ Jesus. ⁵ For in him you have been enriched in every way—in all your speaking and in all your knowledge— ⁶ because our testimony about Christ was confirmed in you. ⁷ Therefore you do not lack any spiritual gift as you eagerly wait for our Lord Jesus Christ to be revealed. ⁸ He will keep you strong to the end ...⁹ God, who has called you into fellowship with his Son Jesus Christ our Lord, is faithful.

More on this: See Isa 11:2 and elsewhere, when the Holy Spirit rests on someone
Isa 40:13-14; Acts 2:17-21 (quoting Joel 2:28-32); Acts 2:38-39;
Acts 5:32; 8:29, 39; and Acts 10:19-20; 20:22-23; and 21:11;
Rom 8:11, 14-17, 26-27; 1 Thess 4:7-8; 2 Thess 2:13-14; Titus 3:4-7;
Heb 6:4-6; Heb 10:15, 26-29; Heb 13:20-21; Jas 1:5-6; 1 Jn 3:24; 1 Jn 4:1-6, 13

ADDITIONAL SCRIPTURE FOR CHAPTER 4

I LOVE GOD WITH HEART, SOUL, MIND AND STRENGTH.
Mk 12:28-34, citing Deut 6:4-6 and elsewhere: ²⁸ . . . "Which commandment is the most important of all?" ... ²⁹ Jesus answered, "The most important is, 'Hear, O Israel: the LORD our God, the LORD is one. ³⁰ and you shall love the LORD your God with all your heart and with all your soul and with all your mind and with all your strength.' . . . Mk 12:28-34 [For ver. 28–34, see also Mt 22:34–40, 46; Lk 10:25–28]
Deut 30:6-10 NIV The LORD your God will circumcise your hearts and the hearts of your descendants, so that you may love him with all your heart and with all your soul, and live . . . The LORD will again *delight in you* and make you prosperous, just as he delighted in your fathers, if you obey the LORD your God and keep his commands and decrees that are written in this Book of the Law and turn to the LORD your God with all your heart and with all your soul. [Circumcision of the heart – a form of spiritual

"heart surgery" – opens us up to love and to serve both God and man. It is God's doing – but we must cooperate!]

Jer 31:33-34 [33] . . . I will put my law within them, and I will write it on their hearts. [Ps 37:31; 2 Cor 3:3 and cited in 10:16]. And I will be their God, and they shall be my people. [Hos 2:23; Zech 8:8; 13:9; Rev 21:7]   [34] . . . They shall all know me, from the least of them to the greatest, declares the Lord. [Isa 54:13]   For I will forgive their iniquity, [Deut 33:8; 36:3; 50:20; Mic 7:18; Acts 10:43; Rom 11:27; Cited Heb 10:17] and I will remember their sin no more." [Isa 43:25]

1 Cor. 8:5-6 For us there is one God, the Father, from whom are all things and for whom we exist, and one Lord, Jesus Christ, through whom are all things and through whom we exist

Col. 1:26-27 . . . [27] To them God chose to make known how great among the Gentiles are the riches of the glory of this mystery [Eph 1:8; 3:16], which is Christ in you, the hope of glory. [1 Tim 1:1]

We work hand and hand with God.

1 Cor 3:5-17 NLT [5] . . . We are only God's servants through whom you believed the Good News . . . It was God who made it grow . . . [8] The one who plants and the one who waters work together with the same purpose . . . [9] For we are both God's workers. And you are God's field. You are God's building ⋯ [11] For no one can lay any foundation other than the one we already have—Jesus Christ . . . [16] Don't you realize that all of you together are the temple of God and that the Spirit of God lives in you? [17] God will destroy anyone who destroys this temple. For God's temple is holy, and you are that temple.

OTHER VERSES
Lev 26:12; Deut 11:1, 13-15, 22-23; Deut 30:19-20; 2 Kings 23:25; Ps 105:45;
Isa 42:8; Ezek 37:26   cited in Heb 10:16; Hos. 2:23; Zech 8:8; 13:9;
Rom. 3:28; Gal. 3:20; Eph 1:9; 3:3–5; 3:20; Eph 4:4-7; 5:32; 6:19
1 Tim. 1:17; 2:5; 6:16; 2 Tim. 1:9, 10 ; Titus 1:2, 3; 1 Jn 5: 19-20

ADDITIONAL SCRIPTURE FOR CHAPTER 5

Ps 66:1 Make a joyful noise to God.
Ps 66:16-19 I cried aloud to him . . . truly God has listened . . . Blessed be God, because he has not rejected my prayer or removed his steadfast love from me.

Ps 69:30 I will praise the name of God with a song; I will magnify him with thanksgiving.

Ps 146:2 RSV I will praise the Lord as long as I live. I will sing praises to my God while I have being.

1 Cor 14:2 Speaking in tongues is speaking to God, not to men, uttering mysteries in the Spirit.

Be a Bible meditator, marinating and meditating in God's word. (includes reference to meditating in John 17) Ps 145:5 Heb 1:3; 1 Cor 13

Prayer is part of conversation with God!

Jesus says: I will give you the keys of the kingdom of heaven; and whatever you bind (declare to be improper and unlawful) on earth must be what is already bound in heaven; and whatever you loose (declare lawful) on earth must be what is already loosed in heaven. Mt 16:19 AMP ; again in Mt 18:18 (expanding Isa 22:22)

[Please note that some writers see "binding" as binding yourself to God and the things of God, and "loosing" as cutting loose and destroying the things opposing God. Whatever definition you use, Jesus is saying here that our actions are to be completely aligned with God and his purposes, and against whatever opposes God.]

Jesus says: Whatever you ask for in prayer, believe that you have received it, and it will be yours.   And when you stand praying, if you hold anything against anyone, forgive him, so that your Father in heaven may forgive you your sins.   Mk 11:24-25 NIV   Mt 21:21-22

Jesus says: Again, I tell you that if two of you on earth agree about anything you ask for, it will be done for you by my Father in heaven.   For where two or three come together in my name, there am I with them. Mt 18:19-20 NIV

Jesus says: . . . Keep awake then and watch at all times [be discreet, attentive, and ready], praying . . . Lk 21:34-36 AMP

Jesus says: . . . There are many people to harvest but only a few workers to help harvest them. Pray to the Lord, who owns the harvest, that he will send more.

And he told them a parable to the effect that they ought always to pray and not lose heart. Lk 18:1

Jesus says: Be ready; for the Son of God is coming at an hour you do not expect. Lk 12:39-40 Mt 24:42-44   and also in Mk 13:35-37

Jesus says: Why are you sleeping? . . . Get up and pray. Otherwise temptation will overpower you. Lk 22:46 NLT

Jesus says: . . . I gave you this work: to go and produce fruit, fruit that will last. Then the Father will give you anything you ask for in my name. Jn 15:16 NCV

Jesus says: I tell you the truth, anyone who has faith in me will do what I have been do-ing. He will do even greater things than these, because I am going to the Father. And I will do whatever you ask in my name, so that the Son may bring glory to the Father. You may ask me for anything in my name, and I will do it. Jn 14:12-14 NIV

Ps 37:4-5 [First . . .] Take delight in the Lord and [Then . . .] he will give you the desires of your heart. Commit your way to the Lord; trust in him, and he will act.

Jer 29 11-13

Acts 10, where we see that God hears the prayers of those who earnestly seek him, even before they know the entire truth of Jesus

1 Cor 14:15 I will pray in the spirit and I will pray with the mind also. I will sing with the spirit and I will sing with the mind also

Phil 4:6-7; 1 Thess 5:1618; 1 Tim 2:1-2,; Jas 1:5-8; 5:13-18

Jas 4:2-3 NLT You want what you don't have, so you scheme, and kill to get it. You are jealous for what others have, and you can't possess it, so you fight and quarrel to take it away from them. And yet the reason you don't have what you want is that you don't ask God for it. And even when you do ask, you don't get it because your whole motive is wrong – you want only what will give you pleasure.

1 Jn 3:22 ; 1 Jn 5:14-15. . . if we ask anything according to his will he hears us

ADDITIONAL SCRIPTURE FOR CHAPTER 6

Additional thoughts about our self-worth or self-image: Mt 6:19-21, 25-34; Jn 13:1-3; Rom 12:3, 16; Phil 2:3-5 ; Phil 4:7, 8; Col 3:1-4, 10

"In Colossians 1:15-20 Paul mentions seven unique characteristics of Christ, which fittingly qualify him to have "the supremacy" (v. 18). No comparable listing of so many characteristics of Christ and His deity are found in any other Scripture passage."

1. Christ is the image of God. (Heb 1:3; Jn 14:9)
2. Christ is the firstborn over creation. (Ex 13:2–15; Deut 21:17; Rev 1:17)
3. Christ is creator of the universe, (Jn 1:3; Heb 1:2),
4. Christ is head of the body, the church,
5. Christ is firstborn from the dead. (Rom. 1:4; Heb 7:16; Jn 1:1, 14; Phil. 2:8)

6. Christ is the fullness of god. Col 1:19 is one of the most powerful descriptions of Christ's deity in NT (cf. Heb 1:8) Jn 1:16; Eph 3:19; Gal. 4:4

7. Christ is the reconciler of all things. Rom 5:10-11;8:19–21; 2 Cor 5:17–20; cf. Eph 2:11–19). (Notes from Geisler, 1985)

Scripture says we are * The apex of God's creation (Gen 1) * Created in the image of God (Gen 1:26-27) * Each of us having the potential of becoming a child of God (Jn 1:12-13) * Created a little lower than the angels (Ps 8:5) * Given a special purpose by God (Gen 1:28) * The objects of God's redemptive purposes in this world (Jn 3:16) * Redeemed people with angels watching over us (Heb 1:14; Ps 91:11-12; Dan 6:22; compare Mt 4:11) * Jesus himself is preparing a place for us in eternity (Jn 14:1-3)

A healthy self image rests on what McDowell calls a three-legged stool - three basic emotional needs common to all persons . . . three pillars around which the input from our childhood is structured and our self-image is developed.

1) The need to feel loved, accepted; to have a sense of belonging
2) The need to feel acceptable; to have a sense of worthiness
3) The need to feel adequate; to have a sense of competence

If one pillar is underdeveloped or damaged, a person's entire self-image is lopsided, unstable and shaky. The stronger the pillars of our self-image, the more they will withstand trauma in later life. (Even the healthiest of adult self-images can be shaken by severe tragedy or trauma, however, forcing a person to lean on someone or something else.) McDowell 100 [In footnote, McDowell says "these concepts are developed in detail by Maurice Wagner, The Sensation of Being Somebody, Grand Rapids, Michigan: Zondervan Publishing, 1975, pp 32-37]

Heb 13:20-21 AMP [20] Now may the God of peace [Who is the Author and the Giver of peace], …[21] Strengthen (complete, perfect) and make you what you ought to be and equip you with everything good that you may carry out His will; [while He Himself] works in you and accomplishes that which is pleasing in His sight, through Jesus Christ (the Messiah); to Whom be the glory forever and ever (to the ages of the ages). Amen (so be it).

When you become a believer, God "installs" all sorts of "equipment" in you. We need to understand that and fully utilize everything he has given us. And we should ask him for whatever we need as we follow him... wisdom, peace, grace, etc. And God also gives me courage and confidence in him, so I can move forward.   Eph 3:16-19

More on pursuing righteousness

Ps 23:3 and 24:3-5; Isa 1:16-17; and Isa 2:5   ... Walk in the light of the LORD

Isa 49:6 and 58:6-12; Jer 6:16 ; Ezek 33 :11; Hos 10:12 ;

Amos 5:14-15, 24

Rom 3:22 AMP ... the righteousness of God which comes by believing with personal trust and confident reliance on Jesus Christ . . .

Rom 6:10-11, 16 and Rom 12:1-2, 11-12; Rom 16:19-20

Rom 13:12-14 ... Cast off the works of darkness and put on the armor of light . . . put on the Lord Jesus Christ

2 Cor 7:1 ; 2 Cor 9:10-12 AMP And [God] Who provides seed for the sower and bread for eating will also provide and multiply your [resources for] sowing and increase the fruits of your righteousness [which manifests itself in active goodness, kindness, and charity]. (Reflecting imagery from Isa 55:10 a 10:12)

Kingdom of God and pursuing righteousness

Heb 12:5-11 AMP ... For the time being no discipline brings joy, but seems grievous and painful; but afterwards it yields a peaceable fruit of righteousness to those who have been trained by it [a harvest of fruit which consists in righteousness – in conformity to God's will in purpose, thought and action, resulting in right living and right standing with God].

Ezek 18:31 [God speaking] ... Get yourselves a new heart and a new spirit . . .

Amos 5:14-15, 24

Micah 6:8   ... What does the LORD require of you but to do justice, and to love kindness, and to walk humbly with your God?

Mal 3:1-3 ... the LORD . . . is like a refiner's fire . . . [to purify us]

Rom 13:12-14 ... Cast off the works of darkness and put on the armor of light . . . put on the Lord Jesus Christ

Rom 16:19-20; Phil 4:12-14 ... I can do all things in him who strengthens me.

1 Pet 2:1-3, 9-10 ESV . . . . You are a chosen race, a royal priesthood, a holy nation, a people for his own possession, that you may proclaim the excellencies of him who called you out of darkness into his marvelous light. . . . (reflecting Ex 19:5-6 and others)

More on this:

Heb 12:13-14, 28; Jas 1:4 and 4:8; Phil 2:14-16 and 4:8;

Col 1:9-14, 21-23; Col 2:6-7 and 3:1-17

1 Thess 2:12; 3:12-13l 5:23-24; 2 Tim 2:21-22; Titus 2:11-14;

Eph 4:13, 15, 22-24 and Eph 5:1-5 Be imitators of God;

1 Pet 1:15-16 (reflecting Lev 11:44-45; 19; 2; 20:26) ; 1 Pet 2:15-16, 24 and 4:17;

2 Pet 1:5-8, 10-11 and 3:11-14 ; 1 Jn 3:1-3 ; Rev 19: 6-8

I am God's partner in his great plans and work, not a passive onlooker. I am a disciple of Jesus.

In Colossians 1: 1-14, Paul lists seven characteristics that mark an alive church and alive followers of Christ even today. This is God's work in us and through us. He generates; we cooperate. And here are the results:

Compelling Faith (Col 1:4a; Rom 10:17); Compassionate Love (Col 1:4b Jas 2:1ff; Jn 13:34f); Confident Hope (Col 1:5); Changed Lives (Col 1:6 ; Mt 23); Committed Believers (Col 1:7, 8); Constant Prayers (Col 1:9–11 AMP); and Continual Appreciation (Col 12–14) and gratitude as a part of our lives (Stone 1995, 51-52).

Of course God should be our priority! A few more verses

Deut 30:1-20; Jer 29:13-14 ESV ... When you seek me with all your heart, I will be found by you . . .

1 Cor 8:3, 6; Heb 3:12 AMP . . . Take care, lest there be in any one of you a wicked, unbelieving heart [which refuses to cleave to, trust in, and rely on Him], leading you to turn away and desert or stand aloof from the living God.

Jas 4:8 Draw near to God and he will draw near to you.

More on this: Deut 4:29; Deut 10:12-22; Deut 11:1, 13-15, 22-23;

Jer 9:25-26   Rom 2:28-29; Phil 3:3; Col 2:11

CHAPTER 7 ADDITIONAL SCRIPTURE REFERENCES

God permits trials and painful circumstances in our lives.

If you want a perfect Bible example of all this, check out the Old Testament hero [but oh so human] King David. "David knew the trials of all classes and conditions of men. Kings have their troubles, and David wore a crown. Peasants have their cares, and

David once held a shepherd's staff. Wanderers have many hardships, and [so do] warriors. (2 Sam 3:39) ... Yet his worst foes were those of his household, for his children were his greatest affliction." Spurgeon 2008 -Morning Aug 20

God can be a great comfort and source of wisdom and peace during our trouble.
2 Samuel 22:26-29 MSG [David's song of deliverance] ... [26-28]You stick by people who stick with you, you're straight with people who're straight with you, ...You take the side of the down-and-out, ... [29] Suddenly, God, your light floods my path, God drives out the darkness.
Ps 34:4 I sought the LORD, and he answered me; he delivered me from all my fears.
Ps 37:23 – 24 If the LORD delights in a man's way, he makes his steps firm; though he stumble, he will not fall, for the LORD upholds him with his hand.
Ps 57:1-3 Have mercy on me, O God, have mercy on me, for in you my soul takes refuge. I will take refuge in the shadow of your wings until the disaster has passed. I cry out to God Most High, to God, who fulfills his purpose for me. ...
Isa 25:4 You have been a refuge for the poor, a refuge for the needy in his distress, a shelter from the storm and a shade from the heat . . .
Isa 41:13 – 14 For I am the LORD, your God, who takes hold of your right hand and says to you, Do not fear; I will help you . . . declares the LORD, your Redeemer, the Holy One of Israel.
Isa 49:13-16 NLT [13] Sing for joy, O heavens! Rejoice, O earth! Burst into song, O mountains! For the Lord has comforted his people and will have compassion on them in their suffering. ... [15] ... Can a mother forget her nursing child? Can she feel no love for the child she has borne? But even if that were possible, I would not forget you! . . .
Jeremiah 31 - God bringing us from mourning into joy — is a favorite of mine. It has some great verses where, over and over, God expresses his desire to bring his people from mourning into joy.
God says, [9]They will come with weeping; they will pray as I bring them back. I will lead them beside streams of water [See Nu 20:8; Ps 1:3; Isa 32:2] on a level path where they will not stumble. . . [13b]I will turn their mourning into joy; I will comfort them, and give them gladness for sorrow. Jer 31: 9, 13b NIV
God says, Keep your voice from weeping and your eyes from tears, for there is a reward for your work, declares the LORD . . . Jer 31:16

God says, [17]There is hope for your future," says the Lord. "Your children will come again to their own land. [18] . . . [Saying] Turn me again to you and restore me, for you alone are the Lord my God. [19]I turned away from God, but then I was sorry. I kicked myself for my stupidity! I was thoroughly ashamed of all I did in my younger days.' Jer 31:17-19

God says [20] "Is not Israel still my son, my darling child?" says the Lord. "I often have to punish him, but I still love him. That's why I long for him and surely will have mercy on him. [21] Set up road signs; put up guideposts. Mark well the path by which you came. [where you made your mistakes] Jer 31:20-21 NLT

ADDITIONAL SCRIPTURE FOR CHAPTER 8

Be strong in the Lord. Ephesians 6:10-18 (with additional references)
[10] Finally, be strong in the Lord and in the strength of his might. [11] Put on the whole armor of God, that you may be able to stand against the schemes of the devil. [12] For we do not wrestle against flesh and blood, but against the rulers, against the authorities, against the cosmic powers over this present darkness, against the spiritual forces of evil in the heavenly places.

[13] Therefore take up the whole armor of God, that you may be able to withstand in the evil day, and having done all, to stand firm. [14] Stand therefore, having fastened on the belt of truth (Isa11:5; Lk 12:35; 1 Pet 1:13); and having put on the breastplate of righteousness (Isa 59:17; Isa 61:10; 1 Thess 5:8; 2 Cor 6:7), [15] and, as shoes for your feet (Ex 12:11; Isa 52:7; Rom. 10:15) having put on the readiness given by the gospel of peace. [16] In all circumstances take up the shield of faith (1 Jn 5:4), with which you can extinguish all the flaming darts of the evil one (Mt 13:19); [17] and take the helmet of salvation, and the sword of the Spirit, which is the word of God (Isa 49:2; Hos 65; 2 Cor 6:7; Heb 4:12;), [18] praying at all times in the Spirit, with all prayer and supplication.

(For more see Lk 22:53; Rom. 4:20; 1 Cor 9:25;
Eph 1:19-21; Eph 2:2; Eph 3:10, 16; Eph 4:14; Eph 5:16;
2 Tim. 2:1; 1 Peter 4:1; Col. 1:13; 1 Jn 2:14).

Jesus says: If your right eye causes you to sin, pluck it out . . . if your right hand causes you to sin, cut it off. . . . It is better that you lose one of your members than that your whole body go into hell. Mt 5:29-30 and again in Mt 18:7-9 Mk 9:43-48

See ourselves with clear eyes – as God sees us.   Col 2:15

COMMON STUMBLING BLOCKS TO A LIFE WITH GOD.

1.   **PRIDE** IS A HUGE OBSTACLE BETWEEN ME AND GOD.
     Proverbs 3:34   Prov 18:12; Isa 5:15-17 and 57:15; Amos 6:8
     Isa 66:2 But this is the one to whom I will look: he who is humble and con-
     trite in spirit and trembles at my word
     Jer 9:23-24 . . . [24] let him who boasts boast in this, that he understands and
     knows me, that I am the Lord who practices steadfast love, justice, and righ-
     teousness in the earth. For in these things I delight, declares the Lord.
     Jesus says– about pride and humility:
     Jesus says: . . . All who exalt themselves will be humbled, and those who
     humble themselves will be exalted. Lk 14:10-11 and 18:14b; Mt 23:11b-12 (re-
     flecting idea in Prov 25:6-7)
     Jesus says: Unless you turn and become like children, you will never enter
     the kingdom of heaven. Whoever humbles himself like this child, he is the
     greatest in the kingdom of heaven. Mt 18:3-4 and again in Mk 10:15 Lk 18:17
     Jesus says: [Repeatedly,] Whoever would be great among you must be your
     servant . . .   For the Son of man also came not to be served but to serve, and
     to give his life as a ransom for many.   Mk 10:43-45 Also in Mk 9:35 Mt 20:26
     and again in Mt 23:1-12 and in Lk 22:26-27
     Jesus says: Blessed . . . are the meek (the mild, patient, long-suffering), for
     they shall inherit the earth! Mt 5:5 AMP (quoting Ps 37:11)
     Jesus says: [on the night before he died] Now that I, your Lord and Teacher,
     have washed your feet, you also should wash one another's feet . . . You should
     do as I have done for you. I tell you the truth, no servant is greater than his
     master, nor is a messenger greater than the one who sent him. Now that you
     know these things, you will be blessed if you do them. Jn 13:14-17 NIV
     Isa 2:5-22 NLT ... let us walk in the light of the LORD!   [6] For the LORD
     has rejected his people ... they have filled their land with practices from the
     East and with sorcerers, as the Philistines do. They have made alliances with
     pagans. [7] Israel is full of silver and gold; there is no end to its treasures. Their
     land is full of warhorses; there is no end to its chariots. [8] Their land is full
     of idols; the people worship things they have made with their own hands. [9]

So now they will be humbled, and all will be brought low— do not forgive them. ...[11] Human pride will be brought down, and human arrogance will be humbled. Only the LORD will be exalted on that day of judgment. ... [20] On that day of judgment they will abandon the gold and silver idols they made for themselves to worship. ... [22] Don't put your trust in mere humans. They are as frail as breath. What good are they?

Prov 16:5,18 KJV . . . Pride goeth before destruction, and a haughty spirit before a fall.

See also Rom 12:3; 1 Cor 4:6-7: Phil 2:3-11; Jas 3:13-18

2. **PLAYING GOD** – Taking the reins when I should let God lead.

3. **MAJORING ON THE MINOR/ LACK OF PROPER FOCUS IS ANOTHER BARRIER THAT CAN CAUSE US TO TAKE OUR EYE OFF THE SPIRITUAL BALL.** Here is just one example (of many): Jesus says to Focus On God Not On Material Things.

Jesus says: Don't worry about everyday life . . . Your heavenly Father already knows all your needs, and he will give you all you need from day to day if you live for him and make the Kingdom of God your primary concern. Mt 6:25-33 NLT Lk 12:22-31

Jesus says: Do not work for the food which perishes, but for the food which endures to eternal life, which the Son of Man will give to you, for on Him the Father, God, has set His seal. Jn 6:27 NASB (builds on Isa 55:1-3)

Jesus says: You cannot serve God and mammon (deceitful riches, money, possessions, or whatever is trusted in) Mt 6:24b AMP Lk 16:13

Jesus says: . . . Give to Caesar the things that are Caesar's, and . . . to God, the things that are God's. Mt 22:21 NCV Mk 12:17

Other Scriptures focus on the error of focusing on material possessions include Eccl 1:14 and 6:7. And the bottom line?

Fear God [revere and worship Him, knowing that He is] . . . and Keep His commandments, For this is the whole of man [the full, original purpose of his creation, the object of God's providence, the root of character, the foundation of all happiness, the adjustment to all inharmonious circumstances and conditions under the sun] and the whole [duty] for every man. Eccl 12:13 AMP; Prov 11:24-25; Isa 55:1-3; Heb 13:5-6;

The love of money is root of all evils 1 Tim 6:6-19; ; Jas 4:1-8; 1 Jn 2:15-17

4. **OVER-RELIANCE ON FEELINGS INSTEAD OF FACTS/ GOD'S TRUTH CAN SIDE-TRACK OUR WALK WITH GOD AND CAUSE LOTS OF PROBLEMS.**
Fear is a feeling. Trust is a choice.
Ps 56:3 When I am afraid, I will trust in you. God knows that sometimes fear and trust share the same heartbeat. This verse is definitive: My will can change my condition…My choice to trust God will inevitably change my feelings of fear. [Rothschild, 23]
"God has not given us a spirit of fear" (2 Tim 1:7).
It is God's power in us – not our own – that gives us the ability to triumph over fear. The Bible also says "perfect love drives out fear" (1 Jn 4:18). Choosing to trust God gives us the resources we need to cast out fear. [Rothschild, 23]

5. **LACK OF RESTRAINT AND SELF-DISCIPLINE (TWIN SISTERS) - ANOTHER OBSTACLE TO LIVING GOD'S WAY IS A.** We'll work with one example – watching your mouth
Jesus says: It is not that which comes into a man's mouth that causes trouble, but what comes out of it. Mt 15:11 WMF   Mk 7:15
Jesus says: A good person produces good words from a good heart, and an evil person produces evil words from an evil heart. Mt 12:35 NLT   Lk 6:45
Jesus says: I promise you that on the day of judgment, everyone will have to account for every careless word they have spoken. On that day they will be told that they are either innocent or guilty because of the things they have said. Mt 12:36-37 CEV

More scripture examples: Prov 10:18-20, 31-32; Prov 12:18-22; Prov 15:1, 2, 4, 28;
Prov 16:21-32; Prov 17:20, 27-28; Prov 18:4, 6-8, 21; Ps 34:12-14; Jer 9: 3, 5, 8; Jer 15:19 ; Gal 5:14 15; Eph 4:29-32

6. **A JUDGMENTAL AND CRITICAL SPIRIT CAN BE AN OBSTACLE TO CHRIST-LIKE LIVING.** God is quite clear about how much judging, criticizing and condemning he wants us to do!
Jesus says: The Father . . . has granted the Son . . . authority to execute judgment, because he is the Son of man. . . . I can do nothing on my own authority; as I hear, I judge; and my judgment is just, because I seek not my own will but the will of him who sent me. Jn 5:26-32

Jesus says: Do not judge according to appearance, but judge with righteous judgment. Jn 7:24 NKJV (reflecting Isa 11:3-4)

God's word tells us that God will judge his people. Never avenge yourself. Leave it to God who says, 'Vengeance is mine.' Here are a few examples:
Deut 32:35-36; Ps 50:4-6; Ps 75:7; Prov 24:29 NIV; Ex 23:6-8 ; Lev 19:15-18; Deut 32:35; 2 Chron 19:5-7; Ps 82:2-4: Prov16:10-11; 24:29; Isa 56:1: Ezek 33:11-16; Zech 7:9-10 and 8:16-17
Jas 4:11-12 NLT . . . [12] God alone . . . has the power to save or to destroy. So what right do you have to judge your neighbor? Rom 12:17-19; Rom 14:4, 10-13 NIV
. . . Why do you judge your brother? Or why do you look down on your brother? For we will all stand before God's judgment seat .
1 Cor 2:15-16; 5:12-13 through 6:3; 1 Cor 11:32; Heb 10:30

JUDGING, CRITICIZING AND CONDEMNING OFTEN PARTNER WITH THEIR BUDDIES HYPOCRISY AND SELF-RIGHTEOUSNESS!

Jesus says: When you do good deeds, don't try to show off. If you do, you won't get a reward from your Father in heaven. Mt 6:1 CEV and again in Mt 23:5

Jesus says: When you pray, go into your inner room, close your door and pray to your Father who is in secret, and your Father who sees what is done in secret will reward you. Mt 6:6 NASB

Jesus says: [regarding the religious authorities whom he called hypocrites] . . . You can't keep your true self hidden forever; before long you'll be exposed. You can't hide behind a religious mask forever; sooner or later the mask will slip and your true face will be known. Lk 12:1-2 MSG

Jesus says: Judge not, that you be not judged. For with the judgment you pronounce you will be judged, and with the measure you use it will be measured to you . . . Mt 7:1-5

Jesus says: You hypocrites, rightly did Isaiah prophesy of you: 'This people honors Me with their lips, but their heart is far away from Me; But in vain do they worship Me, teaching as doctrines the precepts of men.' Mt 15:7-9 NASB (quoting Isa 29:13)

Jesus says: The teachers of the law and the Pharisees have the authority to tell you what the law of Moses says. So you should obey and follow whatever they tell you, but their lives are not good examples for you to follow. They tell you to do things, but they themselves don't do them. Mt 23:2- NCV

Jesus says: Make sure that the light you think you have is not really darkness. If you are filled with light, with no dark corners, then your whole life will be radiant, as though a floodlight is shining on you. Lk 11:35-36 NLT   Mt 6:23

Jesus says: [A warning for the Pharisees and for us] You are careful to tithe even the tiniest part of your income, but you completely forget about justice and the love of God. You should tithe, yes, but you should not leave undone the more important things.   Lk 11:42 NLT   Mt 23:23-24   [Thus tying together the need for tithing from Genesis 14:20 and 28:22, Lev 27:30-32; Mal 3:8-10 – and – the need for justice and love from Amos 5:24; Mic 6:8 and many others.]

Other scripture references share Jesus' impatience with hypocrisy
And there are many warnings against sacrificing, praying and fasting as external exercises instead of a turning of the heart toward God. Here are just a few examples.

1 Sam 15:22 and 16:7; Ps 50:7-23 ; Ps 51:15-19; Ps 147:10-11;

Isa 1:11-17, 58; Jer 2:8: 7:22-23; and 11:15;

Ezek 22:26 to 26:6 (echoed in Mt 9:13 and 12:7)

Amos 5:21-24 and 6:4-8, 12b; Zech 7:5-10; Mal (all)

Rom 2:3 NRSV   Do you imagine, whoever you are, that when you judge those who do such things and yet do them yourself, you will escape the judgment of God?

1 Jn 1:5-10 ESV . . . If we say we have fellowship with him while we walk in darkness, we lie and do not practice the truth . . .

1 Jn 2:4-6; 3:10; 2 Jn 9 and 3 Jn 11

ADDITIONAL SCRIPTURE FOR CHAPTER 9

JESUS IS THE LIGHT OF THE WORLD. AND WITH HIS HELP, I AM SUPPOSED TO BE A LIGHT TOO.

Jesus says: I am the light of the world. Whoever follows me will never walk in darkness, but will have the light of life. . . Jn 8:12 NIV

Jesus says: While I am in the world, I am the light of the world. Jn 9:5 NASB

Jesus says: I have come as a light to shine in this dark world, so that all who put their trust in me will no longer remain in the darkness. Jn 12:46 NLT

Jesus says: YOU are the light of the world . . . Let your light so shine before men, that they may see your good works and give glory to your Father who is in heaven.
Mt 5:14, 16 (using the imagery of Isa 60:1-3)

Jesus says: Put your trust in the light while you have it, so that you may become sons of light. Jn 12:36

Jesus says: Make sure that the light you think you have is not really darkness. If you are filled with light, with no dark corners, then your whole life will be radiant, as though a floodlight is shining on you. Lk 11:35-36 NLT Mt 6:22-23

Jesus says: [in a vision speaking to Saul on the road to Damascus] I am sending you to the Gentiles [18] to open their eyes, so they may turn from darkness to light and from the power of Satan to God. Then they will receive forgiveness for their sins and be given a place among God's people, who are set apart by faith in me. Acts 16:18

For more references on God's light, see:
Ps 82:3-5; Isa 2:5 Walk in the light of the LORD.
Isa 49:6 . . . a light to the nations . . . ; Isa 60:1-3 and 19-20; Zech 7:9-10
Gal 5:6 . . . faith working through love;
Phil 2:14-16 NIV . . . Shine like stars in the universe . . . hold out the word of life . . .
Jas 1:22 ESV, RSV Be doers of the word, and not hearers only, deceiving yourselves
Jas 2:14-26 . . . Faith by itself, if it has no works, is dead

A CLEAR CHOICE: SPIRITUAL LIFE OR DEATH
We must continually remind ourselves of the purpose of life. We are not destined to happiness, nor to health, but to holiness . . . The only thing that truly matters is whether a person will accept the God who will make him holy - and have the right relationship with him. [Chambers Sept 1]

Life is hard. We all face problems, pain, death. All of creation groans to be set free from its bondage to corruption. Rom 8:21-22

GOD'S DESIRES THAT WE REPENT.
The Bible is full of God's desire that we repent, change our ways, and turn back to him. And day by day, I am learning what Jesus wants me to do and how to follow.
Rom 16:26 I confess - admit my mistakes. And I repent. And I move on with him!
Ps 32:1-5 [1] Blessed is the one whose transgression is forgiven, whose sin is covered. . . .
I said, "I will confess my transgressions to the Lord," and you forgave

Ps 51:1-6 [1] Have mercy on me, O God, according to your steadfast love; according to your abundant mercy blot out my transgressions. [2] Wash me thoroughly from my iniquity, and cleanse me from my sin! [3] For I know my transgressions, and my sin is ever before me. [4] Against you, you only, have I sinned and done what is evil in your sight, so that you may be justified in your words and blameless in your judgment ... [6] Behold, you delight in truth in the inward being, and you teach me wisdom in the secret heart

Prov 28:13 Whoever conceals his transgressions will not prosper, but he who confesses and forsakes them will obtain mercy.

Ezek 33:10-11, 18-19 NLT The Watchman's (Ezekiel's) Message

Rom 12:2 Do not be conformed to this world, but be transformed by the renewal of your mind, that by testing you may discern what is the will of God, what is good and acceptable and perfect.

1 Jn 1:7-10 [7] But if we walk in the light, as he is in the light, we have fellowship with one another, and the blood of Jesus his Son cleanses us from all sin. [8] If we say we have no sin, we deceive ourselves, and the truth is not in us. [9] If we confess our sins, he is faithful and just to forgive us our sins and to cleanse us from all unrighteousness. [10] If we say we have not sinned, we make him a liar, and his word is not in us.

THE RIGHT PATH IS TOWARD LIGHT NOT DARK, LIFE NOT DEATH

Ps 23:3 He leads me in paths of righteousness for his name's sake.

Ps 24:3-4 The Lord blesses those with clean hands and a pure heart.

Ps 51:10 Create in me a clean heart, O God . . . put a new and right spirit within me.

Isa 1:16-17 Make yourselves clean, cease to do evil, learn to do good, seek justice, correct oppression, defend the fatherless, plead for the widow.

Isa 2:5 Walk in the light of the Lord ; Is 49:6 I will give you as a light to the nations.

Isa 58:8, 10 Light and righteousness; Jer 6:16 Walk in the good way and find rest for your souls.; Hos 10:12

Amos 5:14 Seek good, and not evil, that you may live; and so the LORD, the God of hosts, will be with you, as you have said.

Mt 12:36; 2 Cor 7:1 On the day of judgment . . .

Rom 13:12-14 Cast off the works of darkness and put on the armor of light

Eph 4:17-24 ... [20] ... the truth is in Jesus, [22] to put off your old self, which belongs to your former manner of life and is corrupt through deceitful desires, [23] and to be renewed in the spirit of your minds, ²⁴ and to put on the new self, created after the likeness of God in true righteousness and holiness

Phil 2:14-18 NLT ¹⁴ Do everything without complaining and arguing, ¹⁵ so that no one can criticize you. Live clean, innocent lives as children of God, shining like bright lights in a world full of crooked and perverse people. ¹⁶ Hold firmly to the word of life; then, on the day of Christ's return, I will be proud that I did not run the race in vain and that my work was not useless. ¹⁷ But I will rejoice even if I lose my life, pouring it out like a liquid offering to God, just like your faithful service is an offering to God. And I want all of you to share that joy . . .

Heb 12:13-14

Jas 1:4 -8 ⁴ And let steadfastness have its full effect, that you may be perfect and complete, lacking in nothing. ⁵ If any of you lacks wisdom, let him ask God, who gives generously to all without reproach, and it will be given him. ⁶ But let him ask in faith, with no doubting, for the one who doubts is like a wave of the sea that is driven and tossed by the wind. ⁷ For that person must not suppose that he will receive anything from the Lord; ⁸ he is a double-minded man, unstable in all his ways.

1 Pet 1:15-16 'Be holy, for I am holy'. (reflects Lev 11:44); 2 Pet 3:11, 14

1 Jn 2:7-11 . ⁸ ... the darkness is passing away and the true light is already shining. ⁹ Whoever says he is in the light and hates his brother is still in darkness. ¹⁰ Whoever loves his brother abides in the light, and in him there is no cause for stumbling. ¹¹ But whoever hates his brother is in the darkness and walks in the darkness...

I AM BLESSED TO BE A BLESSING.

Ps 39:4-8; Prov 27:1; Jas 4:13

Isa 42:1, 6-7 Here is my servant . . . my chosen one in whom I delight; I will put my Spirit on him and he will bring justice to the nations. . . . I, the Lord, have called you in righteousness . . . I will . . . make you to be a covenant for the people and a light for the Gentiles, to open eyes that are blind, to free captives from prison and to release from the dungeon those who sit in darkness.

GOD IS MY FOUNDATION, MY REASON FOR COURAGE AS I FOLLOW HIS PATH.

He says: I will you. You are never alone. Do not be afraid. Do not worry. This is one of the grand themes throughout scripture! Mt 10 is great for this (as is the book of Psalms). But the encouragement is elsewhere as well.

Here's what Jesus had to say about worrying

Jesus says: Do not be anxious about tomorrow. Mt 6:34

Jesus says: Why are you afraid, O men of little faith? . . . Mt 8:26

Jesus says: Do not worry about what to say or how to say it. At that time you will be given what to say, for it will not be you speaking, but the Spirit of your Father speaking through you. Mt 10:19-20 NIV and in Lk 12:11-12 and in Mk 13:11-12; Lk 21:14-15 (reflects Ex 4:10-12, 15-16; Jer 1:6-9)

Jesus says: Do not be anxious about your life. Mt 6:25, 31

Jesus says: Don't be afraid of those who want to kill you. They can only kill your body; they cannot touch your soul. Fear only God, who can destroy both soul and body in hell. Mt 10:28 NLT Lk 12:4

Jesus says: Don't be afraid of those who threaten you. For the time is coming when everything will be revealed; all that is secret will be made public. What I tell you now in the darkness, shout abroad when daybreak comes. What I whisper in your ears, shout from the housetops for all to hear. Mt 10:26-27 NLT; Lk 12:2-3 and also in Mk 4:21-22 ; Lk 8:16-17

Jesus says: Don't be afraid of those who want to kill you. They can only kill your body; they cannot touch your soul. Fear only God, who can destroy both soul and body in hell. Mt 10:28 NLT Lk 12:4-5

Jesus says: Come to Me, all you who are weary and are heavy laden, and I will give you rest. Take My yoke upon you and learn from Me, for I am gentle and humble in heart, and you will find rest for your souls. For My yoke is easy and My burden is light. Mt 11:28-30 NASB

Jesus says: Blessed are the poor in spirit, for theirs is the kingdom of heaven. Mt 5:3

Jesus says: Blessed are those who mourn, for they shall be comforted. Mt 5:4 NKJV

ADDITIONAL SCRIPTURE FOR CHAPTER 10

GOD CALLS AND EQUIPS ME TO LOVE OTHERS, AS JESUS LOVES US.

This love of God's – and our love for him - is central to the many "fruits of the spirit" (Galatians 5:22-23) that result from a life spent following God.

Jesus says: I give you a new commandment: . . . Just as I have loved you, so you too should love one another. By this shall all [men] know that you are my disciples, if you love one another . . . Jn 13:34-35 AMP (expanding Lev 19:18) [Then he repeated his words later in the same evening, during his last meal with the disciples before he was crucified]

Prov 10:12 Hatred stirs up strife, but love covers all transgressions.

Rom 12:9-10 AMP [9] [Let your] love be sincere (a real thing); hate what is evil [loathe all ungodliness, turn in horror from wickedness], but hold fast to that which is good. [10] Love one another with brotherly affection [as members of one family], giving precedence and showing honor to one another.

Rom 13:8-10 . . . Love does no wrong to a neighbor; therefore love is the fulfilling of the law.

1 Cor 16:14 NIV Do everything in love;

Gal 5:22-23 NLT describes the FRUIT OF THE SPIRIT: But when the Holy Spirit controls our lives, he will produce this kind of fruit in us: love, joy, peace, patience, kindness, goodness, faithfulness, gentleness, and self-control.

Col 2:2-3 NIV My purpose is that they may be encouraged in heart and united in love, so that they may have the full riches of complete understanding, in order that they may know the mystery of God, namely, Christ, in whom are hidden all the treasures of wisdom and knowledge.

1 Thess 3:12-13 ESV May the Lord make you increase and abound in love to one another and to all men, as we do to you, so that he may establish your hearts blameless in holiness before our God and Father, at the coming of our Lord Jesus with all the saints. 1 Thess 4:9 and 5:8

1 Pet 4:8 Above all hold unfailing your love for one another, since love covers a multitude of sins

Jas 2:8 NIV If you really keep the royal law found in Scripture, "Love your neighbor as yourself," (Lev 19:18) you are doing right.

Jas 2:20-26 CEV Anyone who doesn't breathe is dead, and faith that doesn't do anything is just as dead.

1 Jn 2:8-11 ESV . . . the darkness is passing away and the true light is already shining. Whoever says he is in the light and hates his brother is still in darkness 1 Jn 3:11-18, 23-24 ; 1 Jn 4:7-10

1 Jn 3:16 NIV This is how we know what love is: Jesus Christ laid down his life for us. And we ought to lay down our lives for our brothers

More scripture on this: 1 Tim 1:5; Jas 2:8; Heb 10:24 and 13:1;
1 Pet 1:22-23; 3:8-9Lev 19:18, 34; Deut 10:19; Rom 12:10; 1 Cor 8:1;

1 Jn 4:13-21; 5:1-3; 1 Cor 13; Gal 5:6 NIV; Gal 5:13-15; Eph 4:2, 15-16;
Eph 5:1-2 Walk in love, as Christ loved us; Phil 1:9 and 2:1-4

I AGREE WITH JESUS - It is my job to do good, give, and tend his sheep.
This involves caring for the poor, the needy, widows, orphans, the blind, prisoners, and
strangers

Jesus says: Turn both your pockets and your hearts inside out and give generously to the
poor; then your lives will be clean, not just your dishes and your hands. Lk 11:41 MSG
Jesus says: When you give a feast, invite the poor, the maimed, the lame, the blind, and
you will be blessed, because they cannot repay you. You will be repaid at the resurrection of the just. Lk 14:13-14
Jesus says: Whoever receives this child in my name receives me, and whoever receives
me receives him who sent me. Lk 9:48 Mt 18:5 Mk 9:37 See also Jn 13:20 Mt 10:40
Jesus says: He who believes in me will also do the works that I do; and greater works
than these will he do, because I go to the Father. Jn 14:12
Jesus says: Take care! Don't do your good deeds publicly, to be admired . . . Give your
gifts in secret, and your Father, who knows all secrets, will reward you. Mt 6:1-4 NLT

Acts 20:35 ... more blessed to give than to receive
1 Jn 3:17-18 . . . Let us not love in word or speech but in deed and in truth.
Ex 22:21-24; Deut 15:10-11; Ps 82:3-4 ; 146:5-9; Prov 11; 17:5a; 19:17;
Eccl 11:1; Isa 1:16-17 and 58:6-10; Amos 6:4-8; 8:4-14; Zech 7:9-10;
Rom 12:1 ; 1Tim 6:17-19; Heb 13:1-3, 16 ; Jas 1:27 and 2:14-19; Jas 5:1-6;
1 Pet 5:2+ ; 2 Cor 9:10-12 AMP (Reflecting imagery from Isa 55:10 and Hos 10:12)

BE AT PEACE WITH EACH OTHER
Jesus says: These things I have spoken to you, that in me you may have peace. In the
world you will have tribulation; but be of good cheer; I have overcome the world. Jn
16:33 NKJV
Prov 16:28, 32 he who is slow to anger is better than the mighty . . .
Isa 60:17-18 …. I will make your overseers peace and your taskmasters righteousness
Rom 12:16-18 so far as it depends upon you, live peaceably with all.
Jas 3:13-18 [13] Who is wise and understanding among you? By his good conduct let him
show his works in the meekness of wisdom. [14] But if you have bitter jealousy and selfish

ambition in your hearts, do not boast and be false to the truth. [15]This is not the wisdom that comes down from above, but is earthly, unspiritual, demonic. . . . [17]But the wisdom from above is first pure, then peaceable, gentle, open to reason, full of mercy and good fruits, impartial and sincere. [18]And a harvest of righteousness is sown in peace by those who make peace.

More scripture on this: Lev 19:17-18; Ps 34:14; Ps 133:1; Prov 3:29-30 and 6:16-19; 1 Thess 5:13b; 1 Tim 2:8; 2 Tim 2:22-26; Heb 12:14-15; Rom 15:5-6; 1 Cor 1:10 and 3:3; Eph 4:1-6, 25-27; 1 Jn 4:20-21

LOVE YOUR ENEMIES:
Jesus says: If someone strikes you on one cheek, turn to him the other also. If someone takes your cloak, do not stop him from taking your tunic. Lk 6:29 NIV; Mt 5:38-42 (expanding Lam 3:30)
Jesus says: I tell you, love your enemies. Help and give without expecting a return. You'll never – I promise – regret it. Live out this God-created identity the way our Father lives toward us, generously and graciously, even when we're at our worst. Our Father is kind; you be kind. Lk 6:35-36 MSG
More scripture on this: Prov 24:17-20, 29; Rom 12:14, 17-18, and 19-20 (expands Prov 25:21-22)

TREAT OTHERS THE WAY YOU WANT TO BE TREATED. DO GOOD. DO NOT JUDGE OR CONDEMN. GIVE.
Jesus says – about our treatment of others:
Jesus says: Do good . . . expecting nothing in return . . . Lk 6:35
Jesus says: Do not judge, and you will not be judged ,,, Do not condemn, and you will not be condemned Lk 6:37. Forgive, and you will be forgiven; Lk 6:37 NRSV Mt 7:1-5
Jesus says: [Dedicate your inner self and] give as donations to the poor of those things which are within [of inward righteousness] and behold, everything is purified and clean for you. Lk 11:41 AMP
Zech 7:9-14 [9]"Thus says the Lord of hosts, Render true judgments, show kindness and mercy to one another, [10]do not oppress the widow, the fatherless, the sojourner, or the poor, and let none of you devise evil against another in your heart." . . .
More scripture on this: Prov 11:24-25; Rom 2:1-3; 12:14-17; 15:1, 5-6

SHOW MERCY.

Jesus says: Be merciful, even as your Father is merciful. Lk 6:36

Jesus says: Blessed are the merciful, for they shall receive mercy. Mt 5:7

Jesus says: Go and learn what this means, 'I desire mercy and not sacrifice.' For I came not to call the righteous, but sinners. Mt 9:13   and later in Mt 12:7 (Here, he is building on Hos 6:6 where God says, 'I desire steadfast love and not sacrifice.')

Deut 4:25-31 The LORD your God is a merciful God; Jer 3:12; Hos11:7-9

Joel 2:13, 25 gracious and merciful . . . I will restore to you the years which the swarming locust have eaten . . . ; 1 Tim 1:15-16

FORGIVE AND DON'T TAKE OFFENSE (or get else ready to meet "Taking Offense", the ugly little sister of unforgiveness.)

Jesus says: I am warning you! If another believer sins, rebuke him, then if he repents, forgive him. Even if he wrongs you seven times a day and each time turns again and asks forgiveness, forgive him. Lk 17:3-4 NLT Mt 18:21-22

Jesus says: [telling a story about a man who refused to forgive a debt, even though his own debt had been forgiven by the king]   ... Mt 18:32-35 MSG

Jesus says: Her many sins are forgiven, so she showed great love. But the person who is forgiven only a little will love only a little. Lk 7:47 NCV

1 Jn 1:9 -10 NASB If we confess our sins, He is faithful and righteous to forgive us our sins and To cleanse us from all unrighteousness ...

More scripture on this: Isa 43:24b-25; Eph 4:31-32; 2 Cor 2:5+

ADDITIONAL SCRIPTURE FOR CHAPTER 11

All believers are called to share the truth of God – in love – by telling
others about God, and then helping make
disciples. Lk 12:8-9 Mt 10:32-33

Jesus says: [When you go out to preach the gospel] The one who listens to you listens to Me, and the one who rejects you rejects Me; and he who rejects Me rejects the One who sent Me. Lk 10:16 NASB   Mt 10:40 Jn 13:20

Jesus says: [in his first words of public ministry] . . . The kingdom of God is at hand; repent, and believe in the gospel. Mk 1:15   Mt 4:17   (affirming John the Baptist's earlier statements in Mt 3:2)   [and then he sent us out]

Then, in Luke 8, Jesus tells a parable about sowing seeds – sharing the gospel, the word of God. And he warns that some ground is hard or hostile and cannot receive what we have to give.

GOD'S CALL - Related Scripture

Rom 1:5-6 NIV [5] Through him we received grace and apostleship to call all the Gentiles to the obedience that comes from faith for his name's sake. [6] And you also are among those Gentiles who are called to belong to Jesus Christ.

1 Cor 1:26-30 NLT [26] Remember, dear brothers and sisters, that few of you were wise in the world's eyes or powerful or wealthy when God called you. [27] Instead, God chose things the world considers foolish in order to shame those who think they are wise. And he chose things that are powerless to shame those who are powerful. [28] God chose things despised by the world, things counted as nothing at all, and used them to bring to nothing what the world considers important. [29] As a result, no one can ever boast in the presence of God. [30] God has united you with Christ Jesus. For our benefit God made him to be wisdom itself. Christ made us right with God; he made us pure and holy, and he freed us from sin.

1 Cor 7:22 ESV [22] For he who was called in the Lord as a bondservant is a freedman of the Lord. Likewise he who was free when called is a bondservant of Christ. [23] You were bought with a price; do not become bondservants of men. [24] So, brothers, in whatever condition each was called, there let him remain with God.

Gal 5:13 ESV [13] For you were called to freedom, brothers. Only do not use your freedom as an opportunity for the flesh, but through love serve one another [1 Cor 9:19].

Eph 4:1-6 NLT Therefore I, a prisoner for serving the Lord, beg you to lead a life worthy of your calling, for you have been called by God. [2] Always be humble and gentle. Be patient with each other, making allowance for each other's faults because of your love. [3] Make every effort to keep yourselves united in the Spirit, binding yourselves together with peace. [4] For there is one body and one Spirit, just as you have been called to one glorious hope for the future. [5] There is one Lord, one faith, one baptism, [6] one God and Father of all, who is over all, in all, and living through all.

Col 3:15-17 ESV [15]And let the peace of Christ [see Phil 4:7] rule in your hearts, to which indeed you were called in one body [see Eph 2:16]. And be thankful. [16]Let the word of Christ [John 15:3] dwell in you richly, teaching and admonishing one another in all wisdom, singing psalms and hymns and spiritual songs, with thankfulness in your hearts to God. [17]And whatever you do, in word or deed, do everything in the name of the Lord Jesus, giving thanks to God the Father through him. [see Col 1:12; 4:2 and Eph. 5:20]

GO AND PROCLAIM THE KINGDOM OF GOD

Lk 9:60 [like Jesus - Lk 4:42-43]

Jesus says: The gospel must first be preached to all nations. Mk 13:10

Jesus says: When you go out to preach the gospel] The one who listens to you listens to Me, and the one who rejects you rejects Me; and he who rejects Me rejects the One who sent Me. Lk 10:16 NASB; Mt 10:40; Jn 13:20.

Then, in Luke 8, **Jesus tells a parable** about sowing seeds – sharing the gospel, the word of God. And he warns that some ground is hard or hostile and cannot receive what we have to give.

But don't be fearful when you do acknowledge Jesus.

Jesus says: Blessed are you when people insult you, persecute you and falsely say all kinds of evil against you because of me. Rejoice and be glad, because great is your reward in heaven, for in the same way they persecuted the prophets who were before you. Mt 5:11-12 NIV

Jesus says: Have no fear of them; for nothing is covered that will not be revealed, or hidden that will not be known. What I tell you in the dark, utter in the light; and what you hear whispered, proclaim upon the house tops. Mt 10:26-27 Lk 12:2-3 and also in Mk 4:21-22 Lk 8:16-17

Jesus says: Don't be afraid of those who want to kill you. They can only kill your body; they cannot touch your soul. Fear only God, who can destroy both soul and body in hell.   Mt 10:28 NLT; Lk 12:4-5

Jesus says: They will lay their hands on you and persecute you. . . This will be a time for you to bear testimony . . . I will give you a mouth and wisdom, which none of your adversaries will be able to withstand or contradict . . . By your endurance, you will gain your lives. Lk 21:12-19 (Again reflecting Ex 4:10-17)

More scripture on this: Ezek 2:3-7; Ezek 3:10-11, 17-21 and 33:7-11; Joel 2:32 (reflected later in Acts 2:21 and Rom 10:13)

SO, FIRST is telling people about God. NEXT is to disciple and teach new believers and encourage and strengthen other Christians.
2 Tim 2:1-2 and 3:14-17; Titus 2; Jas 5:20; Jude 20 - 23
2 Tim 2:23-26 NLT . . . Don't get involved in foolish, ignorant arguments that only start fights. ... be kind to everyone. ...teach effectively and be patient with difficult people. ... gently teach those who oppose the truth. Perhaps God will change those people's hearts, and they will believe the truth. Then they will come to their senses and escape from the Devil's trap. For they have been held captive by him to do whatever he wants.

Some scriptural basis for supporting missionaries who spread the gospel
Jesus remarks when he sent out the 12 - Mt 10:10 ; Mk 6:8-11 Lk 9:3-5
Jesus remarks when he sent 70 others, 2 by 2   Lk 10:7-8
Paul's reference to these, when he said "the Lord commanded that those who proclaim the gospel should be supported" 1 Cor 9:14 and 1 Tim 5:18; Deut 29:29; Isa 66:18-21; Jer 1:17-19
God said: I will give you as a light to the nations, that my salvation may reach to the end of the earth. Isa 49:6

MAKE DISCIPLES, BAPTIZE, AND TEACH
Mt 28:18-20   Mt 5:19b
Mt 28:18-20, NIV – with some additional cross references:
More references for verse 18 [ch 11:27; Dan 7:13, 14; Jn 3:35; 13:3; 17:2; Acts 2:36; Rom 14:9; 1 Cor 15:27; Eph 1:10, 20–22; Phil 2:9, 10; Col 2:10; Heb 1:2; 2:8; 1 Pet 3:22; [ch 9:6; Jn 5:27] ch 6:10; Lk 2:14]
More references for verse 19 [Mk 16:15, 16] [ch 13:52] [Lk 24:47; [ch 24:14; Mk 11:17; Rom 1:5] [2 Cor 13:14]]
More references for verse 20 [Jn 14:15; Acts 1:2] [ch 1:23; 18:20; Jn 12:26; 14:3; 17:24; Acts 18:10] [chap 13:39]

More references to telling people about God and proclaiming the Kingdom: Acts 2:21; 4:29-30; Acts 18:9-10; Rom 15:18-21; 2 Tim 2:11-13; 1 Cor 9:16-18 Woe to me if I do not preach the gospel.

Jas 5:19-20; Heb 12:18- 29 . . . [28] Therefore let us be grateful for receiving a kingdom that cannot be shaken, and thus let us offer to God acceptable worship, with reverence and awe, [29] for our God is a consuming fire.

ADDITIONAL SCRIPTURE FOR CHAPTER 12

THERE IS A INEXPRESSIBLE JOY OF THE LORD THAT COMES FROM MY LOVE AND MY OBEDIENCE AND MY COVENANT RELATIONSHIP WITH GOD THROUGH CHRIST:

1 Pet 1:3-9 [3] Blessed be the God and Father of our Lord Jesus Christ! According to his great mercy, he has caused us to be born again to a living hope[G1680] through the resurrection of Jesus Christ from the dead, [4] to an inheritance that is imperishable, undefiled, and unfading, kept in heaven for you, [5] who by God's power are being guarded through faith for a salvation ready to be revealed in the last time. [6] In this you rejoice, though now for a little while, if necessary, you have been grieved by various trials, [7] so that the tested genuineness of your faith—more precious than gold that perishes though it is tested by fire—may be found to result in praise and glory and honor at the revelation of Jesus Christ. [8] Though you have not seen him, you love him. Though you do not now see him, you believe in him and rejoice with joy[G5479] that is inexpressible[G412] and filled with glory, [9] obtaining the outcome of your faith, the salvation of your souls.

FOLLOW GOD – OR CHOOSE NOT TO. EITHER WAY THERE ARE CONSEQUENCES.

Jesus says: [27] For the Son of Man is going to come with his angels in the glory of his Father, and then he will repay each person according to what he has done. Mt 16:27

Jesus says: [speaking of the centurion's faith] I've yet to come across this kind of simple trust in Israel, the very people who are supposed to know all about God and how he works. This man is the vanguard of many outsiders who will soon be coming from all directions - streaming in from the east, pouring in from the west, sitting down at God's kingdom banquet alongside Abraham, Isaac, and Jacob. Then those who grew up 'in the faith' but had no faith will find themselves out in the cold, outsiders to grace and wondering what happened. Mt 8:10-12 MSG

Jesus says: . . . There is no one who has left house or wife or brothers or parents or children, for the sake of the kingdom of God, who will not receive many times more in this time, and in the age to come eternal life. Lk 18:29 ESV Mk 10:29-30

Jesus says: 35 The good person out of his good treasure brings forth good, and the evil person out of his evil treasure brings forth evil. 36 I tell you, on the day of judgment people will give account for every careless word they speak, 37 for by your words you will be justified, and by your words you will be condemned. Mt 12:35-37

Jesus says: 23Whoever does not honor the Son does not honor the Father who sent him. 24 Truly, truly, I say to you, whoever hears my word and believes him who sent me has eternal life. He does not come into judgment, but has passed from death to life. Jn 5:23-24

The parables Jesus told show that faithfulness and obedience mean everything .

* the parables of the kingdom of God in Mt 13:24-30, 37-43
* the parable of servants doing their master's will in Lk 12:35- 48
* the parable of the fig tree . . . If it bears fruit, well and good; but if not, you can cut it down Lk 13:6-9 NRSV

[Jesus speaking in John's vision addresses the various churches and their strengths and weaknesses, in the book of Revelation]

Jesus says: Be faithful unto death, and I will give you the crown of life. Rev 2:10

Jesus says: 'I know your works. You have the reputation of being alive, but you are dead. 2 Wake up, and strengthen what remains and is about to die, for I have not found your works complete in the sight of my God. . . . If you will not wake up, I will come like a thief, and you will not know at what hour I will come against you. Rev 3:1-3 [echoing some of the imagery in Mt 24:43-44]

Jesus says: . . . 8 " 'I know your works. Behold, I have set before you an open door, which no one is able to shut. I know that you have but little power, and yet you have

kept my word and have not denied my name. ⁹Behold, I will make those of the syna-
gogue of Satan who say that they are Jews and are not, but lie—behold, I will make
them come and bow down before your feet, and they will learn that I have loved
you. ... Rev 3:7-13

Jesus says: . . . ¹⁵ " 'I know your works: you are neither cold nor hot. ...
you are lukewarm, and ... I will spit you out of my mouth . . . ¹⁹Those whom I love,
I reprove and discipline, so be zealous and repent. ²⁰Behold, I stand at the door and
knock. If anyone hears my voice and opens the door, I will come in to him and eat with
him, and he with me. ... Rev 3:14-22

Jesus says:. . . ¹⁵ "Therefore they are before the throne of God, and serve him day and
night in his temple; and he who sits on the throne will shelter them with his presence.
¹⁶They shall hunger no more, neither thirst anymore; the sun shall not strike them, nor
any scorching heat. ¹⁷For the Lamb in the midst of the throne will be their shepherd,
and he will guide them to springs of living water, and God will wipe away every tear
from their eyes." Rev 7:13-17 (from John's vision)

Jesus says: ¹²"Behold, I am coming soon, bringing my recompense with me, to repay
each one for what he has done. ¹³I am the Alpha and the Omega, the first and the last,
the beginning and the end." Rev 22:12-13

**LIKEWISE, GOD'S HEART IS CONSISTENT: THERE ARE CONSEQUENCES
THAT RESULT FROM OUR BEHAVIOR – good and bad.**

But we also see God's mercy – a promise of hope for those who turn their hearts back
to Him.

Isa 61:2-3 ²The nations shall see your righteousness, and all the kings your glory, and
you shall be called by a new name that the mouth of the Lord will give. ³You shall be a
crown of beauty in the hand of the Lord, and a royal diadem in the hand of your God.
Dan 12:1-3 ¹"... At that time your people shall be delivered, everyone whose name shall
be found written in the book. ... ³And those who are wise shall shine like the brightness of the sky above; and those who turn many to righteousness, like the stars forever
and ever

Rom 1:18–32 ¹⁸For the wrath of God is revealed from heaven against all ungodliness
and unrighteousness of men, who by their unrighteousness suppress the truth . . . ²¹For
although they knew God, they did not honor him as God or give thanks to him, but they
became futile in their thinking, and their foolish hearts were darkened. . . . ²⁴Therefore
God gave them up in the lusts of their hearts to impurity, to the dishonoring of their

bodies among themselves, [25]because they exchanged the truth about God for a lie and worshiped and served the creature rather than the Creator, who is blessed forever!

Rom 2:3–11 [3]Do you suppose, O man — you who judge those who practice such things and yet do them yourself — that you will escape the judgment of God? [4]Or do you presume on the riches of his kindness and forbearance and patience, not knowing that God's kindness is meant to lead you to repentance? . . . [6]He will render to each one according to his works: [7]to those who by patience in well-doing seek for glory and honor and immortality, he will give eternal life; [8]but for those who are self-seeking and do not obey the truth, but obey unrighteousness, there will be wrath and fury. [9]There will be tribulation and distress for every human being who does evil, the Jew first and also the Greek, [10]but glory and honor and peace for everyone who does good, the Jew first and also the Greek. [11]For God shows no partiality.

Rom 11:20-22 ... You stand fast through faith. ... [22]Note then the kindness and the severity of God: severity toward those who have fallen, but God's kindness to you, provided you continue in his kindness. Otherwise you too will be cut off.

2 Cor 5:6–10 [6]So we are always of good courage. We know that while we are at home in the body we are away from the Lord, [7]for we walk by faith, not by sight. [8]Yes, we are of good courage, and we would rather be away from the body and at home with the Lord. [9]So whether we are at home or away, we make it our aim to please him. [10]For we must all appear before the judgment seat of Christ, so that each one may receive what is due for what he has done in the body, whether good or evil.

Rom 14:10-12 [10] ...For we will all stand before the judgment seat of God . . . [and] [12] each of us will give an account of himself to God.

1 Thess 5:2-10 [2]. . . the day of the Lord will come like a thief in the night . . . [3]sudden destruction will come upon them as labor pains come upon a pregnant woman, and they will not escape. [4]But you are not in darkness, brothers, for that day to surprise you like a thief. [5]For you are all children of light, children of the day . . .

Heb 6:7-12 NLT . . . [10]For God is not unjust. He will not forget how hard you have worked for him and how you have shown your love to him by caring for other believers, as you still do. [11]Our great desire is that you will keep on loving others as long as life lasts, in order to make certain that what you hope for will come true. ...

Heb 10:19–31, 39 . . . [22]Let us draw near with a true heart in full assurance of faith, with our hearts sprinkled clean from an evil conscience and our bodies washed with pure water. [23]Let us hold fast the confession of our hope without wavering, for he who promised is faithful. . .

Jas 1:12 Blessed is the man who remains steadfast under trial . . . he will receive the crown of life, which God has promised to those who love him.

Jas 5:1-6 NLT . . . ³ . . . This treasure you have accumulated will stand as evidence against you on the day of judgment. ⁴ For listen! Hear the cries of the field workers whom you have cheated of their pay. The wages you held back cry out against you. The cries of those who harvest your fields have reached the ears of the Lord of Heaven's Armies . . .

1 Pet 1:15-19 ¹⁵ As he who called you is holy, you also be holy in all your conduct, ¹⁶ since it is written, "You shall be holy, for I am holy." . . . ¹⁸ knowing that you were ransomed from the futile ways inherited from your forefathers, not with perishable things such as silver or gold, ¹⁹ but with the precious blood of Christ . . .

1 Jn 2:15-17 ¹⁵ Do not love the world or the things in the world. If anyone loves the world, the love of the Father is not in him. ¹⁶ For all that is in the world — the desires of the flesh and the desires of the eyes and pride of life — is not from the Father but is from the world. ¹⁷ And the world is passing away along with its desires, but whoever does the will of God abides forever.

2 Jn 6-9 ⁶ And this is love, that we walk according to his commandments; this is the commandment, just as you have heard from the beginning, so that you should walk in it. ⁷ For many deceivers have gone out into the world, those who do not confess the coming of Jesus Christ in the flesh. Such a one is the deceiver and the anti-christ. ⁸ Watch yourselves, so that you may not lose what we have worked for, but may win a full reward. ⁹ Everyone who goes on ahead and does not abide in the teaching of Christ, does not have God. Whoever abides in the teaching has both the Father and the Son.

Life with God is not all sunshine and merry-go-rounds. ... but God is with me; I am not alone. Jas 1:12-15; 2 Cor 1:3-5; 1 Thess 5:16-18

More scripture on this: Ex 9:5; 20:6; and 33:8-9;
Deut 4:23-31; 7:9; 11:26-28; 15:4-6; 1 Sam 2:30; 2 Kgs 17:15;
Job 31:3; Ezek 3:17-21; Amos 3:2; Mal 3 and 4; Isa 1:18-20, 27;
Psa 50:14-23 ; 58:11 and 103:17-18; Jer 2:5, 17; Jer 4:14, 18; Jer 6:19; Jer 7:5-15: Jer 10:14: Jer 25:29; Col 3:23-25; Jude 17-23 NLT